We Have Some Notes . . .

We Have Some Notes . . .

The Insider's Guide to Notes, Script Editing and Development

Venetia Hawkes

THE BRITISH FILM INSTITUTE
Bloomsbury Publishing Plc
50 Bedford Square, London, WC1B 3DP, UK
1385 Broadway, New York, NY 10018, USA
29 Earlsfort Terrace, Dublin 2, Ireland

BLOOMSBURY is a trademark of Bloomsbury Publishing Plc

First published in Great Britain 2024 by Bloomsbury
on behalf of the
British Film Institute
21 Stephen Street, London W1T 1LN
www.bfi.org.uk

The BFI is the lead organisation for film in the UK and the distributor
of Lottery funds for film. Our mission is to ensure that film is central to our
cultural life, in particular by supporting and nurturing the next generation of filmmakers
and audiences. We serve a public role which covers the cultural, creative and economic
aspects of film in the UK.

Cover design: Louise Dugdale
Cover image © Venetia Hawkes

ISBN: HB: 978-1-8390-2550-1
          PB: 978-1-8390-2549-5
          ePDF: 978-1-8390-2552-5
          eBook: 978-1-8390-2551-8

Typeset by RefineCatch Limited, Bungay, Suffolk
Printed and bound in India

To find out more about our authors and books visit www.bloomsbury.com
and sign up for our newsletters.

For my father, Mike Hawkes, 1939–2023, who loved books, and had way too many, but who would have been getting this one in any case. Much loved, much missed.

Contents

Illustrations

Acknowledgements

This book would not exist without the immense kindness and generosity of all the contributors featured in it. I am deeply grateful to each of them. Both for their wise words in the book and for their willingness to be part of it. It's been a privilege and a delight.

I also want to thank all the assistants, company colleagues, associates and agents who helped arrange interviews, facilitate contributions or source photos; including Finn Blythe, Karis Winstanley, Leo Thompson, Ludo Graham, Caroline Reynolds, Susan Brophy, Bethan Evans, Arthur Barnard, Siân Fuller, Phillene Newman, Ana Albornoz, Hugh Davies, Emma Hewitt, Bea Cartwright, Lee-Anne Baker, Len Rowles and Will Simmons. Huge thanks go out to all the photographers who generously allowed their beautiful work to illustrate the book. And I'm grateful to Caroline Bartleet for letting us use a glimpse of one of her scripts to create the image on the cover.

Staunch supporters throughout the writing of the book are my wonderful walking buddies Ed Foster, Vicky Hewlett and Steve Hill, who are unfailingly wise, funny, encouraging and understanding of the importance of snacks.

The enthusiasm and encouragement of so many people along the way while developing and writing the book has been an uplifting balloon full of sunshine. I'm so appreciative of everyone who shared a kind thought. Which is pretty much everyone I've mentioned the book to whilst writing it, but especially my brother Elliott and sister Melantha, Celia Hancock, Natasha Ellis, Emma Jackson, Sandra Hebron, Alan Thorn, Ludo Smolski, Dougal Wilson, Briony Hanson, Charlotte Moore, and the good people at Nordisk Film and Creative Alliance who looked after me when I did a talk about the book while it was still being written. With particular thanks to Peter Ansorge for his early and unwavering enthusiasm, encouragement and advice. And to Sophie – best of nieces, an inspiring, bright, brilliant joy. I'm very grateful to the kind friends who generously read sections and gave notes on a book about notes, notably – Emma Jackson, Steve Hill, Ed Foster, John Osborne and Katie Elson. Thanks likewise to those who gave guidance about the practicalities of writing a book, including Alan Thorn, Sara Putt, Peter Bunzl and the Society of Authors. I'm also very grateful to Jon Wardle, Ijeoma Akigwe and Gillian Carr at the NFTS for their support to write the book. I was thrilled when Rebecca Barden of Bloomsbury wanted to publish it, and extremely thankful for her and her team's guidance and support.

Thanks of course to my parents, Mike and Mary. From an early age my mum regularly took me, my brother and sister to the library, enabling me to devour book after book of myths, legends and fairy tales and to develop a love of reading and the shape of stories. My dad took me to see *Star Wars* (George Lucas, 1977), the first film I remember seeing in a cinema, introduced me to the work of Ray Harryhausen and asked questions which prompted me to analyse and figure out why old episodes of *The Avengers* (1961–9) stood out from other television programmes. Between them fostering a lifelong love of learning and joy in knowledge of all kinds of curious corners.

I was fortunate to work for Martin Lamb and Penelope Middelboe at Right Angle, who script and series edited animated adaptations of classic tales from around the world, from their little office by the sea in West Wales. I am ever grateful for their kindness, friendship and inspiring introduction to the art of script editing, notes and development.

Finally special thanks to Finn, without whose repeated requests to go out, and to come back in, and to go out again, the book might well have been finished a little sooner, but who is a most excellent cat.

Introduction

This book explores the art of giving and receiving 'notes' in film and television drama. The feedback, comment and discussion that are an integral part of the process. Yet how can notes, script editing and development contribute to creating successful screen stories? Script editing sounds like it might be going through text with a red pen, correcting spelling mistakes, tutting and sighing. And really, who wants that? To reveal some of the mysteries, award-winning writers and directors and distinguished 'note-givers' – producers, script editors, development executives and commissioners, share their insights and advice. They discuss potential pitfalls and perils to avoid, and advise how to achieve a harmonious, fruitful, creative experience. One that is rewarding both for the writers and directors on the receiving end of notes, and those who give them.

First, for those who enjoy a bit of scene setting:

We all know a good story when we read or watch or hear it. It engages us, entertains us, moves us. Stories transport us from our lives or help us reflect on them, tell us something we didn't know or make us see something in a new way, reassure or challenge us, change how we think or feel about the world, or even about ourselves. Stories stay with us. An essential part of us.

All those once-upon-a-times, myths and monsters, books, films, plays, television and radio dramas, you-will-not-believe-what-happened-last-night conversations over coffee, that we read, watch and hear, embed in us a feeling, an instinct, of the shapes that make a satisfying story. And what feels 'wrong'. We're so story literate that it delights us when our expectations of how a narrative will unfold are surprised. For the surprise to work, it actively counts on us 'knowing' what shape a story 'should' be. Yet having an innate story-sense does not by itself bestow the ability to analyse a story as it is being crafted, fathoming its strengths and weaknesses. Nor to convey, in a helpful way, something that will support its creator to better attain their vision and connect with an audience. Which is what script editing, development and notes seek to achieve.

Script editing, development and giving notes is a craft, a trained skill. A two-fold one. The art of analysing the material and considering how it might more closely realize the writer's or director's vision and engage an audience. And the art of sharing those observations with the writer or director. This book explores the latter: how to convey and receive notes constructively and effectively.

This book looks at the invisible. Because when script editing, development and note-giving is done well, it should be invisible. Script editors, developers and note-givers can help enable writers and directors tell the best version they can of the story they want to tell, contributing to creating drama that resonates with an audience. *Their* story, not the script editor's story, not the developer's story, not the note-giver's story. No one's ever going to watch a film or a television drama and say 'Oh, I bet so and so script edited that' or 'I love how there must have been a note that completely changed my empathy for that character'. It's not a job for egos. But it is brilliant. Being able to say something that unlocks a stuck story door, or fuels a writer to fly is magic. Being invisible doesn't mean it's not creatively crucial. Magic is invisible.

But a bad note, or a badly given note, can crush a writer's confidence or derail a director's vision. Generally, people want to help. Believe that what they are saying will help. Yet sometimes there can be a gulf between intention and reception. Leaving writers and directors furious and frustrated, note-givers downcast that their good intentions went awry, and the film or television project adrift, unsure where it's going.

The following chapters contain advice from experienced practitioners on what makes for a note-giving process that contributes to the success of creative projects. And what doesn't. They discuss things such as the vulnerability writers and directors may encounter when sharing work and receiving notes; and the importance of getting past potential reactions of being hurt, defensive or angry, in order to be open to hearing things that may be useful. For example,

BAFTA and Cannes winning writer-director Lynne Ramsay (*You Were Never Really Here* (2017), *Morvern Callar* (2002)) advises, 'Sometimes someone might come in and they just don't get it. But you've got to try and listen if there's anything in what they're saying. Even if it's points of view that you don't necessarily agree with. But it's really hard, because when you've written something you are vulnerable. You're showing your work and half the time when you're writing you're thinking "God, this is awful!" you're questioning everything. It can be a lonely place. You're your worst critic in a way. I think the key is not to get defensive. And to listen to what makes sense and have the strength to discard what doesn't.' Multi BAFTA winning screenwriter Russell T Davies (*Queer as Folk* (1999 & 2002), *Doctor Who* (2005–24), *It's a Sin* (2021)) observes, 'There are ordinary notes, like cut that location, we can't afford night shoots, she's unfunny, etc. But the real notes about the tone, the purpose, your intent, are asking, why did you write this? What are you saying? Who are you? That's why notes hurt. And why great notes transform.'

The selection of interviewees in the book aims to provide a range of voices and perspectives. It includes Oscar and BAFTA winning writers and directors of authored drama from across the British and Irish film and television industry. The interviews took place over a number of years, and relate to the artist's work at the time of the interview.

There are points of consensus. Such as the recommendation that in the face of bruising notes or rejection the only thing to do is pick yourself up, dust yourself down and keep going. For instance, award-winning director Corin Hardy (*Gangs of London* (2020–22), *The Hallow* (2015), *The Nun* (2018)) shares some advice that he received: 'In terms of rejection, Ray Harryhausen once firmly told me, "You've got to be resilient" and coming from a man who has worked his way through centuries of cinema as an almost one man army of creativity, it is inevitable that he must have experienced a substantial amount of rejection and difficulties in bringing his incredible visions to the screen. So I took those five words on board early on and always try, no matter how negative, disappointing or anger-making a situation is, to 'be resilient', keep doing my best, water off a duck's back and tomorrow is another day.'

A consistent piece of advice for note-givers is to refrain from being prescriptive. As multi-BAFTA winning producer Nicola Shindler (*Nolly*

(2023), *Happy Valley* (2014–16), *Years and Years* (2019)) says, 'Our job is not to suggest changes to writers for the sake of it, our job is to try and help writers make their scripts better. The worst notes are those which suggest how we, the script editors, would have written a scene or a character. We need to understand what the writer intends, hear their voices in our head and then help solve any issues. That isn't to say that everything a writer delivers is right. The script editor's job is incredibly important both for creative development and production.'

Elsewhere the interviewees' different, at times even opposing, views on notes suggest a core principle – that notes are most effective when tailored not just to the project, but also to the person. What suits one might not work for another. Notes are not one size fits all. They are bespoke.

'Giving notes' happens throughout the creative process – from evolving the first germ of an idea right through to the final cut and choices around music, sound and visual effects. Sometimes someone such as a showrunner, producer or executive producer might give notes throughout. Sometimes a script editor or story developer might be brought in to work on a certain number of script drafts. Whoever is doing it, at whatever stage, the function is to draw out from the writer or director the best form of the story that they want to tell. Not to re-write it for them, not to tell them what to do, not to change it to what they think it should be. To support, encourage, question, inspire, analyse, interrogate, discuss, challenge, dare to voice a bad idea that might trigger a good one. To perhaps spark in a writer or director a whole new avenue of thought that the note-giver might never have envisaged, but which the writer or director might not have considered without the note-giver's input. To skilfully contribute to the crafting of a screen story which resonates with an audience. It is the beauty and joy of creative collaboration.

Oscar and BAFTA winning screenwriter Simon Beaufoy (*Slumdog Millionaire* (2008), *The Full Monty* (1997)) sums script editors up as: 'Like the writer's best friend, so that they're able to tell you the unpleasant truths, that are always there, in every script, but in the right way. There isn't a script I've written that hasn't got better from notes. Good script editors have made my work better. Consistently. They're important.' And Oscar nominated, BAFTA winning screenwriter Krysty Wilson-Cairns (*1917* (2019), *Last Night in Soho*

(2021), *The Good Nurse* (2022)) recommends embracing notes as an essential part of the collaborative nature of filmmaking. She says, 'To me, filmmaking is the ultimate collaboration. What you're doing when you write a script, or you step on a set, is that you and between eight and eight hundred other people are trying to make something that's a bit of each of you. You're trying to create something together, and if you can't collaborate. . . . I feel as a writer if you don't want notes, if you don't want to collaborate, go write books. I always think – someone might come up with a better idea, and your name's still going to be on the script. Let's make it the best script possible. I love notes, I'm a big believer that the script is the blueprint for the story so people can build it, and why not build it together?'

Peter Ansorge

Peter Ansorge is a former BBC Drama script editor and producer and Channel 4 commissioning editor of drama. As a complement to the writer and director interviews, he provides some insights into script editing, development and notes from a note-giver's perspective; together with a little context of their history and evolution. In addition to his work in film and television, Peter is a screenwriting and script development tutor, and author of *From Liverpool to Los Angeles: On Writing for Theatre, Film and Television*[1] and *Disrupting the Spectacle: Five Years of Experimental and Fringe Theatre in Britain.*[2]

In conversation he is a blend of avuncular wisdom and school-boyish enthusiasm; sparkling intelligence and genuine fascination with learning about others. He begins by asserting, 'In essence, giving notes on a script or a cut of film or TV drama is the crucial pathway to a successful TV drama or a movie. That role and function of the script editor is absolutely crucial.' He qualifies, 'A *good* script editor.'

After an English degree at Cambridge, Peter became editor of monthly theatre magazine *Plays and Players*.[3] In 1975 he joined the BBC English Regions Drama Department as a script editor and producer. His work there included script editing writer-director David Hare's BAFTA winning *Licking*

---

[1]Ansorge, P. (1997) *From Liverpool to Los Angeles: On Writing for Theatre, Film and Television*, London: Faber & Faber.
[2]Ansorge, P. (1975) *Disrupting the Spectacle: Five Years of Experimental and Fringe Theatre in Britain*, London: Pitman Publishing.
[3]*Plays and Players* (ed. Ansorge, P.), September 1973–December 1974, London: Hansom Books.

Hitler (1978) and devising and producing the UK's first Black soap opera, *Empire Road* (1978). He went on to become a commissioning editor for fiction, and later, Head of Drama at Channel 4. There he worked on TV series including the multi-BAFTA winning *Traffik* (1989) and soap opera *Brookside*.

Peter maintains that understanding something of the history and evolution of notes, script editing and development helps inform how they function in today's broadcasting landscape. He says, 'In a sense, script editing is an invention of the UK. In the mid-1950s, television drama in this country was based not upon series and serials, though they existed, but on the single play. A mini revolution happened when a Canadian producer called Sydney Newman took over drama at ITV. He started a series called *Armchair Theatre* (1958). He wanted to do contemporary work, mirroring some of the issues that were being explored in new plays at the Royal Court Theatre. Up until that point, television drama was controlled by the producer or director. When BBC Drama began, the director was essentially also the producer and the script editor. Sydney Newman broke that up into roles. He was the producer, and he brought in Irene Shubik, who was the first script editor credited in UK TV drama. Sydney Newman was so successful that the BBC poached him, and he took Irene Shubik with him. So then, for the first time, BBC drama had the producer and the script editor, who were on staff, and the director, who was a freelancer. Obviously Irene Shubik would be working on the development of commissioned dramas, but she would also be looking for new writers. So it wasn't just script editing a script, it was also a development job. The notion that it is initially the producer and script editor who develop the script with a writer to a point that then they choose to find a director, and the director will have notes, but they will come on after the script is there, that's television and that's really where the script editor begins. Before then, say in those black and white films from the 1940s, shot in UK sound stages, producers like Alexander Korda and Michael Balcon did the script editing themselves. A great producer can also give notes. They did bring in story editors, but it wasn't recognized as a crucial role, which it was to become at the BBC and ITV. In post 1980s UK cinema the same process applies, but it came out of the script editor function in TV drama.'

In 2022 the British Film Institute (BFI) held a season of events to celebrate the fortieth anniversary of Channel 4. Peter, a special guest speaker on panels for that BFI season, recalls the early days of the channel and how its commissioning structure influenced the evolution of notes and development. He explains, 'Channel 4's big commitment was to the single film. And that was very controversial at the time. Jeremy Isaacs, the first Chief Executive of Channel 4, and David Rose – who had been my boss at BBC Birmingham and was the first Head of Drama at Channel 4 – came up with a notion that they were not going to produce their own programmes as a channel, but would commission from independent production companies. People thought it would never work. When I told a friend of mine who worked in TV, that I was going to leave the BBC and go to Channel 4 he said, "You're mad!" he was partly joking, but he said, "This notion of independent production companies, they're never going to make your programmes! You give them money and they'll go off to the Bahamas!"' Peter chuckles to himself, enjoying the memory. He adds, 'It was what a lot of people thought – that it would not work. That as a policy for drama it was doomed to fail. But David Rose was the perfect person to make it work. Because he had a generosity and wideness of taste. He didn't specialize in social realism or period drama or anything, he embraced a whole lot of things. And Jeremy Isaacs was a cineaste, he did know cinema, just before Channel 4 began he ran the filmmaking department at the BFI.'

Peter continues, 'At Channel 4, David Rose, and then Karin Bamborough and I, worked in a very similar way to the way we'd worked with writers and directors at the BBC. The difference was that you were dealing with independent producers. Jeremy, rightly, made it clear that the producers had to have the voice. So if you had a note that you really thought was important, Liz Forgan, who was Commissioning Editor at Channel 4 then, said, "Go down on your knees to them, start crying, but if they really say 'No, that's not what I want to do' then you have to accept it." Jeremy was a visionary; I was fortunate to work for him.'

Peter explains, 'Channel 4 in those days had a very generous development slate. So if a writer came into the office with an independent producer, and pitched something and the idea was quite liked, it was not an issue to develop a full script. Jeremy Isaacs respected the commissioning editors in the same way that we were told to respect the producers. So even if he thought, "This sounds crazy, no one will watch this!" he wouldn't ever say: "Don't do it." I think it was probably around 10:1 the number of scripts they developed compared to what was then made. And that is the key. It was not a problem to develop a full script. I very rarely asked for a treatment, which often happens now, because it's only really when you get a script that you can tell if something will work. Part of the process is you'll think, "Oh that idea is a winner" and another idea will come in and you'll think, "I don't know if anyone will want to see this, but I like this idea and we'll give it a go." It's often that second idea, that when the script comes in works, and the one you thought would be a safe bet doesn't. It's not wholly true, but I've often found that over the years. What Jeremy Isaacs, and then Michael Grade when he took over, basically said was, "Look, you're going to do some things Peter that're not going to work. And that'll be OK. As long as next time you go on and do something that does!" If you only do stuff that flops then you shouldn't be doing that job. But without that notion, it's not creative. It's inhibiting if there's a fear that if you do something that doesn't work you'll be judged on that one thing. I was lucky to be working then. Now, because it takes so long to develop things, if it doesn't work it's harder to get the next thing going.'

Reflecting on the current landscape, Peter says, 'One of the reasons it's changed with Film4 and BBC and ITV is it's much harder for them to fully fund a drama, whether it's a film or a big series. So it's not just Film4 or BBC, maybe with support from the BFI, funding something, but other companies as well. So what happens is that money from those other companies, like say an American streamer, comes with notes. And that has become something a script editor has to take on board, and make a decision about what is important. If they really think these other notes aren't right, they're going to have to find a way to negotiate that. I'm lucky, because back when I was doing it, as commissioning editor we were the ones that had the final say in the script. Those days have changed. And that's partly why it takes longer to develop, produce and create a series or a film than it used to, because there are more voices involved.'

Considering other potential pitfalls to navigate, Peter says, 'Sometimes the script editor was not involved in the actual production!' He laughs incredulously, explaining, 'From the beginning at BBC Birmingham we, the script editors, were involved in production. How can you not be! You need to be involved from beginning to end. Similarly the script editors now, when they come through the independent production companies, can be attached to the production throughout and see the script through.' Peter expands, rebutting any misconception that notes only happen at script stage: 'When I was at the BBC, if there was a problem during production, say the director was running behind or there was a scene the director wasn't happy with, then the script editor would go to the set, talk to people and if necessary then call the writer. It's crucial, absolutely crucial, that the note-giver is involved. And of course then there's the editing stage, watching the rushes on screen, they need to be involved in all of that. And if there were issues, then the commissioning editor or whoever would go and talk to the director or the writer.'

Peter goes on to summarize the key elements of the role: 'Giving notes takes in not just obvious knowledge of craft, but it's very important to give the *right* note. To be able to specifically give a note that makes it better. If you give the wrong note, writers will lose trust in you. I think that goes the whole way through the process, from beginning to work with the writer to the end, the final cut.' But he says, 'I don't believe there is any scientific way that guarantees you will give the right note to a writer or producer or director. The best script editors I've known are first of all great readers. You can't be a script editor unless you've read a lot of scripts and you've read a lot of novels and you keep up with what's going on in the world. That's sometimes forgotten. Because writers, even if they're writing period pieces, have something to say – the good ones. And they say it through metaphor. In other words their story has to be compelling, you have to engage with the characters, in order for the writer or director to get their point across. And that's why the role of the script editor is crucial to the creation of television drama and film – to help draw out from the writer or director what it is they want to say and to ensure it is coming across.'

Peter emphasizes the collaborative nature of the process: 'In the relationship with the writer it's not like you are the genius giving notes, and they are sitting there taking them. It's not like school! Which some script editors, not the good ones, do apparently. You have to talk, so it comes through a conversation.' He cautions, 'There are people working as script editors, or giving notes in some other capacity, who secretly want to be writers. It does happen, but the job should not be considered as a writer's job. It is part of the creative pulse, but the script editor is not there to re-write lines.'

Getting into the practicalities of the job he explains, 'One of the misconceptions about notes is that they are written. Actually a script editor, certainly in my own case, usually doesn't work from written notes, they work with a relationship with the writer. If you're sitting in a room and you give the right note to a writer, they will respect it. They will trust you. If you send them pages of notes, they're not going to be that delighted! If you finish a meeting and the writer says, "Could you send me the headlines, could you send me ten notes?" that's fine because it comes out of the conversation and they'll know what you're referring to. But real creativity happens through the relationship, the conversations. You have to have done your homework, you have to go in there knowing the script, knowing the writer. Of course you do. But you don't arm yourself with it like ammunition. You create the conversation, and out of the conversation – if your notes are right, will come the solution. You don't necessarily have to go in there with a solution, it becomes a discovery. Or you might have a brilliant solution and you wait for the right moment to share it. It's not like marking homework. It's about the relationship. Really you have to have, in terms of the work, an understanding of where the writer comes from. What they're trying to say. What they're trying to do. What is the work they love most? I've always found that if you give a good note the writer will immediately connect with it, but they won't just come back and re-write as you may have suggested, they will make it their own. They will come up with something better than you first thought of, but which they may not have thought of without your input. That's when you know it is working.'

Peter says, 'With notes to a director in the edit, that's absolutely the same thing – have a conversation. There were people who wouldn't go to the cutting room with the director! They'd watch a tape and send notes to the editor and to the director: "Cut this, change that." A good director would go crazy and say, "No, we've got to talk." I think that still happens sometimes. Which is terrible, because an editor is a key to the whole thing. It's as important as the script. The editor's a creator, you can't just go, "Cut that scene."'

Peter shares some insights from his direct experience. He recalls, 'When I started as a script editor at the BBC in the mid-1970s I was fortunate to have David Rose as my first boss. David didn't sit there telling me what I should do.

First of all he took me to video editing, where Mike Leigh was making a *Play for Today – Nuts in May* (1976). Mike was very generous – he welcomed the two script editors in the department, including me, to see a cut and he would say, "Have you got any comments?" If you said something that was relevant, he would listen. We watched a scene and David Rose would make a point in a very courteous but pertinent manner, and I thought, "Oh, right that's how you do it" – you don't pretend you know better; you've got to love what you see, or like what you see, and think "Am I just missing something? Is there clarity?" And that's what you begin with.'

Peter emphasizes, 'I think it's really, really important that you love the work, and that the writer or writer-director understands that you do, and that a note is not a criticism, but you're wanting to help them make it better. You can't sit there and be a critic. You have to engage with the writer's or director's imagination and what they're doing. Therefore you have to have taste and judgement. A good script editor has a broad taste. So they are able to give both Ken Loach and Dennis Potter a note. One of the things you don't do, which is one of the things I learned from David Rose, is you don't come into a meeting or cutting room negatively. If there is a problem, you get to the problem by showing that you understand what the intention is.'

He continues, 'I worked first in an era when television drama went out just once. In fact, if they went out on tape they'd usually wipe the show afterwards! Television drama was regarded as a completely ephemeral medium. But one of the first things David Rose said to me was, "That's a mistake, drama is not ephemeral. If you get it right for the audience, what they will remember are moments. Moments where they laugh, they cry, and discover things they haven't quite seen or thought before. That's what audiences respond to." So when you sit in a room with a writer or a director, it is you and the writer or director, but also somewhere in the background, floating round, is the audience. And it's a mistake to think that the audience is stupid. A real mistake. And people do that. What the audience wants is something new and challenging. And then you also have to do it in a way that engages and entertains them. So when you are sitting in a room with a writer or director and things go well and suddenly there's a note which helps the whole thing, you're not just thinking of yourselves, you're thinking this may delight the audience.'

To illustrate how working relationships can develop, he recalls working with the Oscar and BAFTA nominated writer, Dennis Potter: 'One of the great writers in television was Dennis Potter. When I was at Channel 4 as a commissioning editor, Michael Grade was my boss. When Michael was controller of BBC1 he'd commissioned *The Singing Detective* (1986), which was written by Dennis and is, I think, one of the great TV dramas. Michael championed it and made sure that it went out at 9 pm, prime time on a Sunday night. When Michael went to Channel 4, because Dennis had a great loyalty to Michael, Dennis said he'd do his dramas for Channel 4, and Michael asked me how I felt about doing it – and of course Dennis was one of my heroes!'

Peter recounts, 'The first time we met was at a lunch somewhere posh in the middle of London. Dennis literally didn't say a word to me. He suddenly looked at me as I was fiddling with some peanuts and said, "Why are you so nervous?" Then he said, "Michael, why do you employ teenagers to be script editors? He's probably never seen a drama in his life." I think I was in my early forties. It wasn't like I was a beginner – but I felt like one! As it happened, I knew the director of *The Singing Detective*, Jon Amiel, and Jon said to me that when he first met Dennis he treated Jon in the same way – he was testing us! Now, I don't think all writers do that. But a writer does want to know who you are, something of your character, so that they can connect. As we worked on *Lipstick on Your Collar* (1993), when we looked at the first rough cut I made a few verbal notes with Dennis in the cutting room and he looked at me and he said, "Do you know, you may be right!" and we made changes. From then on we became the best of friends! When Dennis was dying, his agent, Judy Daish, said I was one of the last people he asked to speak to, because I'd just seen a cut of his latest work and he wanted to hear my thoughts. That is a little drama of what can happen as relationships develop, and it never would have happened if I'd sat there and written ten pages of notes to Dennis on his script.'

Peter concludes, 'Having tried to explain in a simple way what giving notes and script editing does, the actual work is very, very hard. Because it's so conversational, people don't always understand the amount of work and analysis you have to do *before* having the conversation in the room. Because you're looking each time to develop a world beater. Something that's going to stand out. And that is not easy. And writers and directors know that. Sometimes if they try and make it easy for themselves you have to direct them a little bit away from that. Not everybody can give a note. Someone who can give a good note will really, really make a difference. But if they give a bad note, which is also common, it can undermine the confidence of the writer or director and the whole project. But if you get it right, you can actually change the world a bit.'

Quick Fire Q&A 1: What's the role of a script editor or anyone giving notes?

'Help. They're there to help. Writing's a lonely job, please help.' – **Russell T Davies**

'They need to be like the writer's best friend, so that they're able to tell you the unpleasant truths, that are always there, in every script, but in the right way. There isn't a script I've written that hasn't got better from notes. Good script editors have made my work better. Consistently. They're important.' – **Simon Beaufoy**

'It's someone looking at the bigger picture when you as a writer are sometimes caught up in the minutiae. I've learned a lot from picture editing when you see how little it takes to express a complex idea.' – **Lynne Ramsay**

'Psychotherapist mixed with a diviner and a miner. Because you have to find what it is that needs to be there, and you need to dig in and get it.' – **Tomm Moore**

'To support the writer to deliver something that has clarity and is focused and best channels the vision of the writer. It's someone who facilitates a writer to reach their full potential. That's what the best script editors do.' – **Amma Asante**

'They're there to hold the story to account in terms of its efficiency. They're basically a kind of script police. In a good way. It's the same as continuity are script police as well, you need those checks and balances sometimes within the process.' – **Ben Wheatley**

'The script editor is there to kind of mentor the writer, to elicit the best version of what their vision is of the story. That is often not the case, that often doesn't happen. But I also think you're there to get it across the line – you've got a little bit of a responsibility to the producer as well. But the prime responsibility as a script editor should always be to the writer.' – **Alice Lowe**

'I have been a script editor in the past. I didn't write on *Spaced* (1999), but I was a script editor on it, and I also did script edits on some of the first series of *The Mighty Boosh* (2003). Your role as a script editor is helping the writer deliver what they intend. I happened to know the writer-performers Simon Pegg and Jessica Hynes as well as Noel Fielding and Julian Barratt, and part of my role as a script editor would be helping them sell it to somebody who didn't know them. In a way, I was saying to them, "This is the best way to get the script across to somebody who doesn't know you." Then you're also looking at length and clarity and whether there's a missed opportunity with something, either with tying up loose ends or cutting anything that feels like it sticks out as not belonging. Here's an example of me at my most brutal as a script editor when I was working on the second series of *Spaced*. Simon and Jessica had written a lot of episodes where Tim and Daisy, the main characters, were separated. For the final script that they wrote, which I think was episode five, they said, "In this one the boys have a night out and the girls have a night out." I read it and said, "I really think you need to do a Tim and Daisy episode, so I would urge you to junk this one and do one where they're together." To their credit they did exactly that. And I think it's the best episode of the series. And I think Simon and Jessica would agree, because it's one that's really focused on them. But that was probably my most nuclear work as a script editor, not saying "this is bad", but rather "you need more of this, so maybe scrap this idea and start again." It can be on as major a level as that, scrap this episode and start again, or it could be really micro stuff. It's really fascinating. The two times that I've done it has been on comedies. Part of it is you're trying to help convey what their vision is, and then if there's room for improvements or suggestions you can throw everything in.' – **Edgar Wright**

'It's the same as with every key crew member, it's the overall team working together that makes the end product shine; streamlining through from the writer's to the director's vision in service of the story. So if a script editor is in tune with the film or TV series and also the director's vision and the writer's intentions, they can really be the glue that supports it all and ensures that it is the best, most solid, effective, smart and coherent version of the story it can be.' – **Corin Hardy**

'You're all trying to share in this dream of what the film you're going to make is, and you're all trying to get on board on the same boat so that you can get to that. It doesn't matter how you do it or what you need to put aside, but that's the whole point of it.' – **Krysty Wilson-Cairns**

'They're the helicopter pilot that's trying to help you reach the summit of a mountain. They're not having to do the hard work of the writing, or climbing in the analogy, and by virtue of not having to do that they have a vantage point that you can't see as the person writing it. So they help by providing a clear perspective, a helicopter's perspective, on where you're heading and what might be the most elegant path to arrive there, and highlight the treacherous areas to circumvent.' – **Michael Pearce**

'A friend? A sensitive, smart, curious friend.' – **Lone Scherfig**

Simon Beaufoy

'The most important thing I could ever say to script editors is you cannot dissociate the work from the person. The person is the work.'

1 *Simon Beaufoy, © Selly Gardner-Morrison.*

'This is Chips.' Simon Beaufoy introduces an eager Bedlington lurcher dog. Chips gazes devotedly up at him and occasionally contributes to the conversation via squeaky toy or the gift of a shoe. Chips' owner, affable Yorkshire-born screenwriter Simon Beaufoy, was nominated for his first Oscar and BAFTA, for Best Original Screenplay for *The Full Monty* (Peter Cattaneo, 1997), aged just thirty. He went on to win both the Oscar and BAFTA for Best Adapted Screenplay for *Slumdog Millionaire* (Danny Boyle, Loveleen Tandan, 2008) and was Oscar and BAFTA nominated again for *127 Hours* (Danny Boyle, 2010).

After studying at Oxford University and then Bournemouth Film School, Simon began working in documentaries; for BBC series *Forty Minutes.* Through his passion for climbing, Simon knew of a group of men who travelled around the country painting pylons, and thought they'd be an interesting subject. Failing to get the idea off the ground as a documentary prompted him to write it as a drama. Emboldened to write fiction, he crafted the script for *The Full Monty*, inspired in part by the way colleagues in a factory he'd worked in talked to one another. The resulting film's success finally enabled him to bring his pylon drama to the screen, eight years after starting to develop it, as *Among Giants* (Sam Miller, 1998).

From the unemployed Sheffield steelworkers of *The Full Monty* to the corrosively wealthy Gettys of *Trust* (2018), his work captures and conveys characters' humanity, complexity, wit and fragility with humour, warmth and understanding, while the drama grips our attention like the most addictive page-turner.

'I used to think notes were very threatening. For a long time. Probably ten years. Before I really, really knew my craft,' Simon begins. 'Now, I know if I can tell a story or if I can't tell a story. I don't know exactly how I'll tell it, but after thirty years of doing it, I have the craft skills to go, "Right, I've got this. I don't know how yet, but if you give it to me I can turn it into a story." There's more craft in screenwriting than art, I think. I see it like carpentry: give me the right wood and I'll build you a table that will have four legs and a flat top, you might not like the finish but I guarantee it'll work as a table. But before I'd really learned my craft, I found notes quite intimidating. I always saw them as a bit of a threat to the storytelling, thought that they'd make the table have one leg shorter than the others.

'It took me a long time to work out that film and stories are incredibly plastic,' he explains, 'they're so malleable, you can turn them around and squeeze them and elongate them. They're like putty. When I wasn't good at my job I thought, "This is the only way to tell the story, and if you don't tell it this way, it'll be ruined." I've realized you can tell it in a a myriad different ways, without that changing my original focus for the story.'

Over coffee, and cake baked by his daughter, which he fondly admits he taught her how to make, Simon describes how it feels as a writer receiving notes on a script: 'Psychologically it's a very odd place to be. You've been working on something for three, four, five, six months or years; a huge amount of time where your brain and emotions are buried in it – writing's a completely immersive experience, obviously, otherwise it's not going to be very good. Then someone reads it, on a weekend, and sends you five pages of notes with their thoughts. And you just think, "Well, you had two glasses of Sancerre on a Friday night and read it wishing you were doing something else, and I spent six months on that!" – I'm already inclined not to listen because they haven't suffered in the way that any writer who has ever written anything has suffered to make that story work. "Suffering" sounds a bit much, but I mean in the sense of absorbing yourself totally in the world of a story to the extent that you're absent from the world around you – your friends and family – the sleepless nights trying to puzzle it out, all that. To write well, you need to be very sensitive, to have a thin skin, to have your antennae receptive to everything – no shield against the world – but to cope with the industry, a business, that is endlessly telling you that the work needs changing, be different, be better, you're required to have a very thick skin. There's a schizophrenia in that which makes for quite an uncomfortable life. So, you have to get over all of that, and that's just getting older, more experienced, less chippy. Though in all the years I've been writing, it's never an easy process to listen to people tell you what's wrong with your work.

'It's just a hard process, throwing your work out into the world for people to comment on,' he says with the stoical acceptance of a veteran. He observes, 'It's very different from other creative processes. If you paint a picture, it's done. People aren't going to come back and say, "Could you change the colour of the sky, because I don't like that colour" or "We want to cast someone a bit younger so could you repaint that person ten years younger" and "If they were ten years younger they wouldn't be sitting in that way and they wouldn't be dressed in those clothes, so could you just change that too. And they wouldn't buy that

kind of furniture, so they wouldn't be in that room, so can you change that."
And suddenly your whole picture's changed. But that often happens with
screenwriting. You've got huge amounts of people who want to change things.'

To prompt a more understanding perspective for note-givers he suggests a
challenge, 'I think every script editor should write a full-length script. Then
they'd know. Writing a script is a really difficult process. Then they'd sit there
and go, "If I give a note it won't just change a scene, it might change everything.
So, I'd better make my notes good." I honestly think it would be a really good
discipline for people to do, because then they would get in the head of a writer.'

Simon adds, 'I mean, I'm assuming we're talking about good notes. Bad
notes are just bad notes. And there are ways of dealing with those as well, which
nobody ever told me about. Whenever I go up to the National Film and
Television School I'm always telling the screenwriting students that you don't
have to do all of the notes. Nobody ever told me that! I always thought it was
like school – you were handed back your homework and you had to do
corrections. So I tried to, and that's really difficult – impossible! If a note isn't
clear or I don't understand it or I think it will make the script worse, then even
with the best will in the world I'll sit there and I won't be able to do it. I mean
literally. It's like a physical inability, my fingers hover over the keyboard and
they will not type. And I can try, because I'll think, "Well it's worth a go, this
person's intelligent, I'll give it a go," but if it makes it worse I have to stop. So
instead I'll go back and continue the conversation with them and say, "I one
hundred per cent know any alternative is going to make this worse, so I can't
do that, so let's think around this, let's have another discussion, let's come at it
from a different direction." And that's what's changed for me over twenty-five
years of writing; that confidence that there will be a way to address people's
problems, just not necessarily in the way that has been first suggested.'

He observes, 'The older I've got, the more I've discovered that generally the
problems people see, if it's a good set of notes, the things people notice and
comment on – their solutions aren't often correct, but the fact that they have a
problem with it nearly always means they've spotted a bump in it somewhere
that needs addressing. That's very valid and in the long run, helpful.'

Simon describes a little more of a writer's emotions around sending in a
script and receiving notes: 'When you've completed something, you send it off

in what you feel is a perfect state – because somewhere in you, you always feel that, otherwise you wouldn't send it off. Of course it isn't, it never is. The creative process is always rolling on, as it should. But when you send it you think, "This is done!" and all you get back is people saying "Well, it's not done actually", "And how about this, and how about that?" it's really hard not to view that as confrontational, or adversarial, because what comes back is what's wrong with it. Script editors have learnt to give you a brief paragraph at the top about how they love it and it's brilliant and you're a star, and unfortunately, though that might be true, writers will ignore that. Because writers, and humans generally, are psychologically attuned to ignoring the compliments and just noticing the criticisms. I've forgotten pretty much all of the nice things said about my scripts, but remember every single bad thing. Honestly, every one. It does help if the person giving the notes recognizes and praises things that they like in a script. It's really bad to just get the problems back. It's incredibly disheartening and you're less likely to respond well. It's really important that people like what you've done.'

Refilling the kettle and bustling with milk and mugs, Simon shares an example from a current project: 'I'm working on a new series and rather than write a pilot I chose to write three episodes, as you needed that to get a full sense of it. Just before Christmas I had this conference call with the broadcaster and they said, "It's just not really working, we just don't get it. It's too complicated and difficult." So that's six months' work that I've basically put in the bin. And that's really hard to hear. And it's really hard to accept when people are right. Because it's six months' work, so you're desperate to believe that they're not right. This particular group of people I couldn't dismiss their comments, because they're clever people. Really smart people, and they're not scared of boldness, and they're not scared of innovation, so it was a genuine creative problem that they had and I respected that. But it took me ages to get over it! It didn't really work, they were right. I hated them being right, but they are people I really respect. From anyone else I'd just go, "Oh, you just don't understand", but these people are really bright and they all said the same thing and I thought in the end, "Oh, yeah, you're probably right." But it hurt!'

As Chips bounces in from the drizzly April garden, the talk turns to handling conflicting notes. Since writing *Blow Dry* (Paddy Breathnach, 2001) around twenty years ago, Simon's contracts specify he'll only receive notes from one source. He explains, 'It's not because I'm difficult and it's not just for me either – it's for them to go, "Do we all agree that this is right?" because what is completely impossible is when you get notes from three different sources. There aren't many stupid people in the film industry, you tend to be surrounded by intelligent people, but they all have different opinions and when you get three different opinions you're thinking – "Well, that isn't clear any more. Who am I listening to here?" So it's important to try and get them to agree first, because if notes are clear, and you agree with them, I find them very easy to work on. I think the industry's changed; when that all happened with *Blow Dry* there weren't script editor courses, it was very loose and casual, so that has got better.'

Chips snuffles about under the table, hopeful for cake crumbs, as Simon discusses what kind of notes are most useful: 'It's not good when people offer solutions. Questions are great. Problems are fine. But the solutions are the writer's job. We've got the whole map of the piece in our head, not just the conundrum on a certain page, in a certain scene. Coming up with solutions is fine in a conversation, I wouldn't put them in writing,' he advises. To demonstrate a helpful type of note, he gives an example: 'For instance, in my pilot for the series I'm writing at the moment, they said, "We don't really understand why the lead character changes her position midway through and does something wholly unexpected and against what she had said earlier she was going to do." I thought I'd made it clear, so I read it again, and it's so nuanced, you miss it. For a pilot you can't possibly understand that the small thing that happens in her life is enough to make her make a big change. If you knew her really well, if it was episode eight, then that would be fine. Episode one, not at all. I completely understand that. For me that was a really good and a really clear note. It was someone saying, "We just didn't quite get why that happened. What is it about her that made her do this?" They had two really big notes that I need to address, the other one was: "Why on this day does this character decide to disappear?" One of the characters just drops out of life, and people think he's killed himself, he's just gone completely off the map: why that day? There's nothing in the script that indicates why. I mean, there is, but again it was too nuanced. And they're just two important questions, which are not solutions – that's my job – but really good questions.'

In terms of types of notes to avoid, Simon says, 'Having line notes I find really offensive – "This page this scene she says this, can she say this?" People trying to write for you is so disrespectful. And just aggravating! People still do it to me and I think, "I've been writing for thirty years nearly, don't tell me how to write dialogue – I'm really good at it! It's what I do." If I'm not good at it after thirty years I should be doing something else. So please don't comment on the dialogue. It's just rude. But absolutely talk about the piece as a whole and the problems with bits of it. Have a few big notes – that to me is really useful. But the massive great shopping list of every little thing they've noticed – all the "Oh is that a semi-colon, should it be a colon on that page?" All of that, it's really wearing, and it makes you respect any of the big useful notes less. It sort of puts up barriers. You think – this is a person going through looking for problems, rather than looking for a really wonderful piece of work.'

As the warm kitchen enables an unwrapping of layers of jumpers to a, somewhat vibrant, salmon-pink t-shirt, it prompts Simon to illustrate: 'If I say, "Ah, Venetia, that top doesn't really suit you", that's a tough thing to hear! And you go, "Wow, that's blunt." It's exactly the same with a script. If you say, "I don't like these scenes, they don't work, I don't like that character", it's crushing, even though you know it's coming from a place of trying to be helpful. But if you forget that, it becomes a really difficult process. If I say to my daughter, "You should do this" or "You need to do that", it's not going to go nearly as well as if I say, "Have you thought about . . .? What about if . . .? Perhaps . . .?" It's a relationship,' he emphasizes, 'and it's not a relationship with a person and a script, it's a relationship with a person and a person who has written a script, and that is really important. The relationships that work and the script editing processes that work, understand that instinctively – that it's two people in a room and a script, it's not a person and a script with this person sitting behind it who writes it. They're the same thing. So you have to treat it exactly the same way as if you're criticizing a person. Or not 'criticizing', but as if you're trying to go forward in a different way with someone. It's not "Don't wear that colour top", it's "Have you tried blue, Venetia? It'd bring out the colour of your eyes." Then you go, "Oh, OK!" If you go shopping with someone, that's the way you go, not "Gah! Don't ever wear that colour!" Which is what some people do. And the barrier immediately is up. If you say, "You need to do that as that's not working" – that's no way to go into any relationship is it? So keep the negatives out of it.'

Simon reflects, 'All the best relationships I've had with people who've edited my work, they're friendships effectively, because they're people who seem to understand both me and the work – which are kind of the same thing. It's an incredibly personal business. I guess the most important thing I could ever say to script editors is you cannot dissociate the work from the person. The person is the work. Even if it's a book adaptation, I'm in every line. So when you say, "I don't like this", how I take it is that you're saying you don't like me. I go, "OK, I'm going to take that I'm in a big, long meeting with someone who effectively doesn't like me because they don't like my work." Of course that's not what they're saying, but I think it's true of every single writer that they are the work. Unless it's just real jobbing stuff. But even then you're in it somewhere. Otherwise they wouldn't be employing you to do it. Your voice is in the work. People want me to do certain pieces because of my voice. My voice is me. So when you comment on the work you're commenting on me.'

For writers receiving notes, Simon advises, 'Read them three times. Probably read them the first time, tear them up and throw them in the fire. Read them a second time with a pen and tick the ones you agree with. Then read them a third time and with a great deal of honesty and soul-searching think which ones you really agree with and whether you can find solutions. Because who wants to be told what's wrong with them? Again – you tell somebody what's wrong with the script you're telling them what's wrong with them. So it's really difficult to sit there and read what your problems are. I've got a set of notes on the current project I'm doing and I haven't even opened the document,' he confesses, 'I just don't want to read it. I will steel myself to read it and these will be good notes, because they're really great people. But I will still be huffing and puffing and going, "Really?" And then the third, fourth read through I'll be going, "Yeah, what they're really saying is. . ., yeah, OK, fair enough, maybe blue does go with my eyes more."'

Conscious of the morning ebbing away, I cut short some of my enthusing about *Trust*, Simon's ten-part series for FX and the BBC about the kidnapping of Jean-Paul Getty Jr. 'No, don't edit yourself!' he jokes, 'All writers need to hear how brilliant they are! I know I'm being facetious, but I'm not. It's really important

– most writing comes from a fundamentally insecure place after all – that writers know that you basically like what they're doing. Because the work and the person are the same. That's the only really useful thing I have to say. That I believe is incontrovertible and works from the day I started writing to the day I stop writing – that if you're commenting on the work, you're kind of commenting on me. So if you think about it like that, you won't go wrong – because you won't say "I don't like that", because you wouldn't say "I don't like you."'

There's a brief interlude to retrieve a proffered toy from Chips, before returning to the development of *Trust*. 'It took me ages to work out what *Trust* was as an entity' Simon recalls, 'Because it appears to be a very easily graspable, obvious story – the richest man in the world's grandson gets kidnapped and he refuses to pay up. But actually it's a story about nothing happening. They don't pay, he doesn't get released – for month after month after month. Nobody talks to each other, it's about a lack of communication – which is terrible for drama! They are literally holed up in their bunkers – the grandfather not talking to the son, the son refusing to take calls from his ex-wife, who is the only person who cares about Little Paul getting released – so everyone's in their silos not speaking. Your lead character doesn't move because he's been kidnapped, locked up and blindfolded. When you finally drill down from what appears to be this wonderful, exciting story – a kidnap story with lots of money – it's actually a story about all the things you shouldn't make drama about: stasis, non-communication, completely unempathetic characters – and I thought how do we make ten hours of this watchable?'

Simon observes, 'The "small" notes are quite often the most devastatingly accurate. On *Trust* it was "Why do we care?" Why do we care about a rich kid who's got himself kidnapped? Brilliant note. And devastating. And it hung over the table for the entire writing process. That was a very early note from FX – "Do we really care about spoilt little rich kids?" Which I thought was really interesting. It made us concentrate endlessly on trying to understand why people behaved the way they did. You couldn't just say "He didn't pay the ransom because he was a horrible person" you have to know why he's a horrible person. The note about "Why do we care?" was fascinating to me. Because it was an absolute problem. A real, completely justified note. And I had to think about it almost for every scene.'

Simon reveals some of the process of developing *Trust*: 'One thing we knew we really needed in *Trust* was humour. Because it's really grim. Both in the story and in the characters. Because they behaved so appallingly, it was sort of funny in a very dark way. The kidnapper trying to get the ransom demand through to the newspaper and not getting put through to the right person, that's true – all that happened. I mean, it was fantastically inept!' he exclaims. Simon appreciatively describes the way the American network handled notes around nuances of humour. He recalls, 'No Americans found the kidnapper, Primo, in *Trust* funny at all. But he had his own sense of humour. The Americans read it and went, "He's really horrible!" and I said, "He's being funny, and I know it's dark, but it is humorous, and that's what rescues him as a character." They'd say, "That's an American-British thing isn't it? Because we're right on the line where we don't really understand this sense of humour." Things like that were really interesting because they said "We don't like the character" I said, "What if he's joking? What if that's a sense of humour?" And they went "Oh, OK!" And they let that go because they trusted that I knew what I was doing. They gave us free rein to be bold and backed us all the way. But they did push it, and that's fine, but it took me a long time to work out what it was they really had a problem with. Conversations can get, heated's not the right word, passionate and engaged; that's fine.

'I've never had a script that hasn't been improved with notes,' Simon says, 'Good notes are brilliant, important things. From the right people. Christian [Colson, producer of *Trust, Slumdog Millionaire, 127 Hours*] was always fantastic at giving notes. Because he's effectively a writer, he thinks exactly like a writer, he just can't write. Thank goodness! So he doesn't try. He doesn't say "Write this, write that." He absolutely understood the process of the scenes and precisely what we were doing in *Trust*, but he never tried to say "Why don't they say this, or why don't they do that".'

Considering notes from directors, Simon says, 'Really born directors, of which there are very few, bring their personality into every shot. It's quite hard to understand how that happens. Someone like Danny [Boyle] won't change a word of my script, because he's not a writer and he doesn't feel that's his place to do that. He's very respectful of the script and yet it's very clearly him behind the camera, behind every shot. There's no mistaking his style. Danny is a unique voice yet he wants you involved in everything, right the way through to editing. He's simultaneously highly collaborative and yet the end product is highly authored.'

Simon advises, 'If people are sensible they do bring writers into the edit. I always think it would be crazy not to. I was talking to my agent about this, and she has to fight to get some of her writers either on the set – just to visit, or into the edit room, just to see. And I think "Why would you not want the voice of the person who created this in the edit room?" Because editing is in reality just a different form of writing. It's just writing with the pictures: it's the same. Editors and writers completely understand each other. And they go through exactly the same process, right down to the nuances of how to get precisely the best out of a character when they're editing, fine cutting actors, so it makes perfect sense and I always have been involved in the edit room because it's crazy not to. But weirdly, writers are often shut out of that process. I don't know whether producers are scared of writers being involved in the edit or they don't care about writers' opinions. It's really odd. Because a writer will just go, "Oh, actually if you did this that could make that work." It's a different stage of the process, but it's still the story. It's still their story.'

As the rain outside becomes steadily more purposeful, Simon reflects on differences in writing for film and television. He explains, 'One of the differences is that film is essentially risk averse and TV embraces risk. Working with Billie-Jean King for *Battle of the Sexes* (Jonathan Dayton, Valerie Faris, 2017) was great. She'd always say, "Follow the money." If you want to know anything, follow the money. That's why she went up against Bobby Riggs, that's why she was instrumental in setting up the Women's Tennis Association, because they were getting paid so little, it was all about money. Her mantra is, "If you really want to know what's going on, find out who is getting paid what." It's the same in the film industry and the television industry. If you want to know why one is risk averse and the other one goes for risk, it's about the financial structure. In film it's like going to Las Vegas. You're raising a huge amount of money and you're gambling it all on red at the roulette table. You're putting it all on an opening weekend's box office. It may fly and you get rich, or you may lose your shirt. TV – completely different financial structure. They've got the money already effectively, and they're looking for ways to spend it. They've got sell-through deals to lots of different territories all over the world, they're not risking their house on your show, because they've kind of got their money back already. So what they need in this environment is to stand out. So they're saying "Take a risk, we want you to take a risk." Whereas in film, when they say that they really don't mean it. When you actually do take a risk, they say, "Oh my God, don't do that, that's really risky! We're already risking everything just making a film." Just the process of making a film is potentially hundreds of millions of dollars of risk. Nobody knows, no algorithm can tell you if you will get the money back or lose it all and get sacked. TV is completely different. They've got their money and they're asking "What are we going to spend it on?" So, the conversation in the room when you're discussing a script or a project is entirely different. You don't have people in a panic going "Don't do that! What if we lose that sector of the audience?" They're saying "How can we make this stand out from the crowd?" Which, to me, is another way of saying "How can we make it really good?" "How can we make it really fascinating and challenging and interesting?" That's catnip to writers. Writers love that.'

Simon's dog looks up at him, knowing that she'll get a walk, despite the rain. Before he heads out with her into the damp day, he muses: 'Storytelling is a great privilege and it's also a great responsibility. It has a magic attached to it ever since we started drawing and painting on cave walls. It's one of the ways we understand our lives, who we are. It's really difficult but that's what keeps it interesting. Writers, storytellers, used to be revered. They used to be the priests. Or the court jesters.'

Oxford, April 2019

Selected credits, awards and nominations

The Full Monty: Writer (1997), [Film] Dir. Peter Cattaneo, UK: Channel 4 Television, Redwave Films Twentieth Century Fox.
    BAFTA nomination – Best Screenplay – Original (1998)

Academy Award nomination – Best Writing, Screenplay Written Directly for the Screen (1998)

Writers Guild of America nomination – Best Screenplay Written Directly for the Screen (1998)

London Critics' Circle Film award – British Screenwriter of the Year (1998)

Among Giants: Writer (1998), [Film] Dir. Sam Miller, Fox Searchlight Pictures.

The Darkest Light: Writer, Co-Director (1999), [Film] Dirs. Simon Beaufoy, Billie Eltringham, UK, France: BBC, Canal+.

Newport International Film Festival, Rhode Island award – Best Director (2001)

Blow Dry: Writer (2001), [Film] Dir. Paddy Breathnach, UK, USA: Miramax.

Slumdog Millionaire: Writer (2008), [Film] Dirs. Danny Boyle, Loveleen Tandan, UK, USA: Film4, Celador Films, Fox Searchlight Pictures.

Academy Award – Best Writing, Adapted Screenplay (2009)

BAFTA award – Best Screenplay – Adapted (2009)

BAFTA nomination – Best British Film (2009)

London Critics' Circle Film Award – Screenwriter of the Year (2009)

British Independent Film Awards nomination – Best Screenplay (2008)

Golden Globe award – Best Screenplay – Motion Picture (2009)

Critics' Choice award – Best Writer (2009)

Writers Guild of America award – Best Adapted Screenplay (2009)

127 Hours: Writer (2010), [Film] Dir. Danny Boyle, UK, USA, France: Fox Searchlight Pictures.

BAFTA nomination – Best Screenplay (Adapted) (2011)

BAFTA nomination – Best British Film (2011)

Academy Award nomination – Best Writing, Adapted Screenplay (2011)

Golden Globe nomination – Best Screenplay – Motion Picture (2011)

Critics' Choice nomination – Best Screenplay, Adapted (2011)

Writers Guild of America nomination – Best Adapted Screenplay (2011)

Writers' Guild of Great Britain award – Best Film Screenplay (2011)

Salmon Fishing in the Yemen: Writer (2011), [Film] Dir. Lasse Hallström, UK: BBC Films.

Golden Globe nomination – Best Motion Picture – Comedy or Musical (2013)

Everest: Writer (2015), [Film] Dir. Baltasar Kormákur, UK, USA, Iceland: Working Title Films.

Academy of Science Fiction, Fantasy and Horror Films nomination – Best Action/ Adventure Film (2016)

Battle of the Sexes: Writer (2017), [Film] Dirs. Jonathan Dayton, Valerie Faris, UK, USA: Fox Searchlight Pictures.

Women Film Critics Circle award – Best Equality of the Sexes (2017)

Trust: Writer, Executive Producer (2018), [TV series] FX, BBC.

The Full Monty: Writer (2023), [TV Series] FX Network.

Sally Wainwright

'They're like your babies, scripts, and you don't criticize people's babies lightly do you? Not without risking getting duffed up.'

2 *Sally Wainwright, © Lookout Point Limited.*

It's 11 am. Sally Wainwright has been up since 4 am writing, and is cheerfully contemplating a canteen sandwich for lunch. Her jeans, checked shirt and relaxed warmth blend easily with the film school students queuing alongside her for coffee. She is a multi-BAFTA winning writer and director, one of the UK's leading television dramatists, awarded an OBE for services to writing and television. Her work, including *Gentleman Jack* (2019–22), *Happy Valley* (2014–23), *To Walk Invisible* (2016), *Last Tango in Halifax* (2012–20), *Scott & Bailey* (2011–16) and *At Home with the Braithwaites* (2000–03), achieving the triple crown of popular, critical and awards success. Her frequently Yorkshire-set dramas are lauded for their addictive storytelling and satisfyingly complex female characters.

After an English degree at York University, and a stint as a bus driver, she honed her writing craft on continuing dramas such as *The Archers* and *Coronation Street.* Heeding the advice of mentor Kay Mellor, Sally made the jump to creating original drama. First writing episodes of other people's series, including Mellor's *Playing the Field* (1999), then having her own series commissioned, *At Home with the Braithwaites*, an idea she began working on when she was eighteen.

At the age of fifty, established as a writer, Sally took on directing as well; starting with episodes of her hugely acclaimed series starring Sarah Lancashire as a West Yorkshire policewoman, *Happy Valley.*

Ensconced in a little office at the National Film and Television School, where she's due to teach a session for the directing students, Sally recounts how she came to write for radio drama serial, *The Archers.* After university, she took the play she'd written for her dissertation to the Edinburgh Festival. 'We got a shit review in *The Scotsman*, but it was a really good experience,' she cheerily recalls. Moving to London, she balanced earning a living with becoming a screenwriter. 'I didn't have any money, so I became a bus driver,' she says matter-of-factly, 'but on the back of having done the Edinburgh Festival I got my first agent, Meg Davis, when I was twenty-one. Looking back, that was a huge thing, to get an agent at that age – the confidence it gives you that someone believes in you, someone who's very intelligent, someone who's excited by what you write. At the time I don't think I appreciated how great that was to get an agent at that age. But I do now. And she got me the opportunity to write trial scripts for *The Archers.* So I resigned from the buses.'

Sally makes it sound, not easy, but achievable, to go from driving a bus to writing for the UK's longest running, much loved, radio drama serial, *The*

Archers. But she doesn't gloss over the grit and graft it took. Nor her appreciation of the chance, and her determination to make the most of it. She says, 'There're two important things I learned from working on *The Archers* – the first was discipline. I remember when I went to meet Ruth Patterson, the series editor, she asked me what I'd been doing. I said I'd been writing a stage play for the last six months and that I was about half-way through it. She said, "Well, you'll have to write five episodes of *The Archers* in two weeks," and I thought "Fucking hell!" But she did also tell me how much I'd be paid for doing it. So I thought, "Right, I'm getting up at 5 am every day. I'm going to put all the hours in".

'The second important thing it teaches you is – take it fucking seriously,' Sally emphasizes, 'I've always had the attitude – it might only be *Emmerdale* (1972), or an episode of *Casualty* (1986) or whatever – but it's an hour of television! It's precious. You make that hour of *Casualty* the best hour of *Casualty* there's ever been. And then people are going to notice you. Turn it into something you love. Turn it into something you're proud of. Turn it into something really exciting. That's the other thing that I learned back then – whatever you get offered, make it the best episode of it that's ever been. Rather than saying, "Oh, I'm just writing this till Steven Spielberg comes along and offers me a film." It's down to whether you really want to tell stories or not. And it's down to working hard.'

With a contemplative sip of tea, Sally considers script notes. 'On *The Archers* I would always get notes from Ruth [Patterson],' she recalls, 'I was really lucky with Ruth. She was a really nice person and she gave me good notes. My attitude at the time was that I was going to show that I could take notes. She gave me notes on my trial script and I realized that if I listened to her notes and implemented them she'd probably give me a job. And that's exactly what happened. But I was lucky, because they were good notes. I think when you're younger you don't know whether notes are good or not, you just know whether you trust the person giving them to you. You've got to listen to your instincts. Because one of the things I've learned over the years is that some script editors are just better than others. Really good script editors are like gold dust. They're like really good writers or really good directors – actually very rare.'

Reflecting on those early experiences with notes on *The Archers*, Sally says, 'I don't ever remember having a problem with Ruth's notes, but they were always very good. One obvious note she gave me early on was – "It's a sound medium, we need more sound effects." That was clear and helpful; to know when you're writing there needs to be more action where you can hear what's going on as well as hear the dialogue. The other great thing about Ruth was she gave me three notes, she didn't give me five hundred notes.' In contrast she says, 'The worst thing is when someone gives you far too many notes – because they don't really know what they want. Or they haven't put enough thought into what they want. Or they haven't put enough thought into how they're going to make those scripts work if they're not happy with what they're doing at the moment. So they kind of overwhelm you with notes. Less is more.'

Sally describes what it's like receiving notes: 'When you get notes it is like a criticism of what you've done. So that's hard. It's hard if you've put your heart and soul into writing it, which I always do. I always aim to hand in a perfect script. So if somebody comes back with notes it means it's not perfect anymore. And that's hard.' She recommends note-givers retain an awareness of how a writer may feel, advising, 'The most important thing for anyone giving notes is sensitivity. It's knowing that hopefully somebody has really put their heart into this. And to assume that they have. If a script is good you should respect it. Any notes that are given should be given on that basis. Whenever I give notes to students on their scripts I always work on the assumption that to have finished a whole script they must have put a lot of thought and passion into it. They're like your babies, scripts, and you don't criticize people's babies lightly do you? Not without risking getting duffed up.'

In practice, Sally advocates 'When you get script notes you should hopefully be in a position where you can go through them individually with the person who's giving them and discuss them. So that it's not just taking away a piece of paper and going "Oh, right, I will now go away and do these." I don't know if some writers go in with the attitude of "I know it's not perfect, but they're going to give me some notes anyway so it'll be fine." There might be some writers that think like that. Most writers work really hard. You have to. You can't do it if you don't work hard. So when you get notes, I think you have to sit down with the person who's given them to you and go through them forensically and discuss them. Some will be really obviously right. Sometimes you get notes and you go, "Oh God, that's brilliant, that's perfect, that's going to make everything so much better." It's brilliant when you get a note like that. When you get a note like that you want to do it because you can see the script could be made better. Then some are more debatable. You think, "Yeah, that is a good note, but I don't know how the hell I can do that. I can see why you want that, but I just don't know how to do it. It's something I already thought about doing and I couldn't find a place to do it." So you can debate that, and then if you debate it together you might come up with a solution. And then there are some notes where it's just misguided, and they've got the wrong end of the stick. That's why you should always challenge notes. Because occasionally,' she pauses and corrects herself with blunt honesty, 'well, not occasionally, it happens all the time, you will get a note where somebody has misunderstood something. So you shouldn't always just take the notes and do them, because you can't assume the person knows more than you do.'

In terms of how notes are best delivered, Sally maintains 'I prefer someone who feels it's a conversation rather than an order. And I prefer somebody who absolutely believes in the note. I've written the script with conviction, so if somebody's giving me a note I want them to have the same conviction about the notes they're giving. You can do both – you can have a conversation about something as a suggestion, but a suggestion you feel strongly about.'

'The trick with script editors is to find somebody you trust. And that's gold dust. Though I know you don't always have the choice!' Sally ruefully acknowledges. Explaining, 'Nowadays I'd take notes from Faith [Penhale, Executive Producer, *Gentleman Jack, To Walk Invisible*] because she's the brains behind the outfit. Now I'd only take notes off people at that level. But earlier on in my career I couldn't do that, I couldn't choose who I worked with. But you'd still have an instinct whether they were any good or not.'

Sally offers, 'I think another good bit of advice for people early on in their careers is to show willing. Even if you feel you've been overloaded with notes, use your instincts about what you believe is a good note, what's a bad note. Try to show willing. But also have the courage to say "I don't agree with you", if that's what's required.

'My aim in life is not to get any notes at all,' Sally declares, 'and as soon as I get them, to bat them all back as quickly as I can.' Qualifying, 'You do want good notes. If they're good notes I will listen to them, but often they're not good, often they're just misunderstood or misguided.' She observes, 'In my time I've taken notes that I didn't necessarily agree with, on the understanding that I might be wrong. I'm willing to go in and have a go at it. Sometimes by choosing to do that and making that effort, you can see what a note was about that you might not initially have been able to get your head round.'

A speckling of rain suddenly descends through the open skylight. Sally, in the cheerful spirits of a writer who's already delivered a script to deadline that morning, stops me jumping up to close it. 'Don't worry, it's quite nice!' she soothes, adding, properly concerned, 'Unless you're cold?' Having established we're both fresh air people, with northern blood in our veins, and sensibly equipped with cardigans, we continue. Sally turns to the question of how hard someone giving notes should push on a point if the writer doesn't initially agree with it. She reasons, 'I'd say it depends if you have a good relationship with someone you trust. Like with Faith [Penhale], most of the time if I say why I don't want to do something she would accept that. But sometimes if she doesn't, and she pushes and pushes, I'll know that I really ought to be listening. Because she wouldn't push like that if she didn't think it was important. So basically it's not doing it too often!'

Famed for her engaging, realistically complex characters, Sally is brisk in her assessment of whether she'd welcome notes on developing them: 'I don't think people can really help with that. Normally the notes I get would be about structure, whether the right beat happens at the right time. My characters tend to come fully formed. By the time I'm writing they're all kind of in place.' She reconsiders; conceding, 'But characters are what they do. A character is defined by how they behave, so you can discuss what they do, what the action is.'

Sally describes some of her development process, and how notes fit into it: 'In an ideal world I will do a really detailed scene breakdown first, and that'll take me between one and two weeks. And I'd send that in to get marked. Then if they have any notes at that stage that's a lot easier to handle, because you haven't committed to dialogue yet. And the shape of the story can be quite raw. Ideally I'll put as much detail and as much information in there as I can. And they'll feed back into that. Once I've written that, actually writing the episode is relatively easy. Because I'll have solved a lot of the problems at that point.

'In my story-line meetings for series two of *Gentleman Jack* at the moment, I've got Faith Penhale, Will Johnson and Stella Merz, who's my script editor, and they're all brilliant,' Sally enthuses, 'they're really, really smart people. When I was writing the first episodes of *Gentleman Jack* nobody else had read the diaries, they're huge and hadn't all been transcribed. But now we're onto the second series they have been, so we'll all have read them, and all be working on the same stories for each episode. Then I'll go away on my own and write a scene breakdown. But then when I've got home on my own I'll want everybody in the room again! And then I'll get everybody in the room and I'll want to go away and be on my own again!' she laughs. 'It's such an unusual project,' she adds, 'it's unique because of the nature of where the material comes from. It's not like an adaptation of a novel, because it's not a narrative, it's a diary, so sometimes it's just boring! Well, it's never boring with Anne Lister,' she says fondly.

Sally's passion for Anne Lister, and her desire to share as much of her enchantment as possible with an audience, influenced the development of *Gentleman Jack*. Sally explains, 'In deciding to use the device of Anne Lister talking to camera, which for me is a cinematic way of evoking that intimate connection the diaries give you, that's the kind of decision where I would always take advice and get notes on. I had a really strong instinct that I wanted to do it. We talked a lot about it as a device because it's one of those things that can go wrong. And can get a lot of criticism. I think the problem is you can start to rely on it, and allow it to give too much exposition. So I was quite nervous about doing it, even though I felt it was the right thing to do because it expressed that intimacy you get with the journals. I was quite nervous of it being irritating, because I sometimes find it irritating myself if it's overused, if you rely on it to get plot points across. So I was quite keen to get Faith's opinion about whether she felt it was working or not before we started filming.'

Thinking more broadly about the series and places notes play a role, Sally says, 'When you're planning out the structure and story across a series and introduce unexpected elements, you can get notes on that. I think there's often a fear, not a resistance as such, a bit of anxiety to make sure it works. Production companies often fear alienating the audience with anything off-kilter. But I always try to do things that are a bit different. Like in episode six of *Gentleman*

Jack there's a nightmare sequence – you cut to this scene where Anne Lister and Ann Walker have been hanged, and then you realize it's a nightmare. Sorry, spoiler!' she laughingly and apologetically interjects, continuing, 'then right at the end of episode seven there's a moment of telepathic connection between Anne Lister and Ann Walker. Those were two of the hardest moments to get right. And it wasn't that people giving notes were resisting them, they just wanted to make sure the audience would get that we were doing something slightly unusual.'

Reflecting on notes later in the process, Sally explains, 'Some notes you get from a producer will be to do with budget. When you see scripts that're production drafts there'll be bits where it says "omitted scene". Often what that is, at a certain point in pre-production you have to lock the script, and at that point you can't change the scene numbers, but then after that point the producer will often call and say "We're struggling with the budget, are there any scenes we can cut?" And they'll suggest a few. And then you'll see you can tell the story without that scene. You know, it felt important at the time, but actually, now that you've got the whole series written you can see that you can do without that beat. But because it's a locked script you can't change the scene numbers. Typically it'll be something like a character walking to a café, an exterior establisher, where nothing significant happens, but where the producer says we could save twenty grand.'

Broadcasters may also give notes; Sally illustrates with an example from the edit of her television directing debut, episode four of *Happy Valley*. She recalls, 'There's a scene set in the cellar, where Catherine, played by Sarah Lancashire, fights with Tommy Lee Royce, played by James Norton. Charlotte Moore, who was Controller of BBC One then, and is a really smart woman, gave the note that we needed to cut down the fight. I was really cross when I got that note, because I felt that it was important to show all of it. I'd been talking to Lisa Farrand, the police advisor on the series, about the scene and she's been beaten up twice in her career. She was nearly killed once. By a gang of lads in Halifax. Some bizarre twist of fate meant she didn't get murdered. I didn't know that, and we were rehearsing the fight scene and I said to her, kind of as a joke, "Have you ever been beaten up this badly?" and she said, "Only twice." So it felt important to show that ordinary women, who are police officers, do get that badly beaten up. So we structure this fight, with this brilliant fight co-ordinator Crispin Layfield, and I did think it was important to see Catherine get kicked between the legs by Tommy, as in the script, because it was a form of rape. He has raped her daughter, this is the worst thing he can do to Catherine, given what he's done to her daughter. I spoke to Sarah Lancashire to see if she was willing, and she was, because she felt it was important as well. But when Charlotte saw the edit of the fight she wanted us to cut it down by about half. And I was cross. Wound up. Anxious it wouldn't have the right kind of impact, if it was sanitized to the extent she wanted it.' But Sally and her editor, Richard Cox, re-cut it; finding ways to keep the tone and story Sally wanted, while taking Charlotte's note. Sally says, 'It was partly a channel decision on Charlotte's part, which is her job. *Happy Valley* went out at 9 pm, and that scene was towards the end of the episode. But retrospectively I think she was right. Not just the channel thing, but from an editorial point of view. I don't think it is sanitized. It is brutal. I think if it had gone out as I had originally submitted it, it would have been gratuitous. It would have been slightly too much. Whenever I've watched it since, and I've seen it a lot as wherever I go that's what tends to get shown, I think it tells the story really well. I think it's not gratuitous. I think it's succinct, which is always a good thing. You get the horror of it without it being too explicit. So at the end of the day I think it was a good call. But again Charlotte's one of those people – you don't ignore notes from Charlotte. Because she doesn't give them that often. So when she does, you listen to them. And she was right. At the time I was a bit cross and didn't want to cut it. But it's one of those times when you have to accept that if somebody at that level is giving a note they're doing it for a reason. She's not doing it to exercise her authority.'

It's nearly time for Sally to go and talk to the directing students. Happily full of energy, tea and canteen sandwich, she concludes, 'Storytelling's atavistic isn't it? It goes back to our primeval selves. I think it is a fundamental part of human nature to want to tell stories and to want to be told stories. I think after basic necessities like food and drink and clothes our ability to entertain each other is very fundamental.

'I love to entertain people,' she says, 'I think of myself as an entertainer as much as a dramatist. If I'm not entertaining people I'm not doing my job. And

I think to entertain people you have to engage people. You have to allow them to forget themselves and believe in what you're telling them. You have to take them out of themselves for an hour. And the best notes anybody can give you are about keeping the story focused so that you don't allow people to wander off to make a cup of tea.'

Beaconsfield, May 2019

Selected credits, awards and nominations

The Archers: Writer, eighty episodes (1989–93), [Radio] BBC Radio 4.
Emmerdale: Writer, episodes '*#1.1508*', '*#1.1509*', '*#1.1521*', '*#1.1521*', '*#1.1537*' and
   '*#1.1538*' (1990–91), [TV soap opera] Yorkshire Television.
Coronation Street: Writer, fifty-eight episodes (1993–99), [TV soap opera] Granada
   Television.
Playing the Field: Writer, episodes '*#2.2*'. '*#2.4*', '*#2.7*', '*#4.1*' and '*#4.4*' (1999–2000),
   [TV series] BBC.
At Home with the Braithwaites: Writer (2000–03), [TV series] Yorkshire Television.
   BAFTA TV nomination – Best Drama Series (2002)
   Royal Television Society nomination – Best Writer (2002)
Canterbury Tales: The Wife of Bath's Tale: Writer (2003) [TV Series] BBC.
   BAFTA TV nomination – Best Single Drama (2004)
Jane Hall: Writer, Co-producer (2006), [TV series] ITV.
The Amazing Mrs Pritchard: Writer (2006), [TV series] BBC.
Unforgiven: Writer, Executive Producer (2009), [TV series] ITV.
   BAFTA TV nomination – Best Drama Serial (2010)
Scott & Bailey: Writer, Executive Producer (2011–16), [TV series] ITV.
   Royal Television Society nomination – Best Drama Series (2012)
   BAFTA TV nomination – Best Drama Series (2012)
   BAFTA TV nomination – Best Drama Series (2013)
   Writer's Guild of Great Britain nomination – Best TV Drama Series (2012)
Last Tango in Halifax: Writer, Executive Producer (2012–20), [TV series] BBC.
   BAFTA TV award – Best Drama Series (2013)
   BAFTA TV award – Best Writer: Drama (2013)
Happy Valley: Writer, Executive Producer, Director episodes '*#1.4*', '*#2.1*', '*#2.2*', '*#2.5*',
   '*#2.6*', '*#3.1*', '*#3.2*' and '*#3.3*' (2014–23), [TV series] BBC.
   British Screenwriters' award – Best British TV Drama Writing (2014)
   Writer's Guild of Great Britain award – Best Long Form TV Drama (2015)

BAFTA TV award – Writer: Drama (2015)
Royal Television Society nomination – Writer: Drama (2015)
BAFTA TV award – Best Drama Series (2017)
BAFTA TV award – Best Writer: Drama (2017)
BAFTA TV Craft award – Writer: Drama (2017)
Royal Television Society award – Writer: Drama (2017)

To Walk Invisible: The Brontë Sisters: Writer, Director, Executive Producer (2016), [TV programme] BBC.

Gentleman Jack: Writer, Executive Producer, Director episodes '*I Was Just Passing*', '*I Just Went There to Study Anatomy*', '*Why've You Brought That?*' and '*Are You Still Talking?*' (2019–22), [TV series] BBC.

BAFTA TV nomination – Drama Series (2020)
Writer's Guild of Great Britain nomination – Best Long Form TV Drama (2020)

Edinburgh TV Festival Outstanding Achievement Award (2016)

Quick Fire Q&A 2: What's the best thing someone giving notes can do?

'Turn you into a better writer or director than you knew you were. And turn the film into a better version of the film than you had in mind.' – **Lone Scherfig**

'Love what they're giving notes on.' – **Krysty Wilson-Cairns**

'Be succinct.' – **Sally Wainwright**

'Give them quickly.' – **Russell T Davies**

'Gently guide you round to an issue that is plain but that you have not noticed.' – **Ben Wheatley**

'Be thoughtful. What may appear obvious will likely already have been thought about by the creative. They are sitting with it every day. What you say may seem like a problem solver but may be much harder in practice.' – **Lynne Ramsay**

'Take the time to say what you think works first.' – **Tomm Moore**

'It's asking the right questions. That's all I really want from a script editor. I don't necessarily want ideas or suggestions or answers. A really good question is enough.' – **Simon Beaufoy**

'Offer a thought process with as much clarity as possible – you have to be able to communicate well.' – **Amma Asante**

'Remind and focus in on the most important aspects of the story that you're telling, within the scenes, characters or overall continuity, and keep honing them to be as efficient, effective and 'honest' as possible.' – **Corin Hardy**

'Identify and help protect the unique strengths of the material, and diagnose the weaknesses of what needs to be developed.' – **Michael Pearce**

'Listen. Be encouraging and positive. Think carrot not stick. Say when you like stuff – that's really important. And don't feel you have to change everything. You can ring-fence certain stuff and tell the writer that you are ring-fencing things – "This is good, it already works."' – **Alice Lowe**

'The best thing that could possibly happen is that someone unlocks you to an absolutely brilliant idea that you haven't yet had. Sometimes when you write the first draft of a script it can come fully formed as a very tight piece, and sometimes it's almost as if your subconscious is on the page and the piece is much more raw as a result. In that sense, there are times where you need the help of someone else to tell you what kind of movie you're trying to make.' – **Edgar Wright**

Russell T Davies

'Do listen to those notes, because sometimes it's not just looking at the page in front of you, they're looking right into your soul. And if they get you, those good people, they're telling you who you are and what you should do and how to write. And you never forget those notes, never.'

3 *Russell T Davies – courtesy of The National Film and Television School, photography by Lesley Posso.*

Ordinarily the disembodied head of a Cyberman does not radiate cosiness. Yet somehow, the one nestled in a corner of Russell T Davies's sofa, does. Enveloped perhaps in the infectious warmth of a man whose conversation flows easily from the serious to uproarious laughter. Much like his scripts. Scripts behind iconic television series such as *Queer as Folk* (1999), *Doctor Who* (2005) and *It's a Sin* (2021).

In November 2021 Russell wrote a series of daily Instagram posts; anecdotes from his thirty-year career. There were enough shows for him to reference a different one each day of the month. Famed now as a writer, he started out as a producer on 1980s children's television show *Why Don't You* (1985). In his spare time he wrote and pitched a sci-fi children's drama, *Dark Season* (1991), which was snapped up by the BBC. He continued writing and producing episodes of *Children's Ward* (1994), wrote for various drama series, and story-lined soap opera, *Coronation Street* (1993). In the late 1990s he wrote what became his first adult drama television series commission, *Queer as Folk*. He is widely credited with re-energizing *Doctor Who* as showrunner of the revived series. He extended the *Doctor Who* world with adult spinoff series *Torchwood* (2006) and children's spinoff *The Sarah Jane Adventures* (2007), bolstering the Welsh television production industry in the process. His work also encompasses the ambitiously interconnecting series *Cucumber* (2015), *Banana* (2015) and *Tofu* (2015); an adaptation of *A Midsummer Night's Dream* (2016); mini-series *A Very English Scandal* (2018), relating the real-life scandal around Liberal MP Jeremy Thorpe; futuristic series *Years and Years* (2019) and 1980s set series *It's a Sin*. His awards include an OBE for services to television drama, alongside a mantelpiece extension's worth of BAFTAs.

As the interview is about to start, the doorbell heralds the arrival of some hand-delivered *Doctor Who* designs, fresh from Cardiff to the showrunner and his sofa-dwelling Cyberman. The designs sit peaceably on the desk, ready for their notes. The Cyberman head gazes unblinkingly at them while Russell chats.

Russell begins, 'Obviously you have to listen to notes. Because you'll learn something good out of them. You have to remember – all notes are trying to make the script better. And you want your name on something that is better. But you've got to balance it. There's no safe option here. It's the tightrope between absolutely believing in something and refusing to let a note damage it, balanced against the question how likely is it you've written something so perfect that other people are going to damage it? What version of your life are you living here? And how much are you the hero of your own events? But sometimes you are! Sometimes a piece of fiction is a really delicate thing and it needs protecting. But equally I've heard of writers who won't change a thing. How you take notes is how you operate in the world, it is all about who you are in the end.'

Reflecting on the attributes necessary for a successful writing career, Russell says, 'I get asked to do a lot of talks, with you at the NFTS, with Channel 4, with John Yorke's new writers' academy. These days, in my big speeches to writers I say: if you want to join in with this industry, go and sort yourselves out. You will never sort yourself out because you're a writer, therefore you're mad, so you will never get rid of all your problems. But I have been in this job a long time, and many years ago I knew wonderful writers who drank too much, I knew wonderful writers who took too many drugs, I knew wonderful writers who just couldn't cope with life, writers who simply couldn't cope with deadlines, to an extent that you don't hear of these people any more. Their careers have vanished, and they were brilliant writers. You've got to be prepared to sort yourself out. If you always deliver late, go and get some therapy. If you want a career, this is hard and you spend all day long with yourself, so whatever kinks you've got in your personality you need to work on. You'll never solve those problems, but you need to make yourself professional and workable and diligent. And you need to be able to face the hard work of it. So that then becomes part of the note-taking procedure as well.

'You've got to take the notes,' he reiterates, 'so if you've picked up this book thinking, "Great, I'll learn tips from experienced writers on how to avoid notes" – go and sort yourself out. Because you shouldn't even have that attitude to begin with. Obviously if someone says to me, "I've got some notes", yeah, my heart sinks, and that's partly because I thought it was perfect. That's pride more than anything. I did not hand it in thinking this is a working draft. I thought it was ready for transmission. But then I get the notes and of course they're making it better, of course they're making it clearer, of course you can cut this whole sequence. I think the best notes you always knew all along. I always get a feeling of that, I roll my eyes, and go "Oh yes, of course! Why didn't I concentrate?" That's why it's a good process. There's very often a chime in your head going, "I knew that bit was wrong!" That's when you know you're with a good note-giver; listen out for those people, where it chimes.'

Russell recounts an experience with notes from early in his writing career: 'The script that changed my life was an episode of *The Grand* (1997). I'd got a job on *The Grand* and somehow I ended up becoming the sole writer on it. Because I could deliver. I eventually wrote one episode that was different. I took the character of a barman and made him gay. The series was set in 1921, so this is a story about a working-class gay man in 1921, and it was stratospherically better than anything else I'd ever written. Because I was finally writing gay. The producers and the script editor, they quite liked the script, but they didn't like it because it broke the format. The format of that show was A story, B story, C story – family story, guest staying at the hotel story, staff story, in varying patterns. This story broke the format completely, by telling one story.' Russell leans forward conspiratorially, confiding, 'I've got to say, it was infinitely cleverer that script, it actually did have stories for all the other members of staff woven into that story, and frankly no one saw that. I'm still angry about it now!' He delivers this last like a joke, yet it is remembered, over twenty years later. He explains, 'I was told very good, pat on the head, but change it. That was the biggest note I've ever had, and I refused to take it. I'm amazed when I look back at myself. But I showed the script to my agent, who said, "It's very good", I showed it to Paul Abbott and he said, "This is excellent, you have to stand by it." I also thought the notes I was getting in order to improve it weren't good. If someone comes up with a note that improves the script, wonderful, I'll have it. But these I absolutely knew didn't make it good. So I refused. I was so rude to them!' He drops his head into his hands in embarrassment at the memory, then continues the story, 'I was called in for a meeting where my only defence was I knew I was the only writer who could deliver this show and we were in a panic. We were shooting. We were into the last three months of production. If I didn't deliver the last episode they were completely fucked. So I kind of knew I had them over a barrel. They couldn't sack me or throw out my script, so I had that as a back-up. You shouldn't be in this position. I mean, I have just written a series of posts on Instagram about thirty years of my scripts, and this is the only time I've been this bullish, or this trapped, it's not normally like this. I thought the only way I can win this is to go ballistic. I still believe in that – if your back's absolutely against the wall then go nuclear, because you might as well! I do think it's a good policy. But I was so rude to them. I sat there and criticized the producer for being in his choir! That winter I was nominated for an International Emmy for *Children's Ward*, the producer was nominated for an International Emmy for something else and we all ended up in New York. I felt so bad about what I'd said that I wrote this apology and walked through New York in the snow to leave it at the desk in his hotel. And he was very lovely about it. The episode went out exactly as I wanted it, and afterwards he did say "You were absolutely right." He was astonished at the mail he got about that episode, saying how much it meant to people, from gay men, from families, from mothers, he showed me the letters saying, "I was wrong and you were right." It's rarely that simple or that victorious, and writers are rarely that right. Literally out of thirty years, it's the one example I can pull up where I can say I was absolutely right and they were absolutely wrong. I thought I'd start with that just to make myself sound good for five minutes!' He laughs that big, infectious laugh, adding, 'Please keep that bit in!

'I've launched into this with stories of villains where I'm inevitably the hero,' he says, 'but most people are nice. That's the fact. Most people we're all soft liberals making lovely dramas intended to make people happy, or sad but glad that they've seen it. We're profoundly left wing, liberal people, and we're nice. It's a very nice industry. People say it's tough at the high end, we're not actually down a mine shaft! It's a nice business to work in. But that infects the notes. Notes are very often delivered politely. And that doesn't always help, because they seem soft then. You can't always sense the importance of a note. When people give notes they don't know what's in your head. They don't know what's wrong with something, but they do know that something is wrong. We all know when a story isn't working. We all come out of a cinema shrugging about a film. We all watch the last episode of a drama and feel it didn't quite work and moan online. And we all have a cup of tea in the kitchen going, "Oh, I've gone off that show." We all know when something doesn't work. It doesn't mean we can give good notes on it. People aren't walking out of a cinema going, "Well, if the inciting incident had been twenty minutes earlier then the character arc would have been more fulfilling." You just come out with a feeling of dissatisfaction.'

He asserts, 'You must listen to notes, but you must know when notes are bad.' He gestures with his hands as though balancing finely weighted scales, 'That's the tricky thing, because how do you do that? I think the first ten or fifteen years of your career are figuring out who to work with. Working out who you trust. I know sometimes from the outside we all look like a club, a bit exclusive, me and Nicola Shindler or me and Julie Gardner, we look like a clique. Actually, it's very hard won that. In every job, in all of life, you find people to spend time with because you agree with them and you get on with them, and maybe they challenge you, but you love them. It's the same with work as in life, you work very hard to find those people. To this day I'm absolutely terrified of getting a bad note off Nicola Shindler. It keeps my standards high. If I handed a script to her and she said "This isn't very good", I'd absolutely die. So what looks like a clique, what looks like chums patting one another on the back is very hard won and very important and keeps me at the top of my game.'

Digging into the detail of receiving notes in practice, Russell advises, 'People who're giving you notes don't know what's wrong, but they know that something's wrong. So you should listen to them. It's very often the case that they'll point at say page seventeen, and it might be a vague, "Is this exciting enough?" or "Am I interested in this person?" Once you go away and think about it, and there's a great power in going away and thinking about notes, you can't always think of it on the spot, you realize actually it's not about the excitement, and it's not about whether that character's interesting. But listen to the fact that there's something wrong on page seventeen. Some of the tension has gone there. And it probably means something was wrong on page ten, or on page one.'

For note-givers he cautions, 'Be aware of the amount of work you're asking someone to undertake if you have lots of notes. But I wouldn't pussy-foot around. If you have a hundred notes, give them. At least then the writer's got some idea of the size of the issue. If you give five notes, the writer's kind of planning their next job let's be honest,' he laughs, 'whereas if you give a hundred notes, generally they know, "Right, set aside a month", or two weeks, whatever schedule you're on, but they know "Oh, this needs a lot of work." No one likes giving a hundred notes, but I think you have to. If the writer starts to cry, then maybe stop around note fifty. It is a sensitive process.'

Warming to the theme of things to be cautious of with notes, for writers he advises, 'I'm very wary of "fixes". An awful lot of writers, and I do this myself,' he puts a forgive-me-for-my-sins hand on his chest, 'you'll be given a note – "Can she explain why she's doing this?" so you put in a speech. And that speech then gets said and that speech gets transmitted and it doesn't work. Putting in a speech explaining why something's happening very rarely works. That's wallpapering over a crack and the crack's still there. But at a very late stage of notes, or post read-through notes, you often get that – "Can you explain why she's doing this?" and they're dangerous those notes, because they undermine things slightly. You end up writing stuff that's not particularly valid or not particularly interesting. Either it's better off without that speech or there's something more profound going wrong where you didn't explain why she was doing X, Y and Z on page one.'

Before becoming a screenwriter, Russell worked as a television producer and script editor, now he is often also an executive producer or showrunner. He reflects on how this extensive experience and depth of understanding of making television influences how he gives notes. 'I think in some ways it makes me a terrible script editor,' he confesses, 'I've lost friends when I'm script editing, because I know every trick, and I know every weakness and I'm quite merciless with it. Half the trouble with notes is that they're couched in very polite language because people are afraid of upsetting the writers. That's correct. Writers are delicate. I can't be bothered with that! If something's rubbish I tell people it's rubbish. I've literally lost friends. One man on *Doctor Who* didn't speak to me for two years.' He confides, 'I was so busy on *Doctor Who* I didn't notice! Until he said, "I'm sorry, you were right, I shouldn't have not spoken to you for two years." I was like, "Oh, didn't you? I missed that bit."' He roars with laughter. 'It was because I'd sat there with this scene and said, "That's a very lazy line. You wrote that at two o'clock in the morning when you were thinking about going to bed, or maybe it was dinner time and you were thinking about dinner, and you dashed that line off with no thought." Which isn't nice to hear. But I was right. That's the kind of note I give. I can smell it, I can tell, and I'm cross when writers haven't been diligent, haven't done the homework. So I choose not to script edit, with the exception of *Doctor Who*. I'll do it as a favour for someone who's new, then I'll be very nice about it. If you're a mate who's written their first script, or if it's via the BFI Flare mentor scheme, I'll be very, very nice about things. If it's for transmission I'll be really tough about it, because millions of pounds are going to be spent on it. Millions. A props man is going to be working till midnight making a prop, and someone's hiring the cars and someone's cooking the tea for everyone, there's a lot of money being spent on it.'

He ponders, 'I don't know if I'm right to always comment strongly. I'm working with Nicola Shindler on something at the moment that we're both exec'ing and hoping will get made. It's by someone who's a very good writer and a friend, so I know him well enough to give very tough notes. I will send him: "This is rubbish, think of something better." It's interesting working with Nicola for the first time giving notes together, she's loving how tough the notes are! She's sitting there saying, "I wish I could say that" but she feels she doesn't have the authority to say that because she doesn't write.'

Russell cites an instance of giving notes to Steven Moffat on a script for *Doctor Who*: 'It's very rare to be able to give notes to a writer of that standard. My god he hands in a script and it's like a little shaft from heaven is shining down on your desk. He did that very famous *Doctor Who* story, *The Empty Child* (2005), that World War Two story with the little kid with the gas mask. It was brilliant. I think some of my notes on that slightly damaged it. I think there was an even better version. With hindsight I think I got rid of something because I didn't quite like it, and now I look back and think, why didn't I quite like it? It was part of collateral damage, there was something else I didn't like and he happily cut that, and this one character went with the cuts. I look back and think that character should have stayed. That character made even more perfect sense of the entire plot. It was a character who never spoke, you thought there was a great big science-fiction reason, and it turns out the character never spoke because the character was German. This is in 1941 in London so of course he wouldn't have spoken. Isn't that good! I cut that character, for other reasons, and it had made perfect sense, so I think I damaged that script. I was talking to Steven quite recently and I said, "Should we have kept John in that script?" I think that was the character's name, and he was lovely about it and said, "Oh, never mind". But we should have. I'm right now, it's taken me fifteen years to work out this note but I'm right now, I wasn't then.'

Russell expands on his role with regards to notes as showrunner on *Doctor Who*: 'It's easier on that in a way. It's a multi-million-pound production; we're spending an awful lot of the BBC's money, so I break all my own rules on that. I'll re-write everyone's scripts, well, except for Steven Moffat's. I'll re-write anyone's scripts, sometimes I'm paid for that, sometimes I'm not. It's a great big public property *Doctor Who*, it's not one writer's cherished vision. In any other circumstance I would say protect the writer's vision, and I do, it's absolutely to protect their vision. That's not true of *Doctor Who*. It's a great big franchise, it's a public property, it's loved, it's loved by children, it's got history, it's also brand new every week. So the rules go out the window. You'll get an awful lot of budget-y type notes, because it's such an expensive thing, so that will weigh down heavily. There's no note session on it without me, because I am the showrunner. No matter how busy I am, the one thing I won't miss is script meetings. I mean, you saw designs have just been couriered to me in the middle of the day from *Doctor Who*, but sod that, nothing is more important than the script. All that CGI, all that effort, all that set building, all those prosthetics are nothing without fixing the script. So yes, I was a very, very heavy script editor on that. And I was not there to protect the vision of the writer, I would trammel over that. I lost friends genuinely, and I know other writers very bruised from going through sessions on that with me. I'm not good, in the sense that I get sarcastic. And that's not good, that's not healthy. I can't help it, I'm tired, you get very tired in that job. I could help it, I should try harder to help it, but I get very cross when writers write rubbish, and that's when I get sarcastic.'

I venture that ordinarily he protects the voice of the writer, but when he's a showrunner he protects the voice of the show, Russell enthuses, 'Yes, yes, yes, that is it absolutely! I've only ever showrun *Doctor Who*, I've worked on soaps as well and I suppose it's the same, you are looking after the show not the individual voice. And sometimes that individual voice is a world class aria. Sometimes Steven Moffat delivers you a script. And then, oh my god. I think on that very first script of his I gave bad notes, after that I learned to kind of dot the 'i's and cross the 't's. I mean *Blink* (2007), one of the finest pieces of drama ever written, a world class piece of television, I think the only helpful note I gave on that was that the house had a really boring name. It was called something like Hargreaves House, and I said "Can't we give it a more dramatic name?" and he went and called it "Wester Drumlins", I still love that!'

We turn to his own writing and how he works with notes. Russell is consistently complimentary about his long-time producer Nicola Shindler, so as part of his early development process does he ever talk things over with her when he's wrestling with something in a script? 'No, I don't,' he says, 'I wait until I trust myself and sometimes I curse myself for this, thinking, "Why didn't I just phone up?" Nicola Shindler would drop dead of a heart attack if I phoned up and said I wanted to talk through a script that I hadn't delivered yet. She'd be like, "What?!" Actually I think she'd love it. I do wonder to myself why I don't. But once it's delivered then it's open for it. At the same time, when someone says "I've got notes" my heart sinks. I refuse to believe anyone looks forward to notes. I read interviews with writers where they go, "Oh good, I can't wait for the notes" and I think, "You liars!" I also think, have some more pride in your work for god's sake. Nicola is just wonderful and honest. Also she delivers them fast. There's nothing worse than waiting two weeks. Nicola will give me notes that day. That's important I think. Writers are never going to know their scripts better than in those days, every single semi-colon is in my head. If you ask me what happens on page twenty-six, I could tell you. I couldn't tell you that weeks after I've written it.'

Russell describes how he sets about integrating notes into a script. He explains, 'I might have a note on page five, on page ten, on page fifteen, but when I go home I start on page one. Overnight I've had better thoughts anyway. So I go through the entire script and I start to re-write things all the way through. If you give me ten notes on a script you don't get a script with ten changes back. I've got a script that's on page forty now, when I go back to it I'll start on page one. Cutting it, cutting it, cutting it.'

For someone giving notes, firstly Russell advocates having the courage to do it: 'Of course the notes are going to make something better. I have had people say, "Oh my god, delivering notes to Russell T Davies, that's hard!" as if I know everything! Well that's just daft, get over yourself. At home we're all critics, we can pick up a book by Margaret Drabble or we can watch a screenplay by Paul

Abbott and we've got notes. We've always got notes. We're always sitting there going, "I love that film, but I would have done this." That's how my sister watches TV, she's a teacher, but she'll watch something on Netflix and go, "I think he should marry her. Oh, I don't like that he didn't marry her." We're all giving notes all the time. So it's completely fine.'

Russell then outlines the types of note he finds most useful. 'I like a note to be honest and precise,' he says, acknowledging, 'and I know that's hard. You get given a note because you're not getting something across – so how do they know what I'm trying to get across if I haven't got it across? So notes are fundamentally guessing, and they might be in completely the wrong area – that's not the note-giver's fault. It's because you haven't said what you mean to say. Or at a deeper level, you haven't worked out what you were trying to say. And we're all full of contradictions, things might be clashing, deliberately or not. So that's why notes are tough, when they're just aiming at a general direction. There are simple notes that are like firing an arrow into a bullseye on a target, you know – "He needs to say he's going to London, you forgot to say that." "Oh right, put in a line." So those notes are lovely. But there are bigger notes – "I don't know why she loves him" and that's hard. But also, that's a nice note because it opens up a door. Sometimes you presume things in your head and you forget to say them. That can happen where you might have lived with characters in your head for years, so you know that she loves him, to the extent that you don't actually say so on the page.'

If people offer solutions or suggestions as part of their notes Russell says, 'I love that; though I rarely accept them. I find people asking questions more annoying. I find that's an arch way of phrasing their note. It's kind of like' (he puts on a wheedling sing-song voice), '"Why do you think Cathy loves John?" and I sit there and go, "What you're saying is, you don't believe it." So tell me you don't believe it. That's me wanting a blunter note. The questions are genuine, but I'd much rather somebody said, "I don't believe these two are in love" rather than, "Why is she so attracted to him?" Oh shut up, that's just a waste of time. But it's very clearly telling me there's something I haven't delivered, without telling me there's something I haven't delivered. So I'd rather things were more direct. I can see why people deliver notes as questions. Anyone that wants to deliver notes that way, carry on doing that, because writers are delicate and these are delicate things we're dealing with.'

He elaborates further on suggestions in notes: 'To be honest I get that less now, people offering suggestions, but Nicola [Shindler] would do it, like, "Why don't they bump into one another?" I'm lucky in that I've got a television shaped brain, so I know instantly whether something works or not. If someone says to me, "Why don't they bump into one another in the shops?" I will say yes or no immediately. I don't have to go away for a day to think about it. I don't have to go away for a second to think about it. If it's great I'll go "Oh, brilliant, they bump into each other in the shops, that's fantastic!" If it's not going to work, people do sit there and talk to me about these two characters bumping into each other in the shops for half an hour, I sit there going, "You're wasting your time, it's not going to happen." But I'll find something else that gives you that "bumping into" effect somehow. We're kind of taught these days not to suggest things to writers, there's a school of thought that says don't do that, but I think you might as well. Otherwise you're just pretending. It certainly wouldn't offend me. I'd rather someone actively engaged with the script and inventing things, rather than somebody questioning things. I find the questions whining. I find the practical stuff fascinating.'

We discuss notes asking for characters to be more 'likeable'. He says, 'It's funny, because of *Doctor Who* I often get accused of being a very sentimental writer. Actually I think it's the opposite, my scripts are often very tough, and I do have to be led towards making it more likeable sometimes.' He recalls, '*Years and Years* went through a very long process of not being commissioned. It was a tough piece of work. Draft one of *Years and Years* was a lot tougher. It's a show in which tough things are happening – immigration's a problem and there's racism afoot and technology's running wild, but the family in the very first draft was a lot more real. The finished version of *Years and Years* is about a very lovely family that loves each other very much, clinging together as the world's falling apart. That wasn't in the first draft. It was a much more real and tough family, who were friendly and lovely, but like all families there were edges and they were arguing. On that first night when the nuclear bomb goes off, they're all gathered for a family barbeque. All the family in the garden eating burgers, having a laugh, but actually they're all kind of falling out with one another. Russell Tovey discovers that Anne Reid has written her will – and I love this story, I will use this story somewhere else – he discovers that she's also left money to the grandchildren. This happens now, people do this, you leave money to your children, and you also leave it to the grandchildren, so Russell as one of four children thought it was going to be split into quarters, but no, it's being split into eighths or ninths. As a childless man, it's not fair. So this all comes out. It was a very good script in that as the world is fracturing, the family is fracturing. And it's also like, "You think you've got problems? They're about to launch a nuclear weapon!" It was kind of putting it all in perspective. But it led to a much tenser afternoon, in which metaphorically the tensions of the world are rising. It made great sense as a script. It was a very believable family story, set against the backdrop of nations falling apart. Also, if you remember, in that episode when the four-minute warning goes off Russell Tovey leaves the house. He goes off to find the man he's fallen in love with. This story about the will really pushed him out of the door. In the finished transmitted version, him leaving is a little bit more of a leap of story. So that was a script that worked. There was no way that this edgy family didn't work. It was a modern family, it was a really good family – we can all be getting on, but money burrows into our hearts, and niggles can become huge. That script got knocked about for a good six months. It went all the way to people like Charlotte Moore and Piers Wenger. And they kept on giving notes and they didn't know what was wrong with it, but they weren't commissioning. We had a dinner in Manchester where we talked about the characters and I was sitting there going, "I don't know what you want from this, I don't know what the notes are, I will re-write anything but I don't know what they are." I think the word "warmer" kept being used, with hindsight this all makes sense, but at the time, before you click that, it's not much good as a note is it, "warmer"? What does that mean? In the end I had to go home and sit there and go, "This isn't being commissioned, I need to do something. It's a really good script. I need to do something about this. I need to work out what their problem is." Because their notes, which again were very polite, and maybe there is a slight hesitation in giving Russell T Davies notes, I had to work out what they meant. In the end I sat there and I worked out what the note was, which was – make the family warmer, make the family happier. Which I hated doing, because I love that story about the will, I think it's so true. But I had to take a deep breath, and to be blunt I felt like I was simplifying it. And I didn't like that. This simpler family where they're friends, but actually, that's what got it commissioned. That cracked it. Suddenly they were a nice British family, while nuclear war breaks out.'

Russell concludes, 'That was a good and bad note session in that they didn't know what the note was, but they were right to keep on giving notes. In the end, I'm the one getting paid and I'm the one that wants to get it made and I had to do the hard work. I can remember sitting at that desk thinking, "Oh, I'll simplify this family, I'll make it sentimental", but when you put it all together, when you put that cast together it's lovely, it's gorgeous, it works. So they were notes I probably did reluctantly. But I wouldn't have done them if I thought they didn't work.'

In *It's a Sin* there's a moment when Keeley Hawes, playing the lead character's mum, says in passing to her son that his grandfather, her father, "was a terrible man". A handful of words. But they can entirely change our perception of, and sympathy for, her character, with its subtle, almost throwaway, revelation hinting at her past. Russell discusses handling notes which might ask for subtle things to be made more overt. He acknowledges, 'Often it does happen, and it's a fair note. The great antecedent of all of these is the end of *Queer as Folk*, where Stuart turns to Vince and says, "It was good enough for me." An entire love story in one line. I remember thinking that wouldn't work. You sit through eight hours waiting for that man to say one nice thing to his best friend, and then he suddenly does when they're talking about *Doctor Who*. I thought that wouldn't work. I give notes to myself, and I sat there going, "Who is listening to one line? Who's involved enough for one line to work?" When that final episode got transmitted in Manchester there was a great big meeting of like two thousand people on Canal Street, where there was a club that got packed out to watch that final episode. That line was said and the entire room sighed. And I went "Oh, it worked."' He folds his hands over his heart as though embracing the memory, adding, 'It was the greatest validation I've ever had.'

He clarifies, 'It does prove you can do an entire plot in one line. I always trusted that with *It's a Sin*. Also it's the final episode, there's an awful lot to pack into that episode. When I do get notes like that sometimes, I get very blunt. When I'm being rude, I sit there going, "Well, what do you want to lose?" And I throw that note back. Because I'm very practical, I'm very annoying about throwing a note back, saying "What do you want to lose then? Because that's going to take three pages. Tell me which three pages you want to cut." I'm so absolutely rude about doing that!' He laughs at himself and puts his head in his hands. 'And then they panic and go, "Oh no! We don't want to cut anything!" so I go, "Well, what do you want to do then?" Oh, I'm horrible! I think the constant note of this conversation is how horrible I am. I'm quite pleased to do an interview where I sound a bit horrible, because all interviews are all, "Oh you're so lucky, it's so lovely." This,' he circles with his finger to indicate everything we've been talking about, 'is also true of the job, it's tough.'

Moving on from merrily attempting to destroy any 'national treasure' reputation, he reflects on notes around tone and balancing humour with darkness. 'I think if you're working with me, you know I'm going to do that,' he says, 'it would be odd to walk into a meeting with me and go, "This scene's funny and then it turns sad" – yeah, have you ever read anything I've ever written? But I learned this very early on – sometimes you get given a note that you carry with you for life. This is why you must listen to all notes, because somehow, somewhere in there you will be told something brilliant. Somewhere you might hear something that will sustain you for your entire life. Very early on in *The Grand*, lovely Tony Wood, who was my producer, said something I've always remembered. There was a really quite shocking scene, where a maid had been gang-raped and had killed one of the men who had raped her. It was quite discretely done, off-stage, but then she kills the one man left in the room. So she has to get out of the hotel, she thinks she can run away. She's gone insane, she's been through the biggest trauma imaginable and is wild. She gets hanged for this in the final episode. But in this episode she has to try and get out of the hotel. So she has to sneak through the kitchen at night. It's about two o'clock in the morning and that night there's been a party in the kitchen, so there's some drunk maids still in the foreground. They have the funniest dialogue I could write, one of them's so drunk she says, "Has that door always been there?"' He laughs, 'I love that line, it's the kind of thing you say when you're drunk isn't it? While in the background a woman who has been gang-raped is sneaking to her room to try and get the last of her tuppence that's under her pillow so she can get out of the country. Quite in passing Tony Wood said, "Only you would write that scene." I've never forgotten that. He said,

"Only you would write something so dramatic with something so funny in the foreground and put them together." It was a passing comment, but sometimes someone says something that . . .' He runs out of words and puts a hand on his chest, marvelling, 'Listen to me, I can still quote it word for word, it goes right to my heart. And that's when I was young, that's someone pointing out: that's what you do and that's what you do well. So do listen to those notes, because sometimes it's not just looking at the page in front of you, they're looking right into your soul. And if they get you, those good people, they're telling you who you are and what you should do and how to write. And you never forget those notes, never. Bless him. Love Tony Wood. To this day I think about it all the time, that sentence will often crop up in my head. I've never told him this, he probably doesn't even know he ever said it.'

After a reflective pause remembering his friend's words, and a restorative sip of tea, Russell turns to handling conflicting notes from different sources. He advises, 'It's very easy to bunker down and make everyone your enemy, and sometimes you are working with idiots! But I think you have to recognize that everyone's there to help you and you have to put up a white flag and say you're getting conflicting notes. You've got a script editor, you've got a producer. If they're genuinely conflicting notes they should see that, don't think you're alone. Because they're there to help. I'm coming back to my thing that we're all nice people. And that's where the producer has to have a word with say, the American network. Do try and sort it out yourself. If you'd talked to me in the middle of those *Years and Years* notes I might have said these are conflicting, because I'd say, "They say they like it, but they don't want to commission it." There's nothing more conflicting than that! But I simply had to focus and find the middle of that, which was "Oh, they want it to be warmer!" So there might be an answer, just do the work. You're being paid to do the hard work. If it's properly, properly mad though – "Cut this character/keep this character", then remember you're not alone with it. Don't think you have to go mad on behalf of your script, it's not worth it.'

Russell considers the arena of notes to do with portraying real-life figures. He says, 'The legal notes are very interesting, that's a whole other world, because you can't ignore lawyers. At the very end of *A Very English Scandal*, before the verdict comes in, Jeremy Thorpe has that conversation with his barrister about why he was involved with Norman Scott. And he flashes back to all those terrible one-night stands with men under the arches. There is no proof of any of those encounters. They say had Jeremy Thorpe taken the stand, the prosecution did have evidence of one-night stands and none of that has survived, so legally …' He tails off, gesturing the muddy situation. In the drama, Russell's solution is to have Hugh Grant, playing Jeremy Thorpe, preface those flashbacks with, 'Hypothetically …'. Russell says, 'It's really on a tightrope. But when I handed that in to Blueprint, the production company, I said, "Lawyers will question that scene, I will never let that be cut." Because actually it's the heart of the drama. That's not any old scene, it's the entire exposing of his soul. I said, "I'll tell you what my proof is for those scenes – every single gay man has had a night like that, and that's in 2018, never mind in 1961. Every single gay man has had a bad one-night stand, no lawyer can tell me that didn't happen to him, and I will never back down from that." I suspect there were battles that never reached me because I didn't even allow them to bring that argument to my desk. Because ultimately what that scene is about is as close as he ever gets to saying "I love Norman." It's the same as *Queer as Folk*, it's coming down to one line. "He was the best" Jeremy says, boiling the whole drama down to one line. I went in big on that because I could see lawyers coming.' Russell braces strong Welsh arms out against an unseen onslaught. 'I know the game well enough to set my stall out, to say "Don't even tackle me on this" – that's a good opening gambit,' he says with a conspiratorial chuckle.

In *Queer as Folk,* the school-boy, Nathan, who has sex with Stuart, is fifteen. Russell discusses channel notes and taking on board the needs of a broadcaster, if they'd had an issue with something such as that. He says, 'It was kind of a test for all of us to see how brave we were. Because that's a very valid question about Nathan's age. Because Stuart is never arrested, he has no downfall because of what he does that night. You simply have to respect that's a very intelligent conversation to have and that they are the broadcaster. If they were walking in going "Can he be a girl?" then you're kind of going "You've just unravelled the entire series!" Whereas if a lawyer had come in and said you cannot transmit this, he has to be sixteen, I would have made him sixteen, because otherwise the entire drama doesn't get made. If you look at the story, exactly the same things would have happened, because it's not a story about legalities, no one gets arrested in it, it's barely even discussed. It's also a very true story. I wrote it because I was seeing those fifteen-year-olds starting to arrive on Canal Street for the first time. They were like comets, they were like peacocks, they were extraordinary. In the end you've got to summon your resources and put an argument forward. You've got to be able to debate intelligently, there's no point in losing your temper. There is no point in storming about and saying, "You can't do this to me, you've ruined my work" because it wouldn't ruin the work, that's the thing. Look at what it essentially is, and *Queer as Folk* is a celebration of gay life and marvellous great big strong gay characters of all ages appearing on screen, it's not about the age of consent. There's a great drama to be written about the age of consent. It's in there, it's a good drama, it's got layers, but do any of us refer to *Queer as Folk* as a drama about the age of consent? No, we don't. So that's when you've got to know your stuff. As it happens I won that argument, but of course I could have changed it. In the American version he's seventeen, and that's fine, that ran for five years. It is picking your battles.'

Russell reflects, 'I'm sitting here thirty years in, I've been in telly longer, but it's thirty years since my own show went out, *Dark Season*. And in all that experience and all that career there has been no note that has ruined anything. I cannot sit here and tell you a story about a show that was ruined by notes. They're never nice. They're always annoying. But they're always trying to help. There's speeches I might not like, little moments that bump, they feel so huge at the time, but trust me, trust the old man, in the bigger picture they're fine. If you think notes are annoying, why do you give them all the time? Every time you sit watching telly, every episode of a soap, every sit-com, every film, there you are, giving notes. So shut up and join in.'

Russell takes a job-well-done sip of tea from his yellow mug as we finish our chat, waving goodbye with warm Christmas wishes and air-blown kisses. But there's a postscript. He emails later: 'I just remembered the best notes. On *Queer as Folk*, everyone was padding politely around episode four, "Could we see more of Nathan? Could they meet earlier? Could Stuart be more centre stage?" Constant, vague notes drip-drip-dripping away, saying, persistently but unclearly, something's wrong. Which only made me dig my heels in. Then, on Nicola's desk, I found a note from the director, Charles McDougall. It said simply: "Ep. 1, good, Ep. 2, good, Ep. 3, great, Ep. 4, rubbish." And that was it.

I went home and rewrote the fuck out of episode four until it was brilliant. That's what I needed to be told! Honest notes are best!'

A couple of days later, some further thoughts arrive from Russell: 'I'm still thinking about notes. It's psychology, really. I had to give notes yesterday. Young writer, only twenty-two. I thought I'd write the notes at first, so I typed out this and that, but then I thought, no, this isn't working, and I had to FaceTime him. And for ages, I didn't talk about the script, it was more like, "Where are you from? When did you come out? What did your mum and dad say? Was school bad? How are you now?" That's the reason notes are hard to give, and why they're essential. Because you're actually asking: who are you? Okay, there are ordinary notes, like cut that location, we can't afford night shoots, she's unfunny, etc. But the real notes about the tone, the purpose, your intent (what idiots call "the theme", but that word is just reaching for the light switch in the dark) are asking, why did you write this? What are you saying? Who are you? That's why notes hurt. And why great notes transform.'

Swansea, via Zoom, December 2021

Selected credits, awards and nominations

Dark Season: Writer (1991), [TV series] BBC.

Coronation Street: Story Associate episodes '*#1.3521*', '*#1.3522*', '*#1.3523*', '*#1.3524*', '*#1.3525*', '*#1.3526*', '*#1.3527*', '*#1.3528*', '*#1.3529*' (1993), [TV Soap Opera] Granada Television.

Children's Ward: Writer, episodes '*#7.1*', '*#7.7*', '*#7.8*', '*#7.9*' and '*#7.10*' (1994), [TV series] Granada Television.
   BAFTA TV nomination – Best Children's Programme, Fiction (1993)
   BAFTA Children's nomination – Best Drama (1996)
   BAFTA Children's award – Best Drama (1997)

The Grand: Writer (1997–98), [TV series] Granada Television.

Queer as Folk: Writer, Co-producer (1999 and 2000), [TV series] Channel 4.
   Royal Television Society nomination – Best Drama Serial (2000)

Bob & Rose: Writer, Co-producer (2001), [TV series] ITV.
   BAFTA TV nomination – Best Drama Serial (2002)

Casanova: Writer, Executive Producer (2005), [TV series] BBC.

Doctor Who: Writer numerous episodes, Showrunner, Executive Producer (2005–24), [TV series] BBC.
    BAFTA Cymru nomination – Best Screenwriter (2006)
    BAFTA TV award – Best Drama series (2006)
    BAFTA TV award – Dennis Potter award for Outstanding Writing (2006)
    BAFTA Cymru award – Best Screenwriter (2007)
    Writers' Guild of Great Britain Award – Best TV Series (2007)
    BAFTA TV nomination – Best Writer (2009)
    BAFTA TV nomination – Best Drama Series (2009)
    BAFTA Cymru award – Best Screenwriter (2009)
Torchwood: Writer, Executive Producer (2006–11), [TV series] BBC.
    BAFTA Cymru nomination – Best Screenwriter (2010)
The Sarah Jane Adventures: Writer, Executive Producer (2007–20), [TV series] BBC.
Wizards vs. Aliens: Writer, Executive Producer (2012–14), [TV series] BBC.
Banana: Writer, Executive Producer (2015), [TV series] E4.
Cucumber: Writer, Executive Producer (2015), [TV series] Channel 4.
    BAFTA Television Craft award – Writer: Drama (2016)
    Broadcasting Press Guild Award – Innovation in Broadcasting (2016)
    Royal Television Society nomination – Writer-Drama (2016)
Tofu: Executive Producer (2015), [TV series] Red Production Company.
A Midsummer Night's Dream: Screenwriter, Executive Producer (2016), [TV programme] BBC Cymru Wales.
    BAFTA Cymru nomination – Best Feature/Television Film (2017)
A Very English Scandal: Writer, Executive Producer (2018), [TV series] BBC.
    BAFTA Cymru Award – Best Writer (2019)
    Writers' Guild of Great Britain Award – Best Short Form TV Drama (2019)
    Broadcast Award – Best Drama Series or Serial (2019)
    BAFTA Cymru Award – Best Writer (2019)
    Emmy nomination – Outstanding Writing for a Limited Series, Movie or a Dramatic Special (2019)
    BAFTA TV nomination – Best Mini-Series (2019)
    Broadcasting Press Guild Award – Best Writer (2019)
    Royal Television Society nomination – Writer – Drama (2019)
Years and Years: Writer, Executive Producer (2019), [TV series] BBC.
    Broadcasting Press Guild nomination – Best Writer (2020)
It's a Sin: Writer, Executive Producer (2021), [TV series] Channel 4.
    Writers' Guild of Great Britain Award – Best Long Form TV Drama (2021)
    Venice TV Award – Best TV Series (2021)
    BAFTA TV nomination – Best Mini-Series (2022)
    BAFTA TV nomination – Best Writer, Drama (2022)
    Broadcasting Press Guild Award – Best Writer (2022)
    Royal Television Society nomination – Writer – Drama (2022)
Nolly: Writer, Executive Producer (2023), [TV series] ITVX.

British Comedy Award – Writer of the Year (2001)
Writers' Guild of Great Britain Award – Outstanding Contribution to Writing (2016)
Royal Television Society Award – Outstanding Achievement Award (2021)

Lynne Ramsay

'I think you've got to be quite open, but also it's about having the courage of your convictions.'

4 *Lynne Ramsay, photo courtesy of Lynne Ramsay.*

On a warm April morning, Lynne Ramsay is thinking about the icy waters of the Arctic. Specifically the logistics of finding a suitable boat and window of weather to shoot a film there. She is a writer-director game for a challenge. Her previous feature, the Cannes award-winning *You Were Never Really*

Here (2017), was shot in under a month during the blistering New York summer.

Her films are hypnotic works of art. Quietly, devastatingly, drawing you in to their atmosphere. Seeping into your soul. The heritage of her training as a photographer at Napier College in Edinburgh and as a cinematographer at the National Film and Television School is evident in the poetic images she crafts. Sound and music are just as integral to the work she creates, everything intertwining to build moving portraits of fractured characters.

Lynne first won an award at Cannes for her NFTS graduation short film, *Small Deaths* (1996). She won a BAFTA for her debut feature, *Ratcatcher* (1999), and another for her lyrical short film *Swimmer* (2012), commissioned to mark the 2012 Olympics. She is renowned for the depth of performances she draws from actors; directing Tilda Swinton to a BAFTA nomination in *We Need to Talk About Kevin* (2011), Samantha Morton to a British Independent Film Award for *Morvern Callar* (2002) and Joaquin Phoenix to an award at Cannes for *You Were Never Really Here.*

Lynne Ramsay is as sunny as the bright spring day outside. She dives straight in, saying, 'I take notes pretty well I think. But I have a selective process about what notes I want to keep and what I don't. And that takes some experience and a bit of courage on the filmmaker's part. I also like that idea of questioning yourself. You have to look at the notes and try to analyse them and see what they really mean. If there's something you really disagree with, something you instinctively feel is really wrong, I won't go that avenue, but I will look at why someone's saying that. I've got notes on a script right now where some of them are huge. I've spoken to another writer, a really good writer, about them, and he's like "I don't agree with that note!" But I'll still look at them and think, "Well, why are they saying that? Why is that coming up?"'

She advises, 'There'll be things where you can get a bit blind to the material. If more than one person comes back with something about the same thing, it's always something I'll look at. You can get tunnel vision in the writing process, so it does help when you've got trustworthy people around you keeping an eye on it from the outside. It's good to get a selection of notes, not just from people who are about script. If they're people who understand the whole process that's good as well. With note-giving, I think it's about responding to the strong parts of the material and then questioning things where you don't feel sure. In a way, it's like you're digging in like a writer. But I think if you come in really bombastic: "It's got to be like this, it's got to be like that", her hands chop through the air decisively as she speaks, 'that can be destructive to the balance of the thing.'

She says, 'I've been lucky that I've never had a note that's really thrown me, but I have had some strange notes sometimes. With *Ratcatcher* someone read it as some kind of biblical text, and I was like, "Well, I don't know about that!"' she laughs. But Lynne recommends looking for the value in even the most unexpected note, to question what in the material has prompted someone to have that interpretation. She observes, 'You'll have readings of things where people read into it maybe in a way that you didn't intend, and that's interesting as well.'

Lynne is celebrated for the poetic, immersive aesthetic of her work, a distinctive vision and way of storytelling. She recalls an instance with her first feature, *Ratcatcher*, to illustrate that sometimes someone giving notes may simply not 'get' a filmmaker's approach, and that it's possible to still find value in that. She says, 'I remember I went to a brilliant workshop called Moonstone, it was a kind of offshoot of Sundance. They had different mentors there, and Hollywood writers, some really good ones. I was quite close to going into production on *Ratcatcher*, and I had this one meeting at Moonstone where the whole script got pulled apart by a particular writer who was coming from a much more conventional point of view. I felt devastated. And I was questioning everything in the piece. But then I think it was actually quite a good thing, because it kind of made me more resolute that I had a different way of telling stories, and that not everyone's going to get it. But some points he made were good,' she concedes, advising, 'you take what you can in that respect. I think you've got to be quite open, but also it's about having the courage of your convictions.'

Lynne expands, 'Because I make films in a certain way, I write quite visually. I don't write in shots or anything, but I try and very much capture a moment or a detail in the writing, so it feels quite precise. When I was a younger filmmaker starting out, that feedback the person gave at Moonstone was a bit more intimidating, but a lot of other people, luckily, had read that script.' Those other people, fortunately, had 'got' it. Lynne explains, 'Even the treatment I did for it, I didn't really know what I was doing – I did a treatment that was seventy pages, I think they're normally fifteen, but there was a life in it. You could tell it was authentic. An environment I knew and I'd done a lot of research and recorded lots of stories round it that gave me ideas.'

Lynne ponders how someone giving notes can best work with a filmmaker who has a more unconventional approach to storytelling. She looks up, considering, then says, 'I think it's recognizing what they're trying to do. And that's to do with conversation. If you know the work of the person who's writing, or even if they're a first-time writer, it's good to just speak to them about their ideas. Because basically that's where all the nuggets are. Questioning someone is not a bad thing. When I work with great actors they always question everything. And through that process of questioning, questioning, questioning, you get to something quite pure. When it's prescriptive or the note-giver comes in with a really set point of view, I don't think that's necessarily a good thing. But if you get a big question about a script like, "Why does this character do that?" you're either going to start to articulate that, or start to get to the bottom of that through the drafts. I think it's about the note-giver having an openness, and also having quite subtle, precise questions. Coming in with an open mind rather than a "that's how every film works", because some filmmakers don't work like that.'

Lynne continues, 'If you're maybe telling a narrative in a slightly off-kilter way, you're not looking at it in a traditional sense of here's a beginning, middle and end.' She clarifies, 'I mean there is that, there is this three act structure, but it's like being a painter – you know the nuts and bolts, but also you have to have knowledge about how you're trying to approach something. And sometimes people can come in with a really prescriptive set of comparisons to other things, when new styles of narrative don't really apply to those. I've been lucky where I think things have worked enough on paper that people have got interested and wanted to do them, and they've haven't strayed from what they're trying to do too much.' She cautions, 'But there is a traditional or a conventional way of looking at things, a particular way of looking at filmmaking and making stories, and if someone comes in with one point of view it can kind of spin a filmmaker out.'

Lynne illustrates with a current project: 'For instance, there's a script I'm writing which is based on a novel; it's quite a surrealist novel and the rules don't apply. So with approaching a book like that, it doesn't have that structure: "Oh, it's like this film or that film." I find it a little bit boring when something's described as a bit like this a bit like that. Obviously people like to know, people like tag lines and to put things in boxes somewhat. But I think with more interesting and more exciting work, it doesn't fit into those little compartments.' She reflects, 'The only advice I can give to people coming in with notes, is have a conversation about what that filmmaker is trying to do. In fact, more than notes, especially in the beginning, that's really important, those conversations, you know: "Where are you trying to go with this?" And that's really illuminating to you as a filmmaker as well.' She reveals, 'On an original script I'm working on now, I had an, I suppose you could say a script doctor, but it was more like an analyst! It was a guy who came in who looked at all the patterns in all the scripts, asking me lots of questions, it was like going to therapy!' she laughs. Explaining, 'It was actually quite good! He made connections' (her hands pick interesting morsels out of the air) 'and asked me questions. It was really interesting, because it was never about enforcing a point of view. It was more like, "Why is that, that?" So again and again for me, and this applies to actors, it applies to yourself as a filmmaker, you should be questioning what you're trying to get at. Sometimes you don't really know. But then there's pointers.' She adds, 'It's a different process for everybody. Some people need a much more structured way of working.'

Reflecting on her script development process she says, 'In general I try and streamline things. It's always about boiling ideas down and having a good sounding board. A good group of people who are kind of incubating it, all behind you. Often you can get down a rabbit hole with things, if you get really close to it, so sometimes it's good to take a bit of a step back or to talk to someone else about it.' She muses, 'It's a strange process. Often a script is a bigger thing and the more you condense it the more you focus the idea. You can see more clearly what it is.' She illustrates, 'One of the scripts I'm working on right now is an original script written in a way that was a different kind of process from normal writing. I approached it much more in terms of images and ideas. I had some pointers in mind – it's about a photographer, set in 1910, exploring Alaska, and I've done a bit of research. That was an interesting process because I did it much more like as if you were making a piece of music, one thing led to another, and it became a big epic story. Almost like a book. But it's so big! So having someone come in, even another writer, and take a look at that is really useful. I had really good notes back on that script. On some fundamental things like: "Where are you going with it?"' She cautions, 'But then there are some things in it that work in more of an abstract way. So you don't want to kill everything that works. It's a balancing act between you going your own way, and feeling it through and thinking about it as a filmmaker. It's good being a writer-director, because you're thinking in images and thinking about how it's going to be in the end. But also those notes are helpful, especially in the case of this original script which has great ideas and people really love the script, but it needs a bit of focus now. It's good to get other people to come in, but to still retain my own vision.' She crosses her hands over her chest, as though holding close something precious. She reiterates, 'That's the balancing act.'

Lynne considers advice for filmmakers on handling potential feelings of vulnerability when sharing something they've created. She owns, 'Yeah, it's really tough that one. I have had that one experience when something was eviscerated. It was torn apart.' But she says, 'I think you've got to roll with the punches a little bit. You have to look at it from the outside. Sometimes someone might come in and they just don't get it. Sometimes they come from a different angle at it. But you've got to try and listen if there's anything in that. In what they're saying. Even if it's points of view that you don't necessarily agree with. But it's really hard, because when you've written something you are vulnerable. You're showing your work and half the time when you're writing you're thinking "God, this is awful!" you're questioning everything. It can be a lonely place. You're your worst critic in a way. I think the key is not to get defensive. And to listen to what makes sense and have the strength to discard what doesn't, what comes from someone's particular point of view that you might not agree with. And that's a really hard balancing act. There's no formula for that. Unfortunately. The best I can say is get the best group of people round you. If everyone's saying it's great, that's not good either! You want criticism. Be open to it. It doesn't really set you back, it takes you forward. It is a bit like therapy. When you finish a draft you're like, "This is great!" Then in the clear light of day you read it, maybe a while later, or you get feedback and some of the notes you go "Oh my god, they totally haven't got it" but then you have to read into why that is. There's not really any simple solution. It's more having the strength of vision in yourself, and that's really quite hard, a tough place to get to if you're feeling like "Oh gosh, I'm putting my thing into the world." But the only way to go is forward. It brings into focus what you're trying to do. Even if you get notes that you think are terrible, they can often make you feel stronger about the piece of work you're writing, and more committed. Or if there's a stumbling block, even if it comes from different people, and this applies to film editing as well, if many people went, "There's something wrong there" it's ridiculous not to listen to that. Even if you do find the solution is a different approach from what you're being suggested.'

She counsels, 'Sometimes you get lots of suggestions that might seem like an obvious choice, but you will find a solution maybe in a way that you didn't expect. Definitely during cuts and within notes on a script there tends to be something wrong in an area if several people are picking up on it. But I don't think it's anything prescriptive, I don't think notes are going to solve everything. What they're there for is to make you think through why somebody's asking that question. If you think it's a valid question, if you think there's something missing in that respect, or if it's a note that's not relevant in that piece of work. And that takes a lot of courage, you know, looking at yourself. I tend to feel if something works very intuitively, very instinctively. If I do something that I'm a bit unsure of it'll always fall flat. So it's kind of feeling your way through it.'

She warns, 'The worst thing is to go in and take every note on board. Because if you take every note on board you're just going to have something really dilute. And you start to forget why you started writing it. So take a bit of time to take them in. Don't be overwhelmed. Don't take anything as prescriptive. Try and look at why someone's saying that. Try and look if it's relevant. I would say don't go back into a script after a big bunch of notes. I would take a bit of time out, just to look at them. Have a real think about what you're trying to do.' She emphasizes, 'I think it's a real mistake to take every note. I've seen filmmakers or writers get really lost by getting a bunch of notes they think can solve the whole lot and thinking that's the way forward. And you just end up in a big mess! Because it's like you're doing it for other people rather than you.'

If there's real disagreement about a note, Lynne advises, 'It's about communication. Going into defence mode is not good. But if you feel strongly about something, then that tells you something. That's actually leading you somewhere. If you feel really strongly about something, either side of the coin, there's a reason why you're feeling strongly. So cutting out all the stuff about being defensive or feeling vulnerable, if you are like, "This is a great idea, I know it's a great idea" then fight for that idea! Even if it might be hard to describe but it's something you feel very passionately about, try to articulate that as much as possible. And also listen. On the flip side of that, if you're giving a note that you feel super strongly about, but the filmmaker's not too sure, then I think that's all about conversations, about why you feel that way. You've got to remember that you're not the filmmaker, but also you're trying to communicate that idea because you think it's important. And so that's about just having a conversation really.' She says, 'It's often the way when you get a set of notes, at first you're all "Grrrrrr". (She balls her fists up in mock frustration.) 'You're like, "That doesn't make sense!" or whatever. But then when you read into it a bit more, you're like, "Right, hang on a minute . . .". So I think it's taking a bit of time just to absorb it. And also, to me anyway, the ideas that work the best are ideas that I do feel really strongly about but they're not something I feel defensive about.'

Thinking about at what point it's useful to have notes, Lynne says, 'I tend to like to have notes when I feel something is starting to work. Often, you can get just into a muddle if you get notes too early and you don't know where you're at yet. I've been lucky enough to work with really creative producers like Robyn Slovo and James Wilson, and then you can talk through things. Or if you've got an actor early, that's interesting as well. During the writing process if you've got an actor involved and you're talking about it, you're kind of evolving the character together. But I tend to like the notes when I feel something's operating on a level where it might have rough edges, but it's working.'

The talk turns to some of Lynne's development process on *You Were Never Really Here* and how she likes to allow a film space to continue to evolve organically from the script through shooting and post-production. Lynne explains, 'Often the material, when it's breathing and living, suggests other things. Maybe during an edit you can see something that seemed like a brilliant idea in the script doesn't work as well in the film, another scene works better or has more emotional power. I tend to stick quite closely to my scripts as much as possible. But the material dictates where you go a wee bit. So there's maybe some scene you think is really important, but then when you shoot it it's not. And maybe another scene has an emotional crux in it that you were looking for. Or there's been times when I've shot a scene and it didn't quite work the way I wanted it to, and I've worked out while I'm filming that I can put more weight onto something else. Sometimes a scene just lives on paper in a different way than it lives on the screen. Then I've made pretty bold choices to go, "OK I'm going to be a bit more organic in how I work." Realizing that something is not necessary is good as well. Because from script to film, it doesn't matter what you've got on paper, there's always something that happens when you're actually shooting a scene where it's electrifying. It's always subtle changes for me, it's got the same intent, but I've recognized that the scene I thought perhaps was going to be that point doesn't work as well as something else. During scriptwriting you can sometimes think "That scene's so important", but when you come to shoot it you realize it's got a flatness or something. I quite like being organic and reacting to what I've got in front of me. Like if an actor's saying something that's really interesting, or there's something happening off screen that I'm watching and I'm going, "Actually, that's better than what I planned." It just depends on the actors, it depends on the location, it depends on all kinds of things. I think you've got to be aware that it's always evolving. And I don't think you should get too precious on things. But it's easy to do! It's easy to get hung up on certain things. Funnily enough it's the things that you get really hung up about that tend to be the first things to go in an edit. Or sometimes things change through necessity, say where I don't have that much time to shoot, so I can't shoot a big action sequence so I did the surveillance camera.' She says, referring to the sequence in *You Were Never Really Here* where lead character Joe's brutal path past assorted henchmen to rescue a young girl is glimpsed via the impersonal eye of surveillance cameras. Lynne explains, 'That made sense because he's such a mechanical character, he's so in and out. Sometimes necessity is the mother of invention. It never stops at the script. The script isn't the end. When I was working on that there was a lot of reacting to the actor [Joaquin Phoenix], because he's such a good actor. He would play things in a way that you wouldn't expect sometimes, which was great,' Lynne enthuses, alive with energy and gesturing the enjoyable give and take with her hands, 'Having that kind of creative process when you're working with someone like that, you're also looking at your script going, "Maybe it's better this way" where it played in a much less obvious way. So the scriptwriting goes on right through the filmmaking. I was still getting up at like four in the morning going, "OK, right I don't like this scene" having seen the locations, or having spoken to the actors.' She asserts, 'I think the best films come, the best filmmaking is when you've got that room to breathe.'

So how might notes from anyone feed into that type of process? Lynne says, 'I talk to my crew, my close friends and producer. If you're working with a creative producer that's great. I think there was a trust in me as a filmmaker, to go with new ideas in that film. That was great. Because you had this really organic actor and you could go, "Hang on, that was better doing it this way", to react in the situation while you're actually shooting. I didn't get that many notes on that movie. I did from James Wilson,' she says warmly, 'one of the producers, we were always talking about the script every day. We were talking about what we were doing every day. So if new ideas come up I would ask someone really close to me to just kind of take a measure a bit. It's a lot to do with trusting yourself. It's like when you're writing a novel or something, you feel when it's good and you feel when it's not, and you have to go with that. Otherwise you're wasting time and you're wasting resources. I've been lucky enough to keep that writing process going right through the film.' She reflects, 'It's all so interlinked filmmaking. It's editing, it's music. I'll start the sound really early. Some things are too hard to describe and people won't get them till they see them. I learned early on it was really nice to show a pre-mix, because the sound is such a big part of the picture, it does so much to the subconscious. People don't often get things until it's in front of them.'

We turn to a short documentary which Lynne made, *Brigitte* (2019) about photographer Brigitte Lacombe, and differences she may have found with notes on that. Lynne says, 'That was part of the Miu Miu Women's Tales, and you were given quite a lot of freedom to be honest. With a documentary you don't really know where it's going to go. I did have an outline of how we were going to do this shoot over a couple of days. I set it up in a way that we could move round this space and be super free and let Brigitte do her thing and never be intrusive with the camera. I'd recorded some sound first as well, just me and her in her garden, so it was really intimate, and I based it a little bit off those sound recordings. I actually storyboarded something, I had some ideas of shots and frames – that kind of went out the window when I did it. But certain threads came up that were more interesting than others. It's all in the edit in a documentary. You've gathered the material and it's about what direction it takes you. I had a brilliant editor, who I've worked with before, Adam Biskupski. It's good to get notes on the edit. I got lots of people I knew in to screenings to look at that film to ask, "What part do you think's interesting?" And that's good when someone says, "I'm more invested in this part than what you thought you were going to do in the first place." So again it's about going slightly where the film's leading you. It's a really interesting process, it takes you on a different journey, and it can kind of free you up. But definitely I had screenings where someone would go, "Well, that bit seems a bit slow, or a bit clunky or it feels like it's a bit disjointed." I would listen to close friends, people I really trust, people whose taste I respect. I'm lucky enough to have a band of brother filmmakers that would be honest to go "Right, well …". To be really critical. You've got to be critical all the way, of yourself.'

Lynne observes, 'I've learned so much about filmmaking in editing that I'm getting better at editing scripts. So something in a script that I might have thought was really important before, I'll be a bit more hard on myself and go "OK, I think I can lose that". I'll be much more critical, and sometimes you have to be. You've got to find inventive ways of retaining what you love about it. It's interesting listening to that other voice, whether it's yourself, whether it's a producer or a script editor or an editor.' She reveals, 'I'm working on a script that I'm hoping to shoot this year, that was quite a long script, although it really worked, but then you've got things like budget, those other challenges, coming into it. But there were still things in that script that felt a bit flabby in places. They were nice moments and details. But sometimes going in with a super focus, a script edit can be really good. I think – don't be too self-indulgent, you can get really married to some things, you can think "I've got to have that" and interestingly when I started pulling some scenes out that I thought were really important, I realized, "I don't miss that", and it became more focused. Sometimes it's that kill-your-darlings thing. Script editing can be really, really useful to me. I'll often send my script to another writer, or I'll talk to one of these script doctor people, or edit my own script with an assistant – talking through it.'

Lynne concludes, 'To me it's about getting to the emotional core of what you're trying to do. The wonderful thing about filmmaking is you've got all these different layers in it, you've got music, sound, don't forget it's a whole thing.' Her hands layer things up like a cake stuffed full of tasty treats. She emphasizes, 'It doesn't just rely on a script, that's not the finished article. So, allow it to be a movie, allow it to have the magic that's there when you're making something and there's all these different forces that go inside it, the actor, the locations, everything. So the script's an ongoing thing, and it never really finishes. To me it's just being true to yourself. Being true to where you're trying to go to. And if you show that to people and it feels authentic, then they often get it. People can smell authenticity, or when something works really well. Whatever way you work, if it's the most conventional way, or if it's unconventional, or it's documentary, or it's whatever you do, I think when something works in the script and when it works in the film, even if you can't dissect or directly analyse why, it has its own power. I'm always trying to get to what's behind a character, what's inside the character, but to approach it in a slightly off-kilter manner rather than purely through dialogue or exposition or anything like that.'

Lynne wraps up with some final words of advice: 'Filmmakers – take notes and look at them really properly. It might not be the note that you wanted, it might be you really disagree with that, it might make you angry, it might enlighten you. Just have an openness to that process, but also stay with what you feel is right as much as possible, because that'll be the guide. And then for the note-givers – I would say try and understand where that filmmaker is coming from as much as possible. The more dialogue there is between you and that person, the more you understand what they're trying to aspire to, then that's always going to get to a good place. And that doesn't mean imposing necessarily, but it doesn't mean you don't have a strong voice if you really feel something. Those are not arguments, those are great conversations to have.'

Still as cheery as the April sunshine, Lynne bids a warm goodbye, adding with a laugh, 'Now I've got to go back to a really difficult script!'

London, via Zoom, April 2023

Selected credits, awards and nominations

Small Deaths: Writer, Director (1996), [Film] UK: National Film and Television School (NFTS).
    Cannes award – Jury Prize – Best Short Film (1996)
Kill the Day: Writer, Director (1996), [Film] UK, France: Channel 4.
Gasman: Writer, Director (1997), [Film] UK: BBC Scotland.
    BAFTA Scotland Award – Best Short Film (1997)
    BAFTA nomination – Best Short Film (1998)
    Cannes award – Jury Prize – Best Short Film (1998)
Ratcatcher: Writer, Director (1999), [Film] UK: Pathé Distribution.
    Edinburgh International Film Festival award – New Director's Award (1999)
    British Independent Film Award – Douglas Hickox Award, Best Debut (1999)
    British Independent Film Award nomination – Best Screenplay (1999)
    British Film Institute award – Sutherland Trophy for most original and creative film (1999)
    BAFTA Award – Carl Foreman Award for Most Promising Newcomer (2000)
    BAFTA nomination – Alexander Korda Award for Best British Film (2000)
    London Critics' Circle Film award – British Director of the Year (2000)
Morvern Callar: Co-writer, Director (2002), [Film] UK, Canada: BBC Films.
    Cannes award – Award of the Youth – Foreign Film (2002)
    Cannes award – CICAE Award (2002)
    British Independent Film Award nomination – Best Screenplay (2002)
    British Independent Film Award nomination – Best Director (2002)
    San Sebastián International Film Festival award – FIPRESCI Director of the Year (2002)
We Need to Talk About Kevin: Co-writer, Director (2011), [Film] UK, US: Artificial Eye.
    London Film Festival award – Best Film (2011)
    British Independent Film Award nomination – Best Screenplay (2011)
    British Independent Film Award – Best Director (2011)
    BAFTA nomination – Alexander Korda Award for Best British Film (2012)
    BAFTA nomination – Best Director (2012)
    Writers' Guild of Great Britain award – Best Screenplay (2012)

Swimmer: Director (2012), [Film] UK: Warp Films.
    BAFTA Award – Best Short Film (2013)
You Were Never Really Here: Writer, Director (2017), [Film] UK, France, US:
    StudioCanal.
    Cannes award – Best Screenplay (2017)
    Dublin International Film Festival award – Best Screenplay (2018)
    British Independent Film Award nomination – Best Screenplay (2018)
    British Independent Film Award nomination – Best Director (2018)
    British Independent Film Award nomination – Best British Independent Film (2018)
    BAFTA nomination – Outstanding British Film of the Year (2019)
Brigitte: Writer, Director (2019), [Film] Italy, UK: Somesuch.
Die, My Love: Writer, Director (in production), [Film] UK: Excellent Cadaver.
Stone Mattres: Director (in development), [Film] Greenland: Amazon Studios,
    StudioCanal Films.

Sarajevo Film Festival Honorary Heart of Sarajevo Award for Lifetime Achievement, in
    recognition of outstanding contribution to the Art of Film (2023)

Quick Fire Q&A 3:
What's one thing never to do if you're giving notes?

'Prescribe – "Do it like this."' – **Amma Asante**

'Suggest dialogue.' – **Simon Beaufoy**

'Have the solutions down pat – that you think. You're not making it, you're guiding someone creative to find their answers.' – **Lynne Ramsay**

'Say: "You have to do this because I said so."' – **Sally Wainwright**

'Never get too carried away with your own voice.' – **Ben Wheatley**

'It's not being too didactic. Keep it as questions. The worst thing you can do is tell people what they should do. But you can get around that by saying, "If it was my film I'd do this, but you will do something different." Keep it always open that you're just helping them make the film they want to make.' – **Tomm Moore**

'To be underprepared, to have idiosyncrasies, to feel safer when something is like something that has been seen before.' – **Lone Scherfig**

'Don't take the piss! The people I've done that to have remembered things I said to take the piss for decades afterwards!' – **Russell T Davies**

'To impose your vision upon the script. To be overly critical and negative. To get rid of stuff that's actually fine and working, just for the sake of changing it.' – **Alice Lowe**

'As a director who's also working with the development of story, it's when they make an assumption of how you're going to execute or visualize something. Sometimes you want to kind of say, "Leave the story there and this is what I'm going to do with it."' – **Corin Hardy**

'Don't just give a note for the sake of it. Don't give a note so that you can hear yourself speak. Don't give a note so that your boss sees that you've done it. If you don't have anything interesting to say, read it again.' – **Krysty Wilson-Cairns**

'It always needs to be constructive criticism. I'm pretty polite, so I would never be savage and negative. Even if there was something that I thought was really wrong, I would try and couch it in a nice way. There's nothing to be gained from being cold and negative. Even if something is not there, or even if it is not good, find a nice way of putting it, or inspire them into something else that you think they could do. I remember when me and Simon [Pegg] were pitching *Shaun of the Dead* (2004) around, we had this meeting where one of the development people sat there flipping through our script in a very dismissive manner. I saw him doing it out of the corner of my eye, and then at the end he said, "Yeah, I just feel there's nothing in here we haven't seen before" and obviously the thing that you can't say in a meeting is "Fuck you".' – **Edgar Wright**

Alice Lowe

'It's like being a plumber. It's quite technical. And it should be quite ego-less. It's not about you winning your point or going, "That was my idea!" you are simply trying to iron out the problems in the script.'

5 *Alice Lowe, photo by Michael Shelford.*

The warm smile and cosily domestic chat about wall-paint colours does not entirely dispel an instinctive flinch on first seeing Alice Lowe. 'Psychotic serial killer' something whispers. A side-effect of Alice's work as an actor as well as writer and director. Her roles include the homicidal Tina in *Sightseers* (Ben

Wheatley, 2012), which Alice co-wrote, and the equally murderously inclined Ruth in *Prevenge* (2017), which she wrote and directed. Alongside her writing, directing and on-screen bloodletting, Alice also works as a script editor.

Alice began by performing in theatre, then in television sketch shows and episodes of series such as *Black Books* (2004), *The IT Crowd* (2006), *Horrible Histories* (2010) and *Sherlock* (2014). She starred in *Garth Marenghi's Darkplace* (2004) and all female sketch show *Beehive* (2008), and featured in films including *Hot Fuzz* (Edgar Wright, 2007), *The World's End* (Edgar Wright, 2013) and *Paddington* (Paul King, 2014). Determined to create her own work, Alice, together with director Jacqueline Wright, made twelve short films in a year; a crash course in honing their skills while generating a body of work to prove them.

Alice continued to perform comedy on stage, and a pair of characters she and Steve Oram created – an ordinary seeming couple with an unexpected hobby – caught the eye of a television production company. Alice and Steve were invited to film a 'taster' with a view to pitching the idea as a series. It was turned down as a television series idea for being 'too dark'. However Edgar Wright saw the taster, and recognized its potential to be a film. With Ben Wheatley on board as director, the result was *Sightseers*, which won the British Independent Film Award for Best Screenplay.

Alice went on to direct as well as write and star in *Prevenge*, a blackly comic horror. At the time of this interview, she is preparing her third feature, again directing as well as writing and performing; *Timestalker,* a time-travelling epic romance.

Alice recounts how she began working as a script editor: 'It's something I've slightly fallen into,' she confesses. 'I was being offered things to direct when I had a two-month-old baby. I knew I wouldn't be able to do the director hours, but it would be people I really wanted to work with, so I said to my agent, "I'll be their script editor if they want, if that's something they're looking for."' She recommends 'Putting yourself out there and offering is never a bad idea. Specifically mentioning the words "Script Editor".' She laughs, fully aware how awkward the idea of 'putting yourself out there' can be and that you need the skills to back it, as well as the access.

Considering what makes for a good script editor, she says, 'All I want is someone who comes along and goes, "This is great. It's brilliant, but I can see why people have got a problem with this bit, it needs to be fixed and it's not going to change your idea radically, it's not going to ruin it, it's just this and it allows this bit to be more palatable and people to understand this bit." It's like being a plumber. It's quite technical. And it should be quite ego-less. It's not about you winning your point or going, "That was my idea!" You are simply trying to iron out the problems in the script. I often have people say to me, "You've made this work!", and that's all I'm trying to do. You know when you watch a TV show and go, "Why didn't that bit make sense? It's so annoying!" To me, my job as a script editor is to spot that a bit and the same way as a viewer you go, "Why didn't they just make it baked beans instead of fish?", or whatever, it's making that suggestion. Often it's just common sense and a little bit of lateral thinking.'

Alice addresses the, not infrequent, conundrum of a script editor being asked to give something 'a quick read' and share their thoughts on it; meaning, 'Could you provide some notes for free?' Weighing up whether there can be benefits for the person giving notes for free, as well as for the person receiving them, she suggests, 'What you're going to learn from doing it is person-to-person interaction, in terms of how you deliver your notes. If you want to practice script reading there's a billion scripts available online that you could read and have your thoughts about, but it's an opportunity to learn about the interpersonal pitfalls. Because I've done exactly that. I've had people send me scripts that they've obviously not really been ready to receive the notes that I'm going to give them. If I think a script is complete rubbish and I've accepted to read it as a favour, which is quite rare because I don't have much time, I will probably go, "Great, well done, congratulations on writing a feature, best of luck with it, goodbye."' She laughs a little guiltily, admitting, 'That's bad news if you get that back from me! Because I'm basically saying it's a lost cause, this person cannot write at all. If it was a work of genius I might say the same thing, weirdly. I might go, "My god, this is perfection, I can't say anything more about it. It's going to be amazing." But if I think it's worth investigating and the person's clever and they've done a really good job and it's just not there yet, it hasn't had any development yet, I'll probably send quite a lot of notes. And if someone's not used to that, if they're only just getting into writing, that can come across as completely devastating to them. They're like, "You've criticized all of it!" They can't cope with it. Sometimes you can tell because they come back with their own notes on your notes. Which is always a bit like, "Hmm, you're not really getting this."' She tips her head to one side, with an expression uncannily like Poppy the dog from *Sightseers'* puzzled look of bemusement at humans' behaviour. She laughs, 'If you don't want to accept the note you don't need to tell me about it! It's important to introduce people to the idea that notes are something they're going to be getting for the rest of their career. If they are serious about screenwriting and filmmaking, they'll have to deal with notes and decide how they're going to do that. My problem, with this particular incident, is that I spent ages trying to write it in a kind, delicate way. And still he was annoyed about it! And slightly threw it back in my face and I was like, "Oh my god, if you knew the amount of time I'd spent doing this!" So it's really about choosing your audience. I have friends who we do script swaps, and that works really well. Because I know they'll do a free read and a free set of notes and they'll chat with me about it, and I will do the same for them. That's really useful because it's a way of doing it for free if you're not yet earning as a screenwriter or script editor.'

Contemplating whether script editing other people's work influences her own writing, Alice acknowledges, 'I definitely have points where I'm saying something to the person that I'm script editing that I know is a massive problem in my own script and a penny suddenly drops for me. So I find it quite inspirational sometimes. Because it's always easier to fix other people's scripts than it is to fix your own. Of course it is, you've got distance on it, you've got perspective and you're not so emotionally involved. Sometimes you do think "Oh my god, have I gone to the other side?" I've become the baddy. I've become that person who goes, "This-doesn't-work!",' she croaks it out in the voice of an evil Dalek-like being, jabbing the words home with her finger, like a sink-plunger weapon of death. Reverting to being Alice she continues, 'But what I do always say in contrast to that, and this is something that it seems producers or commissioners or execs often do not learn as a skill, why would they, no one ever trains them to do it, is going, "This already works, it's fine, we've bought the idea."'

When navigating notes, Alice cautions, 'Quite often people try and change an idea. As soon as I get notes where I realize they don't actually like the project and they are going to try and change the DNA of it, I run a mile from working with those people. But it's very hard to say to a young person, or someone starting out, how you detect whether someone is giving the right notes for you. If you can find someone who likes the same stuff as you, who likes the same films, they're going to understand what you're trying to achieve that you haven't got down on paper yet. But if you're trying to work with someone who says they hate Wes Anderson films, that person is not going to help you to make your Wes Anderson film! Because they're always going to try to lure you away from the things that you like.

'Finding the right critics is really important,' Alice emphasizes, 'The people who are going to give you the right notes to get to what you're trying to achieve. I always try to say to people, "This is actually quite easy to fix. I'm not telling you to make massive changes, this is tiny changes and then it's done." Whereas a lot of commissioners and execs, you go in there and you feel like you've been to visit some mystical figure who hasn't actually told you what to do, or how to make it better. They've just told you they don't like it, in some mystified language, like,' (she adopts the ethereal voice of a cave-dwelling oracle) '"Well, is she kind or isn't she? I don't know . . ."' Continuing in her normal tones, 'And they don't tell you how to fix it. They don't tell you what to do to make it better. So you come out feeling, "Oh my god, I've got to get rid of the whole thing! I've got to re-write the whole thing, this is dreadful, they hate all of it." Whereas actually you could have preserved ninety-five per cent of it, and really all they were talking about was fixing these tiny little problems that'd make it all work. That's what I try to protect with writers. To say to them, "Your vision is fine, it's good. If they don't like that, then they just don't like the project." You have to stay true to what the project is because otherwise you end up with this chimera script which doesn't help anyone. The worst thing is people end up not caring. People go, "I don't know what this is anymore. I knew what it was at first and then I stopped knowing what it was or caring, so now it's a pile of rubbish and no one cares." It's your baby,' she stresses, 'you're the person who cares. So you're the one who's got to protect it, to protect the vision that it is. The person giving you notes doesn't care that much. Not really. You will get the odd person who does, who says, "I really want to get this made, I really love this project, let's make this happen." But generally you are just another pile of scripts on their desk. They just want you to make it work. That's one of the biggest things I've learnt – that only you can make it work. The writer. Everybody else is giving you advice how to make it work, but only you know. You have to get to that point where you're like, "Ahhhhh . . .!"' She gazes up at an invisible light bulb of inspiration flicking on.

When it comes to being on the receiving end of notes, Alice reflects, 'I've got a lot better at dealing with notes, because I take it less personally now. I try to find the note behind the note. That's what people often say, and I think I've got a lot better at doing that because I'm less emotionally involved with it. You have to do a bit of amateur psychology sometimes and go, "Why do they want me to change this?" rather than thinking "I've got to change this." Sometimes I'll be in meetings now and they'll be saying, "We thought maybe you could do this" and I'm going, "No, I've got completely a different idea, this is how it's going to work." And that's not to say the notes weren't useful. Because they were detecting a problem or something that wasn't quite working, but I'm going to have a completely different solution to what they are going to have. Neil Gaiman talks about this – if you get lots of notes about a particular bit then you know it's a problem, but what they're saying is a problem about it is not necessarily correct. I've got to a point now where I very much hear what they're saying, but I'm going to have my own solution to it.'

She expands, 'I enjoy suggestions. I've got to a point of maturity where I'm not like,' (she puts on a spoilt-kid-refusing-to-eat-its-peas voice) '"Urgh, I don't want *your* idea." Because sometimes you get that, someone going, "Yeah, that is a good idea, but you would have to kill me before I took that on, because it wasn't mine, so I'm not doing it." And you're like, "But your great script provoked that brilliant idea, so you still created it." Again, it's like the viewer at home going, "Oh, it would have been great if she did this at the end, oh she didn't, what a disappointment." All you're doing is recreating that audience experience. So if someone says to you, "I was expecting her to do this and she didn't", that's a great suggestion, go with it. Making stuff is such a more team experience than you realize. When you get really good producers on board you are going to feel like you're making that thing together with those people.

And if you've got great producers you're going to respect what they say, and think, "Oh yeah, great, let's do that." It's nice to feel "let's" rather than "I'll", like all the burden is on me, I've got to make this work – you're going to feel that anyway, so it can be really nice and comforting to feel like it's you and some friends chatting about some ideas and discussing what will be fun to watch. What's great about my producer, Vaughan Sivell, is he enjoys the idea, and he sees the overall vision. That's what I like, someone who sees the broad strokes and goes, "I can see how it's going to work, let's do it." Rather than someone already nit-picking notes before we've really got going. Because you're going to have to change it when you sell it anyway, so there's no point someone nit-picking notes on a scene that might not even make it. As long as it's not really bad! You don't want to be sending out a bad script obviously. But someone going, "Does that word read?" You're like, "What's the point of nit-picking over that?" Film4 or whoever might say they don't like that character and so you cut the whole character and meanwhile we haven't spent hours worrying about what word he used at this point on page thirty-seven.'

She asserts, 'I like people who are very positive. Something I've learned through my time in the industry is that I can get quite easily disparaged. I can have quite low self-esteem about my work and whether it's any good. I don't have that bullet-proof confidence of walking into a meeting and coming out going, "Oh, they're all idiots! I'm not selling it to them." I can quite easily come out going, "Oh my god the whole idea's awful!" So to me it's really important that I've got someone who feels like they're on my side. That they get the idea, they like the idea, they're focusing on making the idea work. And that they trust me. That's massive, someone saying, "You'll make it work." That's what is hard to deal with sometimes when you work with producers and execs, and from their notes you feel like maybe they aren't sure you'll make it work.'

We discuss whether there's an unconscious bias of people having less faith in women, and if that can unwittingly manifest through notes. Alice observes, 'I've spoken to script editors who say women get a much harder time in the room, generally. Their ideas get doubted much quicker. I also think if you're writing from a female perspective, which is quite common for female writers, your voice and your perspective is going to be new. So people get very nervous about it; like, "Why isn't the normal thing that normally happens in these narratives happening?" and you're like, "Well, because women's voice in cinema is still new." So it still feels clumsy and awkward and weird, but at the same time – that's what makes it exciting and fresh and dynamic. So a lot of that is really tricky because you come out going, "Why don't they get what I'm trying to say? Isn't it really obvious?" And it isn't obvious to them. Again that's why I try and surround myself with figures who are really supportive. I think there's also an unspoken thing, I don't want to over-egg the pudding, but the kind of traumatic experiences you've had with script development, you can be dragging those with you. And people don't really understand that. And I'm sure that's the same for Black writers, writers of colour, that you're like: "I've had a lot of rejections. A lot. A disproportionate number of rejections. And I've at some point come to think that it's my fault. Or I've been made to feel it's my fault, that I'm not good enough." And that's very hard to shake. Yet it's almost like the organization is expecting and wanting you to be super-confident. They're like, "Show us that you're going to do this well by being super-confident and almost cocky." Because that's what they're used to directors being like – going, "I know everything and I'm a genius." That's the stereotype: "I'm not changing my idea, I'm a genius, how dare you." And I also hear this from industry people: "Yeah, we did develop all these women's ideas but they didn't quite push it through and they weren't quite good enough." And I think, that was a talented woman who was trying to get a project made and you didn't help her to make it. That's your failure. That's not her failure. Because there's a different set of experiences behind that woman. I was talking to a friend about age as well. Women will quite often be older, because it's taken them a long time to tap into the industry. And there's quite a discrimination about that. I'm only making my second feature as a director, I'd love to be on my fifth feature but I'm not, because of the crap that I have to put up with basically!' She laughs, continuing, 'There's also that thing of as a man in your forties as a director you might be seen as just getting started, whereas there's more ageism towards women. Even a note I had recently saying that having a drugs scene in a film is dated, I was like, "Are you sort of implying that I'm too old to be writing this? I'm not cool or trendy enough or something?" And that's so short-sighted. Look at Jane Campion, she's not kowtowing to anyone's fashion or what's trendy or what young people want to see. She just makes her own vision and that's why she's at the top of her game. There's a lot of short-sightedness you have to deal with in the industry. The best thing you can do is let the work speak for itself, unfortunately, because getting the chance to make it is few and far between.'

Alice addresses the delicate art of distinguishing genuinely useful notes from those which may arise from people not being as accustomed to women's voices and ways of storytelling. 'It's about seeing the note behind the note,' she reiterates. Advising, 'When you come to tackle them, first do all the notes that are the easy ones. Where a joke wasn't landing, do that. Where a scene wasn't working, do that. Then you can take a pace back. Sometimes they say with screenwriting a pain in the wrist can be a problem in the elbow. So you might have fixed some stuff by doing those smaller structural notes, where suddenly the people giving notes go, "Oh, it's not such a problem now that she's dumped him, because you did these other notes and now it makes much more sense." So that's the first stage, to do those. But if the notes are really, really riling you I think you have to be like a barrister for the cause. For a start say: "This is why I'm having a problem with this note. This is what I was trying to say with this and this is why I like it." Then see what that dialogue leads to. That discussion may generate another idea for how to fix it. Often it'll be some completely other solution, it's not A or B, it's Z. Don't be afraid to have a discussion with the person who's giving you the notes if you have that opportunity, as you would with a script editor, but maybe not so much with a commissioner. Say to a producer: "I really want to give this a go and how do we make it work?" But you have to pick your battles. Because if there's five things in there that aren't working and you're sticking to your guns refusing to change any of them, then they're not going to see their way through to that message that you're really trying to give. So it might be that you go, "I'm going to leave this one thing in there, that to me means loads, because it's a new perspective of a female voice that she isn't going to do this, she is going to dump him and I know it seems weird, but that's the message that I'm trying to get across." But you have to fix all those other things. So that it doesn't seem like this old banger of a script that's got loads of problems. Cut the dead weight and then your message that you're trying to get through is much more likely to get through. And that's true too for an audience watching it. If there's something that's weird or new, it needs to feel intentional. If you've got loads of clumsy mistakes all over the script it's not going to feel intentional. Make sure that anything in your script feels like it's meant to be there. So that the audience trusts that, rather than thinking it's an error!'

Alice evaluates how to deal with conflicting notes. 'It's really hard,' she acknowledges. Advising, 'It's worth looking at what tallies together – places where you're always getting notes, it might be you're not getting exactly the same note, but it's a note about the same place, or the same thing. Then you know there is definitely a problem. They might have proposed three different solutions and the answer might be a completely other solution. But you know there's definitely a problem there. I would try and avoid all of those notes coming in at the same time anyway. Because that's not great for anyone. And a producer would quite often protect you from that being the case. Also, there doesn't need to be a sort of panic about it. Because I think a lot of people give notes and then completely forget them. They're not scrutinizing and worrying about these notes. They're not going to look at your script and go,' (she assumes a mock stern, admonishing face, like a schoolteacher from the 1950s) '"You kept in the Ford Fiesta joke. I told you to get rid of that!" They're not going to care, not really. They won't notice. Especially if it's something more of a particularly petty note, don't sweat it. It's not a big deal. What your next step is, is to just make it better. That's my shorthand for everything. The best note that you could have is, "Just make it better." Because you know how to make it better, they don't. They're just critiquing it. So the first thing to do is think what do you want to do with the next draft? Re-reading it, what did you see that was wrong with it? Having left it for a couple of weeks you'll think, "Oh, I've realized this was too long and this was awful and I didn't like that scene." Do all of those changes and then map it with the notes. Suddenly that note about this scene where they wanted you to change the dialogue, that scene has gone because you decided to cut it. Amazingly you will have answered some of their notes without even looking at them. And it's surprising how much of that stuff they're going to forget. Which isn't an excuse to ignore all the notes! You've still got to look at them. But you've also got to realize, this next draft is just going to be better. It's the same with acting, just do the next one better. Don't listen to all the noise, all the details, all the, "Can you do it angry but then sad at the end, and faster and put a pause in there", get rid of all that – just do the next one better. So you do that, as answers your feelings about it, and quite often you'll send it in and they'll be like, "Wow, this is great." Because they've read it before and gone, "Urgh, there's a few problems in this" and then they read the better version and something they might have complained about before they don't mind about now, because it's not an old banger any more. It's suddenly a sleek beautiful model and they don't care as much about all the funny little stuff that was sticking out to them before.'

She ponders whether it's partly human nature, that some of the reason people feel a script has got better is down to the very fact they gave notes, even if those notes haven't been specifically addressed. She declares, 'Notes are an investment. If I've given you notes, quite lengthy notes, I've invested in your idea, I've gone, "It's worth my time to fix because it's a good idea. It's good and you're good so I've invested in it." So definitely there's that sense where people giving notes can feel "Oh, this is all because of me that this is great!"' she laughs.

Alice describes how being an actor as well as a writer and director can feed into notes and development. She says, 'I find reading the script out loud as an actor helps people get the jokes. With *Sightseers* I remember receiving quite a lot of notes and then me and Steve [Oram] did a live read and everyone went, "Oh, we get it now." Basically they'd said there weren't enough jokes in it, but once they heard it read they were laughing. A script can be such an imperfect medium because you don't get intonation, and you don't really get rhythm, you don't get music or sound. So stuff that you can do to bring it to life can help. But you have to accept that if you're selling this script, people reading it aren't going to have all of those things! So if a script editor's working with an actor-writer, it's useful if they say, "I love when you do that, that facial expression is hilarious – can you write it into the script?" We did have some of those notes with *Sightseers*. It was like, "OK, we get now what's happening, but you need to put that into the directions of the script." You don't want it to get flabby, because people skim, I'm terrible for skim-reading directions, but it's finding ways of conveying that stuff.'

Alice was pregnant when she wrote *Prevenge*. Which, as she says, was handy for saving money on prosthetics for the pregnant character she played in the film, but did confer a certain time pressure. She identifies benefits in that necessarily speedy development process: 'It helps people to focus on the broad strokes. Rather than these weird petty little notes that you get because someone's sat behind their desk thinking, "Oh, I should probably spend some time looking at this script and reading it" with no urgency whatsoever, so they're like, "Uh, I don't really like that joke." If there's real urgency, like we're filming it next week, they are going to go, "Forget the note about the joke, this whole scene needs fixing because this is in the wrong place!" So they give you much broader stroke notes, which are actually much more useful. Because a lot of the things that are crap and don't work, there's no way you're going to film them. A rubbish joke – you get onto set, you realize, "This joke doesn't work" and you change it. That's the reality, everything gets fixed in filming anyway, or you hope it does. Obviously no one's going to take a punt on that being the case! Because that would be ridiculous. But I do think that's the reality of it – so much stuff gets fixed last minute. When you work on a big production they're sending new pages all the time. Because they're going, "Oh we found the location where we're filming and the line about the staircase doesn't work because there is no staircase so we've changed that line." And that will be happening up to the eleventh hour, those kinds of changes, that's the reality of it. So the idea someone's nit-picking over some weird little thing can be ridiculous. So doing development really quickly can be great in that sense. But equally I've done short films where people do send you the most ridiculous notes because they're having a panic about you filming. They're sort of freaking out and that can send you into a bit of a tailspin. I did a short film with Jacqueline [Wright] years ago and in development they said, "Ooooh, you've got a scene in a car, it's very difficult to shoot in a car, you should not shoot in a car, don't shoot in a car, put that scene somewhere else." And we were like, "It'll be fine, we'll just shoot in a car." Then at the last minute we decided let's not shoot it in a car, we'll shoot it somewhere else, not a big deal. And they had a massive panic. Phoning us the day before shooting going, "You can't change things last minute like that! If it's scripted as being a car it's got to be in a car." And we were like, "You were the people who told us to not put it in a car!" We'd finally stopped resisting and set it somewhere else, set it on a beach, and they had a massive fit about it! And that can send you into a bit of a tailspin. You have to realize they're human these commissioners, they have a panic because their neck is on the line about this project. And I think in those situations you have to talk them down, and kind of go "It's OK, we're going to do this. It's fine. We know what we're doing." And they go, "Oh, OK." Basically they do not know whether they've hired an idiot or not, that's their worst fear. So they're like, "You might be an idiot and that would be my fault and I'll lose my job!" And you're like, "How can you not know whether I'm an idiot or not?" I don't understand. But anyway, that's why I'm not a commissioner.'

As we come to a close, Alice reflects on the importance of telling stories. She says, 'To me it's about different perspectives. Some people say books are empathy machines, but I think film is even more so, because when you lock eyes with a character, even though they're not looking at you, you still sort of step into their shoes, you become them. So I think it's a chance to show people a different perspective to what they have. Or it might be the same perspective they have, but it's validating their perspective. It's going, "It's alright to feel this, it's alright to be this person." And really, the way that I work as a script editor is I want to convey that writer's perspective, the perspective that they're trying to put across. And do that as truthfully and as well as you can.'

London, via Zoom, February 2022

Selected credits, awards and nominations

Stiffy: Writer, Actor (2005), [Film] Dir. Jacqueline Wright, UK: Sister Films.
Out of Water: Writer, Actor (2007), [Film] Dir. Jacqueline Wright, UK: Ignu
    Films.
Beehive: Co-writer, Actor (2008), [TV series] E4.
Sightseers: Co-writer, Actor (2012), [Film] Dir. Ben Wheatley, UK: StudioCanal UK.
    British Independent Film Award – Best Screenplay (2012)
    Sitges Film Festival award – Best Screenplay (2012)
    London Critics' Circle Awards – Breakthrough British Filmmaker (2013)
    Writers' Guild of Great Britain nomination – Best First Screenplay (2013)
Solitudo: Writer, Director, Actor (2014), [Film] UK.
Prevenge: Writer, Director, Actor (2017), [Film] UK: Western Edge Pictures.

British Independent Film Award nomination – Douglas Hickox Award for debut
  directing
British Screenwriters' Award nomination – Outstanding Newcomer for British Feature
  Film Writing (2017)
Brazil Fantaspoa festival award – Best Director (2017)
National Film Awards nomination – Best Thriller (2018)
Timestalker: Writer, Director, Actor (in production), [Film] UK: Western Edge Pictures.

FrightFest – Screen International Horror Rising Star Award (2016)

Michael Pearce

'When you're writing you're in the thick of it; you don't have a clear perspective of the mountain you're trying to climb. Receiving notes is like radioing to a helicopter pilot who can help you on your journey to the summit.'

6 Michael Pearce, photo by Kerry Brown, courtesy of Ivana MacKinnon.

'Excuse the boxes,' Michael Pearce gestures apologetically at the books and lamps flotsam of life indicating a recent move. Behind him the wide windows of his new home look out onto a bright East London skyline. A striking contrast to the sedate island landscape of Jersey where he grew up, and which he used as the setting for his debut feature, *Beast* (2017). Michael discovered his passion for filmmaking as a teenager, studying art and media on the island before specializing in directing, first at Bournemouth Arts Institute, then at the National Film and Television School.

Today, as well as unpacking, Michael is busy with the run up to release of his second feature, *Encounter* (2021). Yet, kindness and consideration spilling out of him, he's keen to ensure we have enough time to chat, offering a follow up time to talk further. Such deep-seated compassion and understanding of others are ingrained in his films. *Beast*, his BAFTA winning debut, and the about to be released *Encounter,* both use genre, thriller frameworks to explore complex character psychology. Art-house films in commercial skins.

It's no mean feat to win a BAFTA for your debut feature. Yet writer and director Michael Pearce is self-deprecatingly amused at himself for the ten years it took him after graduating from the National Film and Television School to make that first film, *Beast*. He shares his journey to making the film and the role notes, script editors and development played in the process.

Michael recalls, 'The thing I struggled with most was the transition from writing short films to writing something feature length.' He explains, 'The difference between writing a ten-page script and a hundred-page script is not just length, they operate in a completely different way. A short film can be an exercise in tone and mood, it can be one event that you're observing in real time, the development of a character can be quite minimal, and so it's a different form of engagement with the audience. I was developing several feature ideas and I realized at some moment with each of them that they didn't have a deep enough story engine. They could have made a very slight seventy-five-minute micro-budget film, but I didn't want my first film to be slight. It took me a while to find the story, character and themes that warranted a feature format.'

Michael credits his participation in a development programme as a turning point. He says, 'Getting into the Torino Film Lab really helped me, it accelerated my understanding of what a feature script needed. The lab's explicit purpose is to help short filmmakers transition into developing their debut feature script. It had a similar format to the NFTS, in that you would pitch your story verbally to other filmmakers in the room and they would give you feedback on it. Then you would write a treatment, and drafts of the script, and everyone had to read each other's work and comment on it, and your assigned script editor would provide their feedback and bring their experience to the table. It could sometimes be a bruising experience, because as much as we were all trying to be encouraging, it was only really going to be helpful if you were very candid with your thoughts.' Michael explains, 'A lot of development is failing as a writer, and so much of writing is re-writing, so there wasn't always a nice warm embrace and praise every time you pitched your story or delivered your treatment or script. It was more often than not people picking it apart and finding the weaknesses.' Michael highlights the value of being receptive to notes and feedback during development, remarking, 'It's hard to make a generalization, because it was also dependent on the personalities in the room, but I felt like I observed that the filmmakers who had gone to film school found that an easier process than people who hadn't. Some people who hadn't been through that experience of pitching stories and then getting feedback from everyone, could struggle to hear and integrate feedback into their script. I saw people who had a great premise, a project with a lot of potential, but when they received feedback they struggled to engage with it and their project became quite static, developing only incrementally over the year. I also saw people who had started out with a so-so premise, but they really engaged with the process and were curious about how people responded to their work, and they ended up developing really compelling material.'

Michael recommends striving for an attitude of open receptiveness to notes. He suggests, 'The person giving notes is your first audience, and I think it'd be counterproductive to not be curious about how an audience reacts to your story. You can reject what isn't helpful and integrate what is. If you're seeing it as a tool for you to continue to develop the story, then there's not much bad that can come out of receiving notes. Ideally it's going to shine a light on weaknesses that you're going to want to solve. Because if you make the film and they're not solved, it's only going to hurt you more later down the line. If you see it as a painful hurdle to get over, it won't be enjoyable and it'll be hard to get much out of it. I try to see it as an opportunity to recalibrate my perspective on the material. When you're writing you're in the thick of it; you don't have a clear perspective of the mountain you're trying to climb. Receiving notes is like radioing to a helicopter pilot who can help you on your journey to the summit. They can have insights by virtue of not being on the difficult step-by-step journey. Not listening to notes is like choosing to throw your radio down a crevasse and just ploughing on through what could be blind alleys and might mean you never reach the peak.

'Try to leave your ego at the door when you go for script meetings,' Michael advises, conceding, 'You can never completely do it, but try do it as much as possible. Go in being very open-minded and curious about people's ideas. Because really those script sessions are an opportunity to strengthen material. I think some writers can see it as an adversarial relationship, almost like they've decided that someone's trying to ruin their material so they need to defend it. They might be willing to accommodate the smallest notes, the ones that are unambiguously beneficial, like a logic error in the story, but anything beyond that they're sceptical of. I'm sure there are some writers that are so good they don't need notes, but for most of us, if the notes are smart and thoughtful and if the person giving them understands what the film is trying to do, then there's nothing to lose by engaging with them.' He adds, 'I don't think anyone giving notes is expecting that you do all of them. They'd probably find it a bit strange if you did all of them! Anytime I've given notes there's maybe only a third of them where I could say hand on heart with full confidence that this will make the material stronger. Another third I might have identified a problem but I might not be providing the right solution, those notes need creative interpretation. The last third are more wildcard, and I try to caveat them as such. And some notes shouldn't be integrated, or can't be, but they helpfully initiate a deeper conversation. The conversation around the note can sometimes be more helpful than the note itself. Notes aren't instructions, at best they're often a catalyst for a creative discussion.'

When it comes to dealing with a note you may not agree with, Michael reflects, 'It depends on the note.' But he suggests the key is 'Knowing what you want the film to be, even in somewhat abstract terms – not what happens, but how you want it to affect the audience, what their relationship with the film will be, how they will engage with the characters. Do you want it to be a subjective experience where the audience goes through the same emotional or psychological experience that the characters are going through? Or do you want the audience to be positioned in a more objective state where they're scrutinizing what happens? Which is a bit of a colder experience, but in some ways a more intellectually engaged one. Whichever way you conceptualize the film and the audiences' relationship with it and the characters, will provide a filter for which notes are helpful.'

Looking back to the process of development of what was to become his BAFTA winning debut feature, *Beast,* Michael recalls, 'The first day of the Torino Film Lab I had a twenty-page treatment for another idea, the idea that had got me onto the Lab. Then the first day, I changed my mind. I only had a paragraph for the new idea. It was going to be loosely "inspired" by the Beast of Jersey case, focusing on a woman who falls in love with the psychopath and what her emotional journey would be during an investigation. That was pretty much it. During the first year of the Torino Film Lab it was about fleshing that out into a thirty-page treatment. Once I had that, I condensed it down to a ten-page treatment, to make it more readable as I was meeting producers. Agile Films came on board and with their support I developed that treatment into a script. Myles Payne and Kristian Brodie at Agile Films were a great fresh pair of eyes. Once we had a draft we were happy with, we applied to the BFI for funding. After working on several drafts with them we started to look for some other producers to join the team. I felt the script was close to being done, maybe four-fifths of the way there, but that there was still work to do. When we met with potential producers, many said the script didn't need any work, and it made me hesitant to go with those producers because I knew it wasn't there yet. But because I'd been working on it for so long, I found it difficult to identify what the weak areas were, so I was looking for creative producers who could help with that. Ivana MacKinnon and Lauren Dark pitched not only what they would do to produce the film, but also how they would want to continue to develop the script, and they had many astute observations about the material and that's part of the reason I wanted to work with them. Shortly afterwards Film4 came on board. So it was Torino Film Lab, Agile Films, BFI, Ivana and Lauren, and Film4.' He counts them off on his fingers as he lists them: 'Five stages of people coming on board and feeding into the notes.'

Michael recounts a specific instance of how development informed the script. He recalls, 'I remember Ivana [MacKinnon] being very keen that we dig into the character background more. She encouraged me to write a sort of biography for each of the main characters. I think I might have been a bit resistant at first, because it felt like homework, like an exercise that wouldn't necessarily directly translate to something in the script. But she convinced me of the value of it, she said at the very least I was going to be able to speak to the actors with more authority. So for Jessie [Buckley]'s character I wrote around six pages: what her upbringing was, what her status was within the family, within the wider community, and how it all affected her. It forced me to articulate her place within the world and the events that shaped her. When I wrote that she lives this Cinderella-type existence, where she's kind of maligned and overlooked within this family and is on the periphery of it looking in, it translated into an image at the beginning of the film where she's standing on the periphery of her own birthday party, not speaking to anyone and she gets upstaged by her sister who announces her engagement.

'The mystery at the centre of the film isn't necessarily who the killer is, it's what kind of person Moll is,' Michael explains, 'what's motivating her and what moral boundaries she will cross, and how far will we stick with her. Part of the project of the film was to test the audience's identification with the lead character. I was very curious how audiences would react. Some filmmakers go into a test screening kind of kicking and screaming. I have some sympathy with that, because it is a really painful process. But I was listening to a Denis Villeneuve podcast the other day and he said he used to hate test screenings, but another director once said to him that test screenings are like a time machine – they allow you to go into the future and show your film to an audience and you get to hear what their response is, and then you get to go back in time and change your movie. You could also apply this to script notes – it's like having a time machine that can go even deeper into the future.'

At times Michael also gives notes to other writers. Examining the detail of his approach he says, 'When I give notes I try to articulate to the writer what it is I think they're trying to do – the story that they're trying to tell, the theme that they're trying to explore, and see if they agree with my interpretation. If they do, that's great because I've understood their intention, and I can measure how successfully or unsuccessfully I think that's coming across on the page. And if the writer doesn't agree, then that's also interesting because there's a discrepancy between their intention and my interpretation. So before going into any kind of structural notes or looking at character I would take a macro view and see if your perception of the material is aligned to the writer's. That's always a very enlightening conversation and it helps you filter the notes which you think are going to be most helpful to the writer. Sometimes being brutally honest helps to get your point across. It can be totally legitimate to say: "The middle of your script is fucking boring" if you think that's going to be a quicker, sharper way to convey that it's dramatically inert for forty pages. Providing you know the person you're speaking to and you can make a good assumption they're going to appreciate the directness. There are different schools of thought about whether you should offer suggestions or not. I've always appreciated it when people have, because you can take or leave them.'

When it comes to how hard someone should push a note if a writer is resistant to it, Michael reasons, 'I think every writer is guilty of having blind spots and of burying our heads in the sand when it comes to feedback, especially feedback that might necessitate a more dramatic rewrite or re-conception of the story. In those cases, I think it's good to be incessant. If someone doesn't hear it the first time round, then the onus is on the person giving feedback to make an even more compelling case, to reframe and articulate their point in a different way. But the person receiving the notes has to go into that conversation with a genuine openness and curiosity. If they're not open to any notes except the very modest ones, it's not really a good faith conversation. And as mentioned, notes shouldn't be instructions, they're a catalyst for creative discussion. Usually it's through a dialectical back and forth that the right idea is landed upon. But it needs to be both parties – the writer to come in with an openness, and the note-giver to come in with a sense of investment and creative generosity. Even then it doesn't mean people will see eye to eye. We've all got different taste, it's not an objective science.'

Reflecting on his own work and at what point he likes to share things for feedback he says, 'It depends on the relationship. If it's someone that you're generating ideas with, a really close collaborator like a co-writer, or a producer or a script editor you have worked with before, you can share material at a very early stage. If you're sharing it with a producer you haven't worked with before, or a new financier, you want it to have found its feet to some degree in terms of the story shape, who the character is, what they're about, what the theme is. It's totally contingent on the relationship. Generally the more developed something is, the more useful the feedback is going to be, they've got more to feed back on and dig into. If it's a half page treatment it's going to be quite a short conversation.'

One big difference with Michael's second feature, *Encounter*, was that the idea and screenplay were originated by writer Joe Barton. Joe's script had been in development for a while before Michael came on board. By that time Joe was busy writing what was to become the hugely acclaimed television series, *Giri/Haji* (2019), and Michael continued developing and re-drafting the script for *Encounter* on his own for a further couple of years. Michael puts the relative number of notes on each of the films down to that genesis as much as to *Encounter* being his second feature. 'I probably did get less notes on *Encounter* than on *Beast*,' he acknowledges, 'but it was a different case, where that script had already been developed seven years before I came onto it. So honestly speaking, if I had originated *Encounter*, I could imagine a scenario where there was as much scrutiny on it as there was on *Beast*. I think the reason it took so long with *Beast* was because it took me a while to find my voice and the story I wanted to tell. I wrote versions of *Beast* that were more austere and art-house, and I realized they didn't feel right to me; and I wrote more explicitly genre and commercial versions which also didn't feel right, I needed to get those versions out of my system. Whereas now, I'm a bit quicker to know the direction I want to go in.'

Both *Beast* and *Encounter* are character focused dramas within genre frameworks. Michael discusses how he works with the actors responsible for bringing those characters to satisfyingly messy, complex life, and being open to integrating their notes: 'I've always said to actors I've worked with that they should feel welcome to give their thoughts on the script. Predominantly, actors' notes have been about calibrating dialogue, finding nuances that would be more natural for them or for how they perceive the character. And I'm always happy to do that. Perhaps some writer-directors might be more particular about certain words, phrases or lines of dialogue. I want an authentic performance; that overrides specificities of a particular phrase or a way of speaking. Then there's also been discussion about beats of behaviour. Riz

[Ahmed] for example was really good at that. Scrutinizing every beat in *Encounter* from his character's perspective: "If I'm walking into this house and there's a light on, how hesitant should I be? Am I taking a gun with me? Maybe I shouldn't have it, maybe I shouldn't be holding it because that's too explicitly threatening, it puts my character on the offensive, I don't even know if someone's in there, they could be friendly, what kind of message does that send? I'm going to take it with me but it's in my back pocket. I'm taking a torch with me, I don't know where the lights are, I'm a trained Marine, so the first thing I'm going to do is scan the room . . .". He'd really walk through the beats. It was very interesting to see that process, because he was projecting himself forward four months to being on set. Jessie [Buckley] and Johnny [Flynn] were also like that in different ways.'

Michael describes how actors' input can contribute to script development. He says, 'I think actors appreciate that I want to continue to explore the character with them. As with Jessie in *Beast*, I wrote a backstory for Riz's character and we talked quite a bit about what his character's childhood upbringing was like, because that was the furnace that forged this sword that was Malik. Malik had been in very vulnerable situations as a child and had gone through some traumatic experiences and he'd never had a protector, which usually is fulfilled by the role of the parent.' In the film, all this backstory is alluded to in a single line from Octavia Spencer's character. Michael explains, 'It was only one sentence in the film, that some audiences might not pick up on, but for us there was a rich history. Then Riz and I got up to the crime Malik committed for which he was court-martialled and sent to military prison. Originally in the script I had written that Malik had executed an enemy combatant, a Taliban fighter, who they should have taken as a prisoner of war. I was very interested in the case of a British Marine who killed a Taliban fighter and then was court-martialled. There was a fascinating discussion around the Marine's culpability because of what they had experienced up until that point. They were obviously very traumatized by going on so many tours, they were fighting in the most dangerous square mile on the planet and had witnessed many of their friends being killed, but they'd also broken the Geneva Conventions. It felt like a unique type of guilt and shame that he was experiencing from that, and a dramatic fall from grace, to go from being a revered and honoured Marine to being someone that was cast from that group. Riz and I had quite a few discussions about race and Malik's ethnicity and how that plays into the script and what kind of messages the audience might extrapolate from the film. We were often discussing that, and Riz said there was something that concerned him about Malik's crime. He was worried about using a "Brown life" as the biographical footnote of the lead character. We had interesting discussions about what the ramifications were once the film was finished, because either the film's going to have to make Malik confront this crime that he committed and the film is going to have to reckon with it, and given that the film takes place over a weekend do we have the space in the story-world to do that justice? And how does that impact the audiences' relationship with the character? It could damn Malik in the audience's eyes. Or there's a version where the film doesn't reckon with his crime and the audience's sympathy is very much with Malik, in which case are we kind of morally exonerating him for this crime and what's the ethics of that? In the script the crime is alluded to in a few lines of dialogue, but we put it under intense scrutiny. Ultimately I decided it's too complex a subject matter and it's such a moral quagmire, which needed space to be explored in a nuanced way. And in our story we don't have the space to do it justice. So that's an example of where I changed something that I wouldn't have without those conversations with Riz.'

Continuing thinking about notes around characters Michael says, 'It's useful when someone is doing a read focusing specifically on the characters. So the story beats or any kind of plot mechanics or the architecture of the story is set aside for the moment. You're putting aside everything that isn't behaviour. Sometimes you can do a read focusing on just one character, or if the film focuses on two characters, it could be about their relationship and tracking that through the course of the film.' He illustrates, 'What I found helpful during the development of *Beast*, was when we were scrutinizing the audience's relationship to the character – when are you aligned and have sympathy for her and when are you starting to doubt her and when that identification becomes more tested. Because that was part of the project of *Beast*, to create this almost shameful pact between the audience and character. So that by the time you're three-quarters of the way through the film you might be starting to regret the empathy you feel towards her, and the identification you have with her, but by that point it's too late. You can't retroactively go, "I wish I didn't like them as much." With notes focusing just on character we would look at the beginning of the script and look at Moll. We knew at the beginning it was about creating this bond and connection between audience and character. I described it as wanting to create an umbilical cord between the audience and the character, that you cared so much for, who you're spiritually invested in. I'm sure earlier in development there were things in the first thirty pages which jeopardized that investment and made you look at Moll as a "case", you were perhaps fascinated by her, but you weren't identifying with her. Our film needed to operate by putting the audience in the character's subjective emotional world early on so we could test it later. So we were careful about which beats of behaviour to show the audience. We wanted the audience to be intrigued by Moll's behaviour, but also emotionally drawn towards her. For example, we kept in the moment where she breaks a glass and then she self-harms, because that's an indicator that she's troubled, but you immediately have sympathy for someone who is self-harming because you know there's trauma and pain there. We don't know yet that she was culpable of a crime and that she's still wracked by guilt and that crime was quite horrific in its own way. We're going to leave that till the second half of the script, but we're going to let you know that she is someone who has some kind of painful trauma and she hasn't found a healthy way to deal with it. This brought us closer to Moll at the beginning, and the messy complexity of her is gradually revealed later in the story.'

Michael describes *Beast* as a 'dark, adult fairy-tale'. He reflects on whether it's useful for people giving notes to talk in fairy-tale or mythic terms: 'There's a danger that if you use that terminology it can feel quite general and detached from the specifics of the script that you're discussing. It can feel quite removed and abstract. However, it can be helpful and it can enlighten a problem or a solution in a script, it just shouldn't need an academic knowledge of that school of thought or those archetypes to really receive the message. If it's contingent on knowing the book *The Hero with a Thousand Faces*[1] then I don't think it's useful. Whereas if referring to them can make your case more compelling,

---

[1]Campbell, J. (1949), *The Hero with a Thousand Faces*, New York: Pantheon Books.

even to the uninitiated, then yeah. I think writers can be, understandably, a bit cynical that you've taken a 'how to' screenwriting template and tried to apply it onto their script.' He summarizes, 'Sometimes it fits in a very elegant way and it will provide you with a solution and sometimes it doesn't.'

Before heading off to his next meeting about the release of *Encounter*, Michael concludes, 'For me stories are a creative vehicle to explore human behaviour. So what I want from a script editor is that they have a real curiosity about human behaviour, and how it comes across on the page; to have a deep interest into the characters and how they act and react, and what they're consciously wanting and subconsciously need. It's hard to come up with a tasty premise and a unique story-world, but beyond that, it's really about the characters; what do they want and why, how are they going to get it, and what are they hiding from themselves? It's about the emotional engine underneath the hood, what's driving the behaviour.'

London, via Zoom, October 2021

Selected credits, awards and nominations

Rite: Director (2010), [Film] UK: DigiCult.
    BAFTA nomination – Best Short Film (2011)
Keeping Up with the Joneses: Director (2013), [Film] UK: Incendiary Pictures.
    BAFTA nomination – Best British Short Film (2014)
Beast: Writer, Director (2017), [Film] UK: Altitude Film Entertainment.
    British Screenwriters' Awards nomination – Outstanding Newcomer for British
        Feature Film Writing (2018)
    British Independent Film Award nomination – Best Debut Screenwriter (2018)
    British Independent Film Award nomination – Best Screenplay (2018)
    British Independent Film Award nomination – Douglas Hickox Award for Best Debut
        (2018)
    British Independent Film Award nomination – Best Director (2018)
    British Independent Film Award nomination – Best British Independent Film (2018)
    BAFTA award – Outstanding Debut by a British Writer, Director or Producer (2019)
    London Critics' Circle Film Award – Breakthrough British/Irish Filmmaker of the
        year (2019)
Encounter: Co-writer, Director (2021), [Film] UK, US: Amazon Studios.
Echo Valley: Director (2024), [Film] USA: Apple Original Films.

Quick Fire Q&A 4:
Can you reveal any comically bad notes you've had?

'Oh god, in thirty years of writing I've had so many bad notes! Including a bizarre misunderstanding on *Blow Dry* – some hairdressing salons went through a phase of the hairdressers sitting on sort of saddles, like movable, backless chairs, so that they didn't have to stand up all day. I'd written for Alan Rickman to be sitting on one of those in the hairdressers in *Blow Dry*. Then somehow, this got back via Harvey [Weinstein] to Alan Rickman that he was going to be on a horse, in the hairdressing salon. And I was faced with the possibility of having to do a re-write with a horse in a hairdressing salon!' – **Simon Beaufoy**

'When we were writing *Shaun of the Dead,* someone read the script and basically said, "I guess my one note is – does it have to be zombies?" I think he just didn't care for zombies full stop. But that was his main note. And because me and Simon [Pegg] were writing our valentine to the zombie genre, this was not a very helpful note because we couldn't do anything about it. We wanted to make a zombie film. So throughout the entire production, and for years afterwards, every now and again, me and Simon would say to one another,

"Does it have to be zombies?" That's a note that still haunts me to this day.' – **Edgar Wright**

'On *Kill List* (2011) we got a request for a drawing of the map of the tunnels, to make sure that they understood which way they were going through the tunnels. There's quite a lot of bad notes! Or during the edit, asking for dialogue that doesn't exist, that was never in the script – "Can we put this line in?" I mean, no, it doesn't exist. That seems to be one I get quite a lot and this confuses me every time.' – **Ben Wheatley**

'I'm lucky to have had pretty good experiences. There have been strange interpretations though. Like, is James in *Ratcatcher* Jesus?

'I was on a workshop once where a Hollywood writer and advisor was confounded by my script as it didn't play by the rules – it was pretty far advanced at that point, it was a wobble but it made me more determined I was doing something I believed in even if not to everyone's taste.' – **Lynne Ramsay**

'Notes where you can't do anything – "I wish that dress had been blue." Criticizing something at a point where it's too late to change it, but you'll still remember the criticism every time to get to that scene.' – **Lone Scherfig**

'I was once asked by a producer what gave a Black female character the right to speak the way she did to a white male in the story. I responded to the note by saying "Would you ask the same question if the Black character's white female counterpart did the same?" I didn't really get a response back. But the question went away, let's put it that way.' – **Amma Asante**

'One on *Beast* was – "Since they're both singers, shouldn't Jessie Buckley and Johnny Flynn play a song together in the film?"' – **Michael Pearce**

'I've probably blanked a lot of the worst out! I got one note that the end of *Wolfwalkers* (2020) should be that the whole town had been bitten and everyone had turned into a wolfwalker. It was like some kind of Sam Raimi zombie apocalypse movie!' – **Tomm Moore**

'Oh my god, so many. There's too many to choose from! Well, recently someone told me having a drug scene in something was dated. And I was like, "How can that be?" When someone says something's old-fashioned it sets alarm bells ringing, because there's no bad ideas, and nothing's out of fashion – if it's out of fashion, let's bring it back! These are the sort of notes that alarm me because I think they're trying to please what they conceive of as being fashionable to an audience rather than what makes a good script.' – **Alice Lowe**

'I tend to just quickly forget the bad notes!' – **Corin Hardy**

Ben Wheatley

'There's a difference between starting from a place of being critical and starting from a place of wanting to help the filmmaker get their voice out.'

7 Ben Wheatley, photo courtesy of Ben Wheatley.

With a click Ben Wheatley appears on the computer screen; entirely mellow about accidentally being kept in a Zoom 'waiting room' and nice enough to chuckle at a weak joke hoping there were decent tea and cakes in it. It is four months into the pandemic. Zoom has become a familiar tool, if with unexpected secret rooms. And with typical industry, Ben has not only finished post-production on *Rebecca* (2020), an adaptation of the Daphne du Maurier novel, but also written a new script that he's prepping to shoot. 'I've been writing since 6am' he says happily.

After art school in Brighton, Ben began creating short gags and animations to post on early internet forums. One in particular, *Cunning Stunt*, in which Rob Hill appears to jump over a car only to be hit by another car as he celebrates, generated a huge number of views. His internet work caught the attention of ad agencies and Ben worked for a while in commercials, winning various awards, before moving into writing and directing episodes of television series.

Rather than follow the well-worn path of making a short film to persuade people to finance him for a feature, Ben decided to simply make one; *Down Terrace* (2010), which he directed and co-wrote. Together with Rob Hill and producer Andy Starke, Ben put together a budget of £6,000, tailoring the script so it could be achieved on that amount. He shot *Down Terrace* in eight days, calculating that was the maximum time you could take off freelance work in a month and still pay the mortgage. With a tight group of key collaborators, including his writing partner and wife Amy Jump, *Down Terrace*'s cinematographer Laurie Rose, and producer Andy Starke – with whom he co-founded Rook Films; Ben moves seamlessly back and forth between lower budget independent films like *A Field in England* (2013), episodes of television series such as *Doctor Who*, and bigger budget features *High-Rise* (2016) and *The Meg 2* (2023).

'Notes make me immediately furious. I almost can't even read them because I'm so cross,' Ben Wheatley observes in an amiable, matter of fact sort of way. Then explains how he handles them: 'What I tend to do to take the sting out of the tail of a note is I'll re-write the notes. I take out any descriptive stuff, and reduce them down to single points or words. Then you can deal with them. If they're clever about notes there'll be a fat blurb about how much they like what you've done, then there'll be a thing about these are the potential changes. So you strip it all back. And this is what some actors do to scripts as well – they take out all the description except for lines that they're saying. I've seen actor's versions of scripts which are just . . .'. He mimes concertinaing something right down, 'So you have to do that. And once you've taken the poison out of it, you can analyse it in terms of "Oh, really what they're saying is X. What they're really saying is the middle of the second act's a bit slow." Now that's a note. I like that note. I can deal with that note.'

He adds, 'Sometimes I'll write the notes back to them and go, "So this is what you're saying?" And in the process of doing that it makes you less cross. To a degree. Then you can go, "OK, that's a constructive point. I'll take the constructive bit and work with that."

'I've always maintained that it's the continuity of thought idea,' Ben explains, 'which is that each of the decisions that are made in a film can be made by anybody, and anybody can reasonably ask to change any reasonable amount of the film at any point. And it'd be very difficult to argue against if someone says for example, "I don't like those trousers. Could they be green rather than blue?" You go, "That's a reasonable thought, I suppose they could be." But the problem is, once a few of those ideas start to creep into the project then it dilutes the thinking process. And some of the things in a film are a web of thought, and once you start unpicking it through other people's ideas it ruins your train of thought and your general image of what you're doing. I think that is the danger of notes in general.'

He asserts, 'There may be mistakes in my work, but they are my own mistakes. They're not the mistakes of a script development person or a group of people. I guess that's a wabi-sabi kind of idea of how to do things – that problems aren't necessarily problems, bugs are features and so on. I think that's really important for making stuff which has a voice in it.'

Ben continues, 'The other point of view I have about it is from when I've given notes on stuff myself, in a commercial realm when I've been working as creative director. If I heavily note people, I find then what I get back is a version of myself. If I break their back when they're trying to make something for me and go, "I don't like this and I don't like that and I don't like all these things", eventually they'll give up and they'll give me what I want; but I'm not a designer, so why am I not designing it myself, and why did I hire them in the first place? I learnt that quite early on. I realized "Oh, this thing I've got back is a bit rubbish a and it's my fault because I've done it to them." If I want to be creative, my creative act is hiring them, not telling them what to do.'

Illustrating further he says, 'In painting if there was a job where someone rocks up at the studio, sits in the corner and goes, "Hmmm, I don't know, have you thought about putting a bit more heavy paint on the cape?" is that a real job? Doesn't sound like one! The idea that the artist doesn't know what they're doing and they need help. But if they ask for help – that's a different thing. Because there's no right and wrong way of process. So someone's process might be "I'll give my work out to people, I'll get the feedback and I'll work through the feedback because I can't see it myself." Someone else's process might be "I'm going to write this thing, I want to make it and I have to get money for it, but now I've got to jump through all these hoops because the people who might give the money for it want to tell me what they think about it." One of the reasons I didn't try and get money for *Down Terrace* is how the regional funding bodies seemed to be very intent on telling you what to do. Giving you notes and making you jump through hoops and having opinions. Tons of opinions! It feels a bit like they act like a studio. I think they just get into their roles. I mean, it's a hard job, they can't just give money out to people without some kind of process.'

He distinguishes, 'It's different when it's a commission. If they're saying we've got a space and our financial side needs something that fits this particular space, then you have to fit that space. And that's when you get stuff that's a bit more prescriptive. If they've got a commercial imperative that they feel they've got an agenda for, then you come along and they go "Maybe you can help us with this thing", and you give them the script and they go "That's not what we want, we want it a bit more like this", then that's a different thing. That's more like client and creative. It's more like the set up you get when you're doing stuff for an ad agency. And you feel it when you're making stuff. Like when you do an advert, you have the creatives on set who've written the script, you have the agency producers and you have the client. And then there's a tension between all those positions and you. So you're kind of negotiating all those to get the thing out. But at the end of the day it's selling butter! And sometimes that's the case with the channels; because they've made a decision about what their audience is, very specifically, and they use that as the big stick – "Our audience says they want this", and you go, "Really? Is that a thing? But OK."'

He recalls, 'I'd always had people giving notes in ads, then I'd worked on *Modern Toss* (2008) and *Wrong Door* (2008) and all those TV shows, so I'd been on the receiving end of the BBC process as well. I think I was lucky that I'd worked in both sides of it already, so I knew what it was when it came, and I wasn't that bothered. But the films, because they were low budget and independently produced, were a much freer place, like the web work really, where I did whatever I wanted and just made it. Then if people liked it, they liked it.'

Ben explains, 'We'd had a unique experience doing *Down Terrace,* being as independent a movie as you could ever make. So we had a blueprint then for how to work. Which you don't get if you go and apply for money, you become part of the system of notes and beholden to people; because you can never say after your first short goes through that system that it's your short, because someone else has told you what to do to a degree, or you've had to navigate through that. We were arrogant enough to go, "We're right. If you want stuff like we've just made, then we know how to do it."'

He advises, 'As long as you go into it with your eyes open and you bring that your position is to make it better, and everyone's position is to make it better, then it's alright. My big bugbear is contradictory notes. Or notes from separate groups of people and they're horse trading their own notes between them and it's all a big political game. That's really harmful and pointless.'

Ben reflects 'There's a difference between starting from a place of being critical and starting from a place of wanting to help the filmmaker get their voice out. There's a world of encouragement. It becomes a tropey thing that I say all the time about what directing is – directing is not telling. If I approached actors in the same way that note-givers sometimes approach the director, there would be a bloodbath on set. People do do this I know, but if you rock up after each take and break the actor going, "You did this wrong and that wrong and I'm disappointed and this doesn't work."' He leans back expressively with a half shrug and an amused eyebrow at the thought of what would ensue, concluding, 'They would walk off. Or their performances would be really awful and everyone would wonder why, and it'd be because you've upset everybody. It's really about how you deal with creative teams. How you talk to creative teams is the key to it. Sometimes you need to trust the people who're making the thing. You cast actors because you know they can do it and you want what they can give you, you don't then break them and tell them to do it how you would do it.'

Ben's image freezes mid thought, and there's a brief interlude as we try to fix it, followed by a cheer as the advanced technique of turning the picture off and on again brings it back to life. Elevated to Zoom masters we continue.

Ben appreciatively describes the hands-off approach of his producer, and partner in Rook Films, Andy Starke. 'He never gives notes. I mean, we're all very tight, so we talk about things all the time, every day. Before *Down Terrace* I think we talked every day for about ten years. So we already know what each other's understanding of film and story is. He's just really super supportive. That's one of the big things about Rook, and where we get into trouble with financiers, is that we support final cut for the directors. It's up to them. When I exec produce Peter Strickland films I don't write to Strickland about what he should put in his film or how he should cut it. No fucking way. I wouldn't dare. I can't imagine what a note would be like from Strickland to me. It'd make me flip a table over,' he laughs, 'Why would I put my big podgy fingers into his film? What do I know? We're in collaboration with Strickland so that you get a Strickland film, not a hybrid.'

He counters, 'I think it's a different thing if you're in a production company and you're beholden to the financiers and you have to get them a certain thing and there's a pressure on you to deliver it. It's very different from what I do on Strickland's films. I mean, maybe if it was my own money and I was on the hook for it then I might be a bit different – if I'd given a load of money to some genre filmmaker and they'd come back with some kind of esoteric tone poem, I might be the person writing some quite harsh notes!' he laughs, 'But if your thing is to get as good a Peter Strickland film as you can get, then that's that.

'I think there's ways of developing scripts that aren't irritating,' he concedes, 'It's an odd old job. I'm not saying there's no role for them. And I think that the role is certainly there within the more commercial ends of things. They're the backroom team that're part of a production company that's got a big slate. So they have to make sure that all the scripts make sense from all the different drafts they're getting through from all the different people. It's a consequence of studio filmmaking that you have to have that many people working on stuff, because no one person can hold it all in their head. Which, you know, you get a film like *Casablanca* (Michael Curtiz, 1943) out of that system, which is not necessarily a bad thing!' he laughs, 'But you also get all sorts of unnameable, terrible films too.'

Ben advises, 'The most important thing for someone to be conscious of when they're giving notes is that there's another person at the other end of it. Writing notes itself is blunt. They end up a bit like texts the way they're written. All of these things are diffused as soon as they're done face to face. I'm dealing with something at the moment and we got a load of long notes, and I'm like "Well, at least talk about them!" Because the other thing you can do is write back to the notes, which is just a long "Fuck you", he laughs, 'it's pointless! You've got to get to the bottom of what the notes are about. I think the Walter Murch thing's right, the doctor analogy – where if you've got a problem with your wrist, it's probably because your shoulder's buggered. So, often in a script they go, "Oh the third act doesn't work" but it's really something that's happened in the second act that you've got to fix and that sorts everything out. Certainly I found it with *Sightseers* for instance. We had early versions of it which we had a problem with, it kind of sagged in the middle and didn't work. But it wasn't that the stuff after the middle was broken, it was there was something specific in the middle that was broken. Once we took that out it was like electricity, the lights all just came back on in the rest of the film. And that's interesting, because you can panic and kind of smash everything up if you're not careful.'

Considering notes more broadly, Ben says, 'A lot of this stuff around notes is wrapped up in ego and the battle of egos and whether you think you're right. The worst kind of note is when you realize they're sliding away from what you wanted to do. You're thinking, "Ohhh, right, so even though these notes are actually positive from my viewpoint, they are the ones that they're saying are negative." And then you're in trouble. You're thinking "Oh fuck it's broken, and how do we join that back together again?" But that's in the more commercial end of the street. Because also there's no set way of making films particularly. And it changes all the time as well. But you want to try and find a way where everything is up front and everyone agrees on everything.'

He advises, 'If there's a note you don't agree with, I think it's making the case for it, and against it. My first position is usually, if I can, to say, "This is why this was done this way, and this is why it's working." Basically it's about how many people are disagreeing with you. If they gang up and they stack up and you get the dreaded "Everybody says . . ." then you're into the world of what card do you play? Is this the hill you're dying on? Are you going to play the card that's "Well, *I'm* the director"? Which is like the doom card and you can't play it that many times. Or if at all really. You shouldn't really play it. Or the "My taste is better than your taste" card? And you don't really want to be in that position either. It more needs to be a negotiation. Or you just back off and go "OK let's do that" and circle round and see if it works, and when it doesn't work you stop it. So there's no real advice,' he concludes, 'because the situation is always fluid.'

Ben's phone rings with a chirpy tone. He kills it immediately to kindly carry on chatting about notes; outlining how different types of projects result in different dynamics. He states, 'Basically you have more independence at a lower budget. It depends as well if you've written it. *Colin Burstead* (2018) and *Rebecca* are chalk and cheese, they're totally different productions. It's a different thing when I'm in partnership with people. If I've come in with a script I've written and I'm producing it and then there's other people involved at a higher level, then yeah, you'd expect it to be a different kind of control. But when you're doing stuff which you haven't written and other people are involved in creating the script, then there are other parties that have to be considered as you go through it. You have an ownership, but also you can't just ride over the top of people. Though some people do. But I'm much more for it being less confrontational, that's better usually for me. Some people are stronger than that. I certainly know people who just don't take any shit from anybody. But I'm always a little bit "Hmm, am I right? I dunno?"' Ben laughs at himself and pulls a mock anxious look. 'I take it all on board. At that stage anyway. There's notes then, and if it's meant to be for a certain audience and a bigger audience, then maybe people who understand that audience, or think they understand that audience, and are speaking up for that audience, ought to be listened to. Then you've got the thing of fighting against your own issues, your own taste, which might get in the way of that a bit.'

The dynamic with notes is different again for a director working in television, Ben explains, 'You just know that as director you're not on the top of the pyramid in terms of your position on a TV show. You're there to do your job and a big bit of your job is craft. Doing the craft bit of it right and as well as you can do it and defending that bit. I've certainly gone into it before that it's not even a question that you would be able to change anything in the script as a director. I like the discipline of it, so it's not a problem. And I've sought out that kind of work because in a way it's a blessed relief not to be responsible for it! You're just doing your bit and you can concentrate on that side of it and there's a whole load of people who're worrying about the rest of it. And you're just trying to make it work day by day, scene by scene.'

Turning to notes on adaptations he says, 'They have their own trickiness, because everybody has access to the text. So everybody's right and wrong at the same time. With something you've written yourself, you're the living expert on it. Whereas if it's Du Maurier everyone can read the book and have their opinion about it, and then we can thrash it all out. So that's different. Certainly with Ballard as well, it was the same thing. But also it means in the final analysis you can always drop back to the book, you use the book as a kind of backstop. When people go, "Well this happened and that happened and this doesn't make any sense" you go, "Go and talk to Du Maurier about it! That's what she wrote. That's her, not us, we're doing the book." Then you get in a sticky situation of someone going "It doesn't have to be an exact version of the book" and then you're like, "Well, doesn't it? Or does it?" There's loads of arguments like that. I think it makes it there's a heavier backstop to fall back to, but it's fraught with all its own problems.'

Wrapping up, he advises, 'Read the room. Try to work out what way the wind is blowing in terms of how much you can get through. So if you're making commercial television and you're the director, then possibly you have less of a say in what happens, because that's just the way that these things have grown up – that a writer, a producer, an actor-star have more sway over what we're doing than you might do. Though that's not necessarily the case, because these things change all the time. But on a director-led kind of indie film that you've instigated, then you should have more say, and notes become less . . .' he tails off expressively, then summarizes, 'You don't have to follow them so much.'

Ben concludes, 'The thing that's always guided me is to find the pleasures in what you're doing. And go into it with your eyes open. If you go and do a project with a company that's got a big story department, then you're going to have to be working with them and that's how it is. But if you're set up as a little Indie that makes your own stuff, and is set up in a very particular way, then you don't. And you can't necessarily take those ways of working from place to place. And maybe there's a reason those things are set up in different ways, because different spaces don't support that.'

Reflecting on why we're so drawn to watch, read and tell stories he says, 'I feel that as creatures we are kind of hard-wired for story. It's how we make sense of things. By joining facts together with stories as the glue of our lives. So in our day-to-day we use narrative to make sense of things, and when we rest we like to hear narratives that reinforce or challenge our positions. That's kind of what it's about, and what it's always been about. I don't know how notes work, what the best way for it is. I guess it depends on the situation that they've been given or the commercial imperative of them and the gap between what they're hoping to get and what they're getting. So it's to try and guide those two things together. But that depends what weight you put on storytellers versus product. If you believe that creative things can be made by large teams, then note away. But if you have any sense that creative stuff may be better from a singular point of view, then you probably want to keep out of the way of it.'

And with a cheery wave of farewell, the most affable and hard-working Ben Wheatley disappears from the screen. Quite possibly to polish off another script before tea-time.

Brighton, via Zoom, July 2020

Selected credits, awards and nominations

Modern Toss: Director, episodes '#2.1', '#2.2', '#2.3' and '#2.6' (2008), [TV series] Channel 4.
The Wrong Door: Writer, Director, episodes 'The World's Most Annoying Creature',

'Njarnia', 'The Smutty Aliens', 'The Wizard of Office', 'Bondo' and 'The Wrong Door: Best Bits' (2008), [TV Series] BBC.

Down Terrace: Co-writer, Director (2009), [Film] UK: Boum Productions.
Raindance Film Festival award – Best UK Feature (2009)
Evening Standard British Film Award nomination – Best Screenplay (2011)
Evening Standard British Film Award – Most Promising Newcomer (2011)

Kill List: Co-writer, Director, Editor (2011), [Film] UK: Optimum Releasing.
British Independent Film Award nomination – Best Screenplay (2011)
British Independent Film Award nomination – Best Director (2011)
Evening Standard British Film Award nomination – Best Screenplay (2012)

Sightseers: Director, Editor (2012), [Film] UK: StudioCanal UK.
British Independent Film Award nomination – Best Director (2012)
Evening Standard British Film Award – Peter Sellers Award for Comedy, Director (2013)
Sitges – Catalonian International Film Festival nomination – Best Motion Picture (2012)

A Field in England: Director, Editor (2013), [Film] UK: Rook Films.
Karlovy Vary International Film Festival award – Special Jury Prize (2013)
Sitges – Catalonian International Film Festival nomination – Best Motion Picture (2013)

Doctor Who: Director, episodes 'Into the Dalek' and 'Deep Breath' (2014), [TV series] BBC.

High-Rise: Director, Editor (2016), [Film] UK, Belgium: StudioCanal UK.
San Sebastián International Film Festival nomination – Best Film (2015)

Free Fire: Co-writer, Director, Editor (2016), [Film] UK, France: Rook Films.
British Independent Film Award nomination – Best Director (2016)
Toronto Film Festival – People's Choice Award (2016)
British Screenwriters' Awards nomination – Best British Feature Film Writing (2017)

Happy New Year, Colin Burstead: Writer, Director, Editor (2018), [Film] UK: Rook Films.
British Independent Film Award nomination – Best Editing (2018)

Strange Angel: Director, episodes 'The Mystic Circle of Young Girls', 'The Fool' and 'The Magus' (2018–19), [TV Series] CBS.

Rebecca: Director (2020), [Film] UK, US: Netflix.

In The Earth: Writer, Director, Editor (2021), [Film] UK, USA: Rook Films.
British Independent Film Award nomination – Best Editing (2021)
Sitges – Catalonian International Film Festival nomination – Best Motion Picture (2021)

The Meg 2: Director (2023), [Film] USA: Warner Bros. Pictures.

Krysty Wilson-Cairns

'Really, what whoever is giving the notes and whoever is receiving the notes has to realize is that neither of them has the correct answer, but between them they can find the correct answer. That, like everything else in filmmaking, it's a collaboration.'

8 *Krysty Wilson-Cairns, photo by Myles Standish Pettengill III.*

'Let me move those so they don't attack you,' Krysty Wilson-Cairns says, deftly hoicking a vase of spring blossom from the little wooden table in her kitchen as we sit down. The BAFTA winning, Oscar nominated screenwriter is the warmest and most thoughtful of hosts. She's even arranged for her mum to take her dog out for the afternoon in case he intrudes on our chat. 'He's a big, over-friendly golden retriever' she explains, 'When we go out for walks, he sometimes steals kids' ice-cream cones. I keep £20 in my pocket now to buy replacements.' Such flat-out niceness may be part of why filmmakers such as Edgar Wright and Sam Mendes are so keen to work with her, but the real reason is her talent. Her BAFTA for *1917* (Sam Mendes, 2019) glows quietly on a shelf, half hidden behind a leafy plant. Her strong work ethic and can-do spirit are reflected in the walls of her flat, which she plastered herself.

After graduating from the National Film and Television School's screenwriting course in 2013 Krysty worked as a bartender in Soho. The script she wrote between shifts, *Aether,* was named among the top ten on The Black List – an industry insiders' annual survey rating the best unproduced screenplays. It impressed screenwriter John Logan, who recruited her to write for his television series *Penny Dreadful* (2016). The series' executive producer, Sam Mendes, invited Krysty to collaborate on a number of projects, ultimately resulting in her co-writing the multi-Oscar and BAFTA winning *1917*. At the time of our chat, early in 2020, *Last Night in Soho* (Edgar Wright, 2021), which she co-wrote with Edgar Wright, is in post-production, and she is writing the screenplay for *The Good Nurse* (Tobias Lindholm, 2022). When they are released, both films receive BAFTA nominations, *Last Night in Soho* for Best British Film.

'To me, filmmaking is the ultimate collaboration,' Krysty begins, 'what you're doing when you write a script, or you step on a set, is that you and between eight and eight hundred other people are trying to make something that's a bit of each of you. You're trying to create something together, and if you can't collaborate . . .' she shrugs eloquently. 'I feel as a writer if you don't want notes, if you don't want to collaborate, go write books. I always think – someone might come up with a better idea, and your name's still going to be on the script. Let's make it the best script possible. I love notes,' she enthuses, 'I'm a big believer that the script is the blueprint for the story so people can build it, and why not build it together? Why not listen to everyone? If someone gives me a good note I don't care who they are. You can give me notes on anything. You can give me notes on my eyebrows if you want!' (She has excellent eyebrows.) She reiterates, 'I like notes. And I like the discussion.

'It's important to learn how to receive notes,' she advises, 'When you write something it drips with you; it's so much yours, your hopes, your dreams, your secret little weird twisted self, you just really want it to be great. And that's OK! It's great to want it to be great. But it's also nice to be: Do you know what? It's OK if it's not great, because I can fix it. In writing there's so much you can do. You never have to stop fixing it. It's not like you've presented someone a finished piece and gone "Please like me." What you're doing is saying "I'm working on this. What do you think of it?"'

For those on the other side of the table, the note-givers, she advises, 'When you're giving notes to a writer you have to realize that they've spent however long – a week, three weeks, three months, three years in their own head, trying their best. No one delivers something thinking "That'll do." They're trying their best. Remember that in everything, so that you approach things with a sense of kindness. I'm not saying lie. Never lie. Be honest. But there's a way of being honest that's not brutal. I always think "brutally honest" people enjoy the brutality more than the honesty. Don't get me wrong, I've had some brutally honest notes and they're fine, you learn to take them on the chin, but it could have been expressed a different way.'

She continues, 'The other thing with notes is – do them in person or on the phone. Written notes are no good to me. And never do them through another person. Notes should be a discussion, not laying down rules. Because sometimes the things you get in notes are "Why don't you do it this way?" and you've already tried it that way and it's not worked for these reasons. Really, what whoever is giving the notes and whoever is receiving the notes has to realize is that neither of them has the correct answer, but between them they can find the correct answer. That, like everything else in filmmaking, it's a collaboration.

'Giving notes is a bit like writing,' Krysty observes, 'you have to be brave to say "I have my own personal opinion here." The worst notes you get are the ones they think their bosses would give. The reason you're in the room, the reason we're sitting together is I want to hear *your* opinion, not "I think what they're going to like is . . ." I don't care about that. What do *we* like? People are paying us to be here. We must have something to offer. So give me those notes – "This is my personal opinion" and that's scary. I don't envy those people, because sometimes they're giving a note to Sam Mendes! Sometimes they're giving a note to Simon Beaufoy! Can you imagine how nerve-wracking it would be? That whole idea of having to say "Yes, you've been paid millions of pounds to come up with this script, and you have awards, but I right now have an opinion which I think could be helpful." I experienced that. I would give Sam [Mendes] notes on our draft, scenes he'd written or re-written, and the same with Edgar [Wright]. At first you think, "Who the fuck am I to say anything?" Then you have to decide "No, actually I think I have an important thing to say here." You need courage to say, "I know I'm like a dog with a bone with this, but there's something important in this." Sometimes you don't know why it's important, but you have to say "There's something in here and can we re-examine it together?" I don't envy people giving notes, it's not easy. I've done it, and you do have to be brave.'

Krysty considers how early on in the development process notes can be useful. She says, 'Treatments are a great place to get notes, a great place to go "We've discussed this project at length, but are we both on the same page?"' She advises, 'Treatments should incorporate tone. Massively. Because that's the one free radical in screenwriting that you can't properly say in a meeting. It doesn't matter how many things you compare it to; you both say blue and then when you write it they're like "But this is pale blue! I was looking for navy." And you're like "Ohhhhh, sorry, I love navy!" She cautions, 'But if you don't have people that you trust, I wouldn't share something too early. I wouldn't share something that made it possible for the project to cease to exist.' Krysty continues talking through her process and where notes fit in. She says, 'I've had hundreds of notes. Notes on scripts, notes on pitches, notes on me as a person! You name it notes. Even now when I finish a script I'll have my mum or one of my friends read it before I send it out, usually to check the spelling – I'm a terrible speller! But also because I'm so in it I have no idea if it's shit or not. I'll get back a "Yeah, it's OK" or "I really liked this" or "You can't send this in! You look like a toddler got loose with a crayon" – which makes you think "Thank you, I will take another week with that!" It's like a litmus test. I want to know if I'm going to embarrass myself by sending it out.'

Krysty recalls, 'When I finished the first draft of *1917*, I read it and I had no idea – might be good, might be bad. I gave it to my mum and she cried, and I thought "Yes! I can send this to Sam Mendes." Because that's what it's like – sometimes you're sending your script to Sam Mendes or to Edgar Wright, or *1917* went to Steven Spielberg, these absolute titans of industry and it's very nerve-wracking. I will send it off, and my house will be a tip – because a clean house is a sign that you're not writing. So I'll send it off and then clean up my house. Then I won't sleep all that night, just waiting. Usually all I want is an email saying "Received." Then you can think, "Oh, O K", and it's in the hands of the gods after that, because you've done your work.' She adds, 'I've learned to do this thing where I have a load of thoughts on the draft after I've finished it, but I'm going to send it in anyway. So I have my own notes, and sometimes, depending on the collaborator, I'll say, "I have some issues with these areas, probably other areas too that you'll have issues with, but just so you know, I'm still working on that, but wanted you to see something." Because also, until it's on paper it's not anything. Until it's a finished thing it doesn't exist. It doesn't matter how much you spoke about it, how many bullet points you put on your wall, it doesn't count.'

Krysty gives an insight of how a writer might feel having sent in a draft, anticipating notes on it: 'So you get all anxious; you wait, you wait, you wait. Then you get the "Received" email, and still I won't sleep. Sometimes I'll start thinking "Maybe I should take up running?" maybe I should do this, maybe I should do that. Then I actually just walk my dog. At four in the morning.'

She describes some of her process during development: 'After I deliver a script I like to have about a week where I don't think about it at all. I'm not going to go over and over it again because there's nothing I can do about it now. I find when I come back to it I've fresher eyes. So usually I'll deliver it, they'll set a notes call for say a week or two weeks away, and I'll not do anything with the script until about three days beforehand, then I'll read it again and be fresher in it and have my own notes on it. Because you should think critically about your own work.'

She emphasizes, 'People who go back and forth with drafts after they've sent one in – you look unprofessional, get your shit together.' Explaining, 'The best people that give me notes, they don't just read the draft, sometimes they'll read it aloud between each other, sometimes they'll act it out, they'll sit and study it line by line. They spend their time trying to work out why you did each thing. For someone to spend the time doing that, for you to then go "Oh, you know all that work you just did? Forget it, here's a new draft, do all the work again because I changed four pages." Frankly, fuck off with that shit. It's my pet hate.'

Krysty continues outlining how her script development process works with notes. She says, 'After a notes meeting I'll do a new draft very quickly. Unless I'm side-tracked by being in production or being in the edit. I'll take notes in the meeting, and then as soon as I'm done with the meeting, either in the car or back at my hotel or back at my house, I re-write everything out so that it crystallizes those thoughts. If you don't do that the water gets out of it. If I do that it doesn't matter if I need to wait a month till I go back to it, because I know what I'm doing.'

Krysty reflects on some of the difficulties that can arise with notes, and how to tackle them: 'I've heard many stories of instances where you've got massive conflicting notes from different sources. You point out to them that they're conflicting and they say, "Oh we'll get together and we'll go through our notes" and then you just get some kind of mad jumble. I think it's always been a problem. I think now more and more people are coming into things, it's tricky. In those situations I like to find who the end authority is on this. Who is the one who decides, "This is what I put in my film"? With film often it's the director. In TV now it's me!' she laughs with a mix of incredulity and delight, self-deprecatingly adding, 'Which is infinitely more difficult, because now it's "Well fuck, I have to make a decision!"' She advises, 'If you get conflicting notes, they still usually all centre over one or two things. So you have to put on your detective hat and go "Well, they're talking about this issue, and that really is about that character; and this other note is really about that character as well." Basically you have to do more legwork when you've got conflicting notes. I think the best way to solve that is for everyone to give notes together and have the conversation. Or for the production team to nominate someone to be the torchbearer of the notes. But then I find people try to go around that!'

Krysty raises other potential pitfalls for note-givers to avoid. She observes, 'I'm trying to say this in a not rude way: sometimes people who don't write, really want to write but instead try to put their stamp on something through notes. They're so involved in thinking "I've got to put *my* impression on it" they forget that actually what we're all trying to do is make something else. Go write your own thing! I want everyone to do it if they want to do it, because it's a fucking great job. Also, sometimes film industry people are desperate to say "I've read *Save the Cat*[1] or *The Writer's Journey*[2] and the inciting incident happens on page twenty-two when really it should be on page sixteen" and that to me is just waffle, waffle, waffle.'

In contrast she says, 'With Neal Street [Production Company founded by Sam Mendes, Pippa Harris and Caro Newling] it's an embarrassment of riches – everyone there will give you great notes. That's why I keep working with Neal Street, because I love them. But you find someone on each job that's your person. You realize, "That's who gets it, that's who I'm going to focus in on." It does become like a relationship. You have to have that ease of being with someone, and a shorthand of how you talk together.'

She advises, 'I don't like when people qualify their notes by saying "Other people might feel differently." I find women do that a lot because they're kind of afraid to put forward their opinion. I did that a lot in my early meetings, then I decided, "No, people have paid me for my expertise, if they want to listen to me, I'm going to speak." I've been in rooms where I'm nervous to speak, nervous to give my opinion, thinking who the fuck am I? But they've got me here so I may as well. And I've been in rooms where you've not been listened to, and that's very frustrating. But they'll listen to any man who says the same thing that you just said! "He-peated" someone called it.' There is a mutual eye-roll of recognition.

She counsels, 'It does help when people say something positive as part of their notes – the compliment sandwich: compliment, note, compliment. Even

---

[1]Snyder, B. (2005), *Save the Cat!: The Only Book on Screenwriting You'll Ever Need: The Last Book on Screenwriting You'll Ever Need*, California: Michael Wiese Productions.
[2]Vogler, C. (1998) *The Writer's Journey: Mythic Structure for Writers*, California: Michael Wiese Productions.

though I know they're just doing it so they can give the note, it's still nice. It's still nice to be told that your writing's good, even if it's not for them. I also think it disarms a writer a little bit. When someone says, "I really, really love what you've done here, I think this character is great, this section you sort of lose me in, but when it comes back round, I feel like the ending lands on its feet, and if you could just fix that middle bit, it'd be really strong." So you go "I will fix that middle bit!"' she says with mock eager-eyed enthusiasm. In contrast she says, 'There's been plenty of times when it's not worked. When it's people giving the wrong notes in a way that gets your hackles up. Then you think, "Well, they just don't understand what I'm trying to do. We're on two profoundly different pages."'

Recommending ways to foster a successful note-giving relationship, Krysty says, 'I find the best way to frame notes is for the two of you to sit down and start from "We're both after the same thing. We're looking in the same direction, we've just got to work out how to get there." As soon as you've got that, you can think "Right, it's not us versus them, this isn't a competition, this isn't who is going to please the ultimate uber boss. It's – how to we get there?" When you have that foundation it lets me be honest about the things I think aren't working. It's important to be able to discuss your notes in a way that allows room for "Oh, that note is wrong. The onus behind it is right, but the actual note is wrong." It's a fluid conversation – is the note right? Is the script right? The answer is usually that they're both wrong. And you need to work out the new way forward together. Then the two of you are working out the solution together. I'm a big believer in if you work with a bunch of smart people, you're only going to have smarter product at the end of the day.

'Notes should diagnose the problem, not offer a solution' Krysty asserts, 'That's the whole point. The best kind of note is "You lose me around this page, I don't know why." Or "I don't really feel like I believe that." As opposed to "I think he should fire a gun here." Because then I have to go and find the note behind the note. Which is twice the work for me.'

Going further into the detail of what works for her, she explains, 'There's two different types of notes. There's the big notes that are about structure, about character, about theme, about tone, and then there's the page notes. Page notes I don't need till we're on our last daft. I know I've misspelled shit, that's not important to me. If it's important to you, I'm sorry. But the fact that I've written Marnie instead of Marine isn't important to me right now, I'll catch it when I go through it again. Forget the page notes. Sometimes you get the big notes and you think "Maybe I'll do the page notes first" because page notes are easy. And then you're just lost in the woods again. On the big notes, I think have loads. Because usually the big notes all intermesh. It's not a case of "First I can fix the tone and next time you can give me the note about structure." No, give me them all together.'

She continues, 'By and large there'll always be a note in there that you don't agree with. You think, "That's a bum steer, it's going to lead me down the wrong path", or "I've tried it and it doesn't work". The best thing to do is to have the conversation with whoever is giving you the notes. It's changed a little bit now, because I have some glimmer of power.' Waving at her half-hidden BAFTA she jokes, 'I've got the shiny gold face! So people respect you. But when I was starting out and I was a twenty-seven-year-old bartender, people were like "What the fuck do you know?" You would get into these positions where you'd say, "Hey, if you would listen to me and we could have the conversation it would make both our lives easier." Sometimes people don't want to listen to you. I've had really bad experiences with that, and that I think is just part of the job. You have to take the knocks every so often. But if you have a good relationship with the person you can say, "Hey, I'm not sure about that note" and they might go, "You know what, I'm also not sure about that note – but this is the reason I gave that note" and you go, "Oh, OK, now I understand it." You're basically always looking for the note behind the note. If someone's given you a bad note, you're looking for the reason they've given you that note. And if you can find that, if you can fix the problem without implementing their solution they won't be angry because they'll think "Oh, I gave the note that led to that." As long as people feel heard, that's the main thing. Take every note you can. Don't automatically dismiss a note thinking it's a bad note. Do examine it. Think it over. Think – what would happen if I did do that? Because sometimes – you're wrong!'

Considering notes specifically on characters she says, 'I've had great notes that unlock the parts of characters. Sometimes, especially in the very rough first draft where everything's a bit more in flux, where you're maybe trying to wrangle four or five different ideas, I find the best notes are – "What I like about this character is that he embodies the theme perfectly because he's trying to do this" and you go "Oh, I didn't realize I'd done that!" People can understand them more from the outside in a way. And they can say, "But this one beat changes all of that and it ruins it", which is also helpful.' She explains, 'Everyone thinks the most important thing in a story is the character, and they're not wrong but they're only half right. It's character and connection. One character is fine, but if they don't connect to something – it can be the audience, it can be a dog, it can be a potted plant, it can be another character, it doesn't matter, but that connection is the thing that resonates. That's the magic in it. It's not "He's a really interesting fucked up man and I want to see him solve crime", it's nothing to do with that, you actually care about his relationship with his best friend, or his relationship with his dog. So when you're giving notes try and remember the key components to making a story fantastic, to making a story live in your head when you're no longer watching it.'

A squirrel suddenly appears outside the window, confidently at home in Krysty's courtyard garden. 'I feed him nuts every day' she confesses. Joking, 'I work from home, so like a Disney princess, I make friends with birds and squirrels. My dog loves the squirrel, he sits and watches him. He'd never chase him, he's not really one for moving. He's a fat golden retriever.'

Tearing ourselves away from the urban nature documentary, Krysty turns to notes that might reveal a writer and note-giver are striving to take a project in different directions. She says, 'There's nothing worse in film or TV than trying to make a different thing from what they want. The biggest lesson I ever learned, and it's true to this day, is – don't write something that you wouldn't want to watch. My one rule is if I wouldn't watch it hungover on a Sunday, I won't write it. No matter how much they pay me. Because I won't enjoy it. And there'll be someone else out there who'll do it better. So I always revert to my "Is this something I would watch hungover on a Sunday?", and if it's not, I won't do it. I'll work at my passes and I'll say, "This is the version I believe in. I understand we've profoundly come off chart from what we discussed at the beginning, but I'm not going to be the best writer for that. I will finish my passes or I will happily give you back the money you gave me." Because it's not worth it. Also, I feel like with that approach you're trying to preserve the relationship, because even though this project might not work out, you might want to work with them again down the line.'

One of many strong working relationships Krysty developed is with Oscar winning director Sam Mendes. Having first worked with Krysty on *Penny Dreadful*, for which he was an executive producer, Sam invited her to collaborate on two other projects, both of which ended up not going ahead due to rights issues. Then, she recalls: 'Sam phoned me up one day saying, "Third time's the charm", and asked if I would be free to do something else with him. Of course I said yes! So he said, "I want to write this First World War movie. It's based on a story my grandfather told me about him delivering a message in no-man's land. Gather some of your ideas, come round to my house Tuesday and we'll talk about it." Then he added, "Oh by the way, it's all going to be one shot" and hung up on me. And I thought, "I don't think I can have heard that right."'

Krysty describes how she and Sam developed the script and how notes fitted into the process. She says, 'I've been fascinated by the First and Second World Wars since I was a teenager, which Sam hadn't known, so I took round all my niche First World War books and out of print diaries to his house, thinking "Haha, I'm going to impress you Sam." But the first thing I asked was, "That one shot thing . . .?" He said, "Well, here's the thing, I want to tell a story where you understand what it is to go every step with them, and I think the only way to do that is to do it in real time and have it all one shot." I said, "That's going to be really hard!" and he went "Yep! But we'll see if it works!"'

She recalls, 'After Sam and I had done a bullet point outline, I went to France and walked the exact route the boys were going to take, to help me get the detail of the landscape. I remember walking through a field and seeing pockmarks on the land; you can tell where it's been shelled, where trenches were. It would have been about this time two years ago, the early spring, and it's when the earth is churning up again – I was kicking these bits of rock and I realized they were grenades. It's called the Iron Harvest – twice a year everything that's been put into the ground makes its way back up to the surface. I found this bayonet just sticking out of the earth!' She fetches a rusted, clearly treasured, bit of metal from its central place on her shelf, where it's displayed far more prominently than her BAFTA. Adding, with a touch of awe at the synchronicity and physical connection to hands that held it a hundred years ago, 'I took it to a historian and they said it's a British bayonet, probably from 1916 or 1917!'

We turn from this poignantly tangible link with the reality of millions of people's experience to the practical responsibility for crafting a story illuminating it. Krysty explains, 'When you're working with a co-writer, usually when you're forming the idea it's less giving notes to each other and more "Wouldn't this be good?" and "Hmm, I don't know about that", that kind of discussion. After I'd written the first draft Sam gave me notes. I would re-write or there'd be scenes he'd write and I would give him notes on those. Eventually it got to the stage we'd re-written so much and given each other so many notes I couldn't tell you what was mine and what was his. Similarly with Edgar [Wright] for *Last Night in Soho*. It always the same thing – you get it down on paper, it doesn't really matter who gets it down, as you've both talked about it at length, and then you go back and forth. When you reach a stage where you're both sort of happy with it, though you know there's still work to do, you'll say, "Right, who do we trust? Who's our next port of call?"'

Krysty says, 'When you're both writers on the same project there's a shorthand in it. So I wouldn't necessarily be giving Sam the compliment sandwich because I don't need to, and he knows he doesn't need to do it to me – we're working together. It's both our ideas, so if I'm criticizing something I'm not criticizing him, I'm criticizing both of us. Collaboration is very tricky. With the right collaborator it's half the work, with the wrong collaborator it's five times the work. With the right collaborator you never worry thinking you might have upset them. You find a way of talking to each other that's not rude, that's not harsh, and where there's respect.'

Discussing notes from historical advisors she says, 'With First World War knowledge, I was obsessed with that since I was fourteen years old. I read hundreds of books about it. I mean, there's always someone that knows more than me about the First World War, but does that mean I can't in some way be any kind of authority on it? No, of course not. I'm writing *this* story and I have researched *this* story. And you're making a movie, you're not making a documentary. We had military advisors on the film, one on set and one on the script beforehand. When Sam sent me the notes on the script from the military advisor he said, "Brace yourself!" Some of them were things like: "April 6th 1917 was the coldest April on record, there would not be flies on the dead horse." Things like that you just go "disregard", because to me that's not important.'

She explains, 'What I'm trying to do is tell this story in an interesting way that becomes entertainment but that also makes people think and that pays respect to the people who've died. When Sam and I sat down with the big bumper of notes from the historical advisors, some of it was interesting, some of it we had to weigh up. For instance, we were very careful with the dialogue because we wanted it to feel a bit archaic but also modern. So the "Pip-pip"s, or "Right-o", or "Buck up" go in. We had a dialogue coach who Sam spoke to at length, trying to craft a hybrid that wasn't entirely 1917. That's a very specific thing to do and we did that with full intention. But the military advisor would give notes on dialogue. And Sam and I sometimes had to consider, "There's probably seven people in the world who are going to be angry that we don't include this one phrase. Do we owe the duty to these seven people, or do we owe the duty to the hopefully millions of other audience?" Ultimately as the writer you need to decide what's best for the story. You have a duty to truth, you have a burden to the people who lived and died. That's the reason that we didn't tell one true story – it's not Sam's grandfather's story, it's an amalgamation of many different stories, we invented these characters, because it wouldn't be fair to give all those to one historical figure. You have a duty to that, it's a tightrope but ultimately you've got to think "What's the most entertaining way to tell this story?"'

Krysty recalls, 'We got loads of great notes on *1917* from Steven Spielberg and Jeb Brody, the executive producer. The producer, Jayne-Ann Tenggren, worked very closely with Sam and I on the script. She's fantastic at development, and there would literally be thousands of notes where she would say, "Have you considered this?" That phrasing is so disarming because you think, "No, I haven't considered that, but now I will consider it!" Because of how we were filming it all one shot, we were staging it, rehearsing it, but also building the set around it, so you'd have cardboard boxes around and the cinematographer Roger Deakins moving in with a small camera. Sometimes you can only be on one person at a time in a particular shot, but in what you've written you've got two very interesting reactions and you want to see both of them, and a pan would just be bad. So you might realize "Actually, we don't need to re-stage the scene, we need to re-write the scene." And Jayne-Ann would be perfect in that case. She'd say,

"You know, this section here is holding up the flow of it. You don't need that even though you've become a bit attached to it. So if you kill that darling you can push those two together, he can move that way and that camera can come round and you can be on the two shot rather than on the one shot" and you'd think, "That makes perfect sense!" Working with Jayne-Ann and Pippa Harris was a privilege. The notes that Jayne-Ann and Pippa gave, I can't even quantify how much they profoundly affected the script. They were hugely, hugely involved creatively. And they are so good at that because they understand that we're all trying to work to get to the same goal. No one had their own agenda. We all had the same agenda, which is actually the most important thing for a producer.'

Krysty was on set for the shoot of *1917*, ready to re-write on the spot for any changes that were needed, which sounds a high-pressure situation in which to respond to notes. She laughs, 'I actually love huge amounts of pressure. I like deadlines. I like to feel there's someone out there that's desperate for it, it makes me feel I need to up my game. If you say to me "We've got twenty minutes to do this" I'll sweat profusely, but I'll do my damnedest. On set, a lot of the time the re-writes would be small. Surgical strikes of lines. Because of the way we made *1917*, every day we would have another two, three, five, eight minutes of footage. So by the end of the first week you could sit and watch the first fifteen minutes of the movie. In doing that, Sam, the editor Lee Smith, Jayne-Ann, Pippa and I began to understand the rhythm of it. So sometimes on set I would say to Sam "Why don't we cut these lines, because the actors are doing it all with their faces and we don't need another talky scene here." Other times he would come to me and say "Hmmm, I don't know about this scene." There were a couple of scenes that we re-wrote, because we'd done them and realized they weren't working. Those are stressful because you know there's five hundred people waiting around. And one of them's Roger Deakins! And you're thinking "I really want him to like me!" you know – Cinema God! And Sam and I would be holed up in his trailer, or in a horse-box, or in the rain in a forest going "Right, what about this? What about that?"'

Krysty was on set for the shoot of *Last Night in Soho* too, and was also involved during the edit of both films. She says of the edit, 'With *1917* Sam often brought me in, or had me watch it and do work on it, the same with Edgar on *Last Night in Soho*. In the edit you're the one giving notes more.

Giving notes to other people is a skill, and it's really good to have that skill in your arsenal. Giving an editor notes is a lot like giving a writer notes; it's "I see how hard you're trying here, I know there are certain things that aren't working, here're some of my ideas, have you tried that? Is that any good to you? Maybe this won't work, but have you considered . . .?"'

One of Krysty's favourite parts in *1917* is when the two young soldiers journeying through no-man's land to deliver a message, walk through cherry blossom at an abandoned farm. 'I know that's not one of the "big" scenes,' she concedes, 'but there's something about that. It's tied up with there being a cherry blossom tree in my garden that my gran and I used to sit and look at. It had to be chopped down when it became diseased, and remembering my gran being sad about that. The reason I really like that chopped down cherry trees scene as well is because I remember talking with Jayne-Ann about it and she had a beautiful note. She said, "It's such a beautiful metaphor for the destruction of youth." Which hadn't occurred to me when I was writing it because I was too busy thinking about the pay-off of it. And I think getting that sort of note made me more fastidious on how important that scene was.'

Concluding she says, 'This is usually writer advice, but I think it applies to both writers and people giving notes – don't be afraid to be bad at it. I know so many people who'd make brilliant writers and they are afraid to do it. They fear the blank page, or they fear that when they get it written down it won't be what they think it's going to be. And it won't be! It never will. What you have to do is get it all down – bleuarghhh,' her hands gesture a messy, abundant, spewing forth of ideas, 'Then, with your iron will, try and shape it into something that you love. And you can spend twenty years doing that if needs be. You don't have to put a clock pressure on yourself. But give yourself permission to be shit. Work with people who also will accept that sometimes you will come up with a bad idea. Or you'll give a bad note. Because only in the bad notes, only by making mistakes will you get better at your job. Also – in that bad note might be something magical. So just do it.'

London, early March 2020

Selected credits, awards and nominations

Penny Dreadful: Writer, episodes *'The Day Tennyson Died'*, *'Predators Far and Near'*, *'Good and Evil Braided Be'*, *'A Blade of Grass'*, *'The World Is Our Hell'*, *'No Beast So Fierce'*, *'Ebb Tide'*, *'The Blessed Dark'* and *'Perpetual Night'* (2016), [TV series] Netflix.

1917: Co-writer (2019), [Film] Dir. Sam Mendes, UK: Neal Street Productions.

BAFTA award – Outstanding British Film of the Year (2020)

Academy Award nomination – Best Original Screenplay (2020)

Writers' Guild of America nomination – Original Screenplay (2020)

Last Night in Soho: Co-writer (2021), [Film] Dir. Edgar Wright, UK: Universal Pictures International.

BAFTA nomination – Outstanding British Film of the Year (2022)

Hollywood Critics Association nomination – Best Original Screenplay (2022)

BloodGuts UK Horror Awards nomination – Best Screenplay (2022)

The Good Nurse: Writer (2022), [Film] Dir. Tobias Lindholm, USA: Netflix.

Quick Fire Q&A 5:

What's the most useful question someone giving notes has asked, that has moved a story forward or made it stronger?

'There's two: "What are you trying to say?" and "How do you want people to feel?"' – **Krysty Wilson-Cairns**

'Sometimes it's the really simple ones. Like "What is driving this character? What's the emotional engine?" Because if you've got a very passive character it's very hard to circumvent that question with an honest answer. And by trying to articulate it, it can really bring into focus, not just what their motivation is, but what's creating the momentum for the whole film.' – **Michael Pearce**

'"If you were to shoot one more scene what would it be?"' – **Lone Scherfig**

'I'm so used to telling stories where I express to an audience how my lead character feels, that sometimes I forget to really say it on paper. And I was recently asked, in the process of writing a bible, to ensure that an audience really understood what it felt like to be that character. And I thought that was a really good note. I'd become complacent, because it's so part of me, that that's what I would do anyway when I shot it, and that's what would be in the script, but I didn't actually have it in the bible.' – **Amma Asante**

'Whenever someone asks "What is your main character's why?" that is always really powerful, because if you can't answer that then you're really back to square one.' – **Tomm Moore**

'A specific example of this was with *Last Night in Soho*. I knew I didn't want to write the screenplay on my own, I was very aware that I wanted to write it with somebody else. When I met Krysty Wilson-Cairns and discovered that she'd been a barmaid in Soho and lived above a strip club there, I said, "Oooh, let me tell you this idea for this film I have." I pitched her the whole story and then months later I asked, "Do you want to write it with me?" My original conception for the movie was that the dream sequences, the 1960s sequences, were silent. When we first sat down together, Krysty said "The lead character Eloise and the audience have to fall in love with the 1960s character Sandie, so I really think you need to dramatize the 1960s scenes and have there be dialogue." It wasn't something I'd ever envisaged and as soon as we started doing it, it unlocked a big part of the movie, and it was some of the most fun sequences to write. So that is an example where somebody comes in with an idea that had not occurred to you, and it becomes a major part of the film. The best kind of interjection of new ideas that you could possibly have.' – **Edgar Wright**

'"Why?" – like a child. I think it brings you back to yourself. Even if you don't agree with someone you have your own compass and it's important to know.' – **Lynne Ramsay**

'When I was writing the first genesis of the *Braithwaites*, Tony Wood at Granada said "Don't write the first episode, write the third one." I think it's a really good note generally – about hitting the ground running. Saskia Abbot, my script editor on *Scott & Bailey*, gave a similar note, she said "You don't need to see somebody buying the milk to see them make the tea."' – **Sally Wainwright**

'Not so much a question as a process. When working with Sam Raimi and the writers on a recent project, I was surprised and excited that the first way we all started to work together (also during lockdown) was to do a group table read of the current draft of the script, each of us, me, the writers, the execs and Sam would play two or three parts each, with me narrating the directions, and it was a great opportunity to feel out the script together, and I was able to interject with my own notes and discuss my own ideas for scenes, additions, adjustments, characters, monster-mythology and continuity in real time along the way. It's a process I strongly advise and it was a lot of fun too!' – **Corin Hardy**

'I think the question they're always really asking is "Why don't I like this?" That's what it's about with everything in the end, whether it's an affair, or a character, or a murder, or a chase – why don't I like it? That's the real question they're asking.' – **Russell T Davies**

Corin Hardy

'Notes are a key part of the script's evolution, and they're incredibly important to be constantly honing your story into its final shape.'

9 Corin Hardy – Martin Maguire Stills.

A visit to award-winning director Corin Hardy's home studio reveals mementoes of a lifetime of fantastical creating. A set of miniature puppet heads here, a life-size changeling monster there, a hand-illustrated macabre book resting on this shelf, a distressed scythe leaning in that corner. Testament to a director famed for his visual flair, attention to detail, love of monsters and inventive action.

Corin's work ranges from BAFTA nominated television series *Gangs of London* (2020) to multi award-winning independent feature film *The Hallow* (2015); from entirely self-made animated short, *Butterfly* (2003) to studio franchise blockbuster, *The Nun* (2018). What unites them, and his multitude of music videos, is a distinctive, darkly flamboyant aesthetic married to emotionally grounded performances. Good humour and a sense of fun pepper his work. Look closely, and a keen eye can spot Corin playing a zombie in his childhood friend Edgar Wright's debut feature, *Shaun of the Dead*, or glimpse an album cover for Corin and friends' band The Conspirators in *The Hallow*, or Corin playing a busker in a *Gangs of London* cameo. Brief moments that reflect a desire to support friends' creative endeavours, foster a buoyant mood on set, and a conviction that work should be entertaining to make as well as to watch.

After a day in the edit for series two of *Gangs of London*, on which he is executive producer as well as lead director, Corin Hardy is back in his London hotel room. Instantly making the room cooler with his rock and roll pirate vibe. His creative energy infusing the space around him. He's up in London from his small Sussex village home, and shows one of the travel essentials he's brought with him – a birthday card made by one of his young daughters. It features four cats – two parents and two kittens; the cardboard cats' heads sculpted in 3-D to stand out from the 2-D drawing. The creativity is strong in this family. It is not unusual to find a giant spider made by his wife perched on top of their roof, or Corin gliding through the lanes at twilight in a cloak and stripes, like a hero from a Victorian-set melodrama, off to perform with his band in the local pub.

From amid the rather more bland environs of an elegantly neutral hotel room, he reflects on notes: 'I've found as I've gained more experience in developing, writing, overseeing and co-writing scripts, you can really recognize the difference between good, informed, helpful notes and bad notes. And that obviously is subject to who you're collaborating with and how in tune with the project and you they are generally. Useful, good, helpful notes can be really gold, and other notes you just … ignore.' He laughs, like the nicest pirate you ever met.

He expands, 'It's to do with the trust you have with your collaborators. Sometimes you're in a position where you know someone and you trust them, you've worked with them before or you've had a long history with them and understand each other's sensibilities, which can be really liberating for you both. Other times you're working with new people you've never met before, and so you're perhaps a little more wary and protective. Hopefully I'm always wanting to be open to new collaborations and other people's input. If you've chosen a good crew and you have that trust with them it's fantastic. Then you're able to achieve a much higher, more successful, end result. It's the same with producers' and script editors' notes. In the situation where you realize for some reason that you're getting notes from someone whose opinions either aren't in line with what you're thinking, or you get the sense that they're maybe not as experienced, or are giving notes just to make sure they gave notes, then it's less helpful and you have to politely skirt around them.'

He considers how to tell if notes are 'good' or 'bad' for your project. 'I find it relatively easy,' he says, 'It sounds selfish, but because I'm thinking about what my perspective and understanding is on any script and the story that I'm going to make, when I read the note my reaction initially might either be "Yes, totally, that's exactly right!" or "Oh god, I really disagree with that." Then I'll maybe have a cup of tea and read it again and go, "Oh, that was just me being reactionary or sensitive, hang on a minute, maybe there's something in it, oh I see where they're coming from" or "No, that's definitely not how I see it." Who's to say what's right and wrong for a story? Some opinions are coming from personal perspectives, and others are more baked into the process and methods of storytelling, so it's open to interpretation depending on the type of story you are telling. But if it's in relation to being a director operating off those notes, it's relatively straightforward. I will always consider the notes and feel it out, weigh up the note and try and remain open to what is being suggested, putting my ego aside. If it helps improve the story, it's a good note.'

Possessing those instincts for whether a note chimes with a directorial vision arises from a lifetime of experience. Corin's first forays into filmmaking were as a horror movie loving teenager. He and a group of friends made their own gore-spattered tributes in their local woods, experimenting with filming, prosthetics and animatronics. He stifles a snigger at the idea of anyone giving notes on those, explaining, 'My early childhood films from the age of twelve to seventeen, I don't know if you'd have been able to give notes on them because, well, aside from the ambitious gore and creature FX, at least story-wise there was only sometimes a vague semblance of an actual script!' He laughs fondly at the memory of them. After graduating from Wimbledon School of Art, where he studied theatre design, he spent five years making every aspect of a thirty-minute stop-motion short film, *Butterfly,* in his parents' garage. He recalls, 'When I wrote the script for *Butterfly*, I was really doing it for the first time, as properly as I knew how, but without having any training or having gone to film school. I had heard of getting notes, so after I wrote the script I organized with a local book group in my village to sort of review it. I asked if I could send them the script and get their thoughts on it. It was to try and open up to see whether the story made sense outside of my own head. It was a relatively mature aged group of people, used to reading books, who were intellectuals and were smart, nothing to do with film or students or producers. I remember them reading it and then having a session at their book group where I sat around in one of their lounges. It was good to hear their interpretation of the story. It wasn't like they were giving specific constructive notes, but it was getting a human response to the story from a group of regular people. Because sometimes it feels really obvious to you exactly what this story's about and what these characters are feeling, and then you hear someone's response and in their response, even if they can't articulate it exactly, you go, "Oh shit, there's something lacking there if they aren't actually talking about the thing that I hoped they would be." That's the earliest example I can remember of getting a form of notes.'

The success of the resulting animated short, *Butterfly,* drew the interest of Music Video commissioners; leading to Corin making videos for the likes of

Keane, Biffy Clyro and The Prodigy. Looking back on that time Corin says, 'My roughly ten years of making music videos was a bit like my film school, and learning about working in a professional industry with crews. One of the skills I learned was balancing the idea I wanted to make with satisfying the band, satisfying the music video commissioner and the record label. Trying not to be defensive and protective, but at the same time trying to make sure that I made the thing that I ultimately wanted to make. Which is similar to when you're thinking about notes. Same thing again, it depends on the personalities and the people you trust. It can be frustrating if your vision for the music video gets compromised by politics or if they're somehow missing the point and it loses shape through adhering to notes in the edit. But hopefully you are working with people who are going to improve it. So I learnt patience and collaboration, and also the importance of trying to work with people that you like and trust as much as possible.'

He advises, 'A part of it is your choice of projects. Whether it's your own independent movie or short film or feature film and what level of budget that is, because obviously the lower the budget the more control you have, because the less of other people's money you're using. The minute you're using other people's money, you're going to have their input. So you have to manage keeping them involved and satisfied while pulling off your own intentions. With music videos, I tended to take on a smaller band with a lower budget that I could try and retain overall more visual and conceptual control, or I'd do a more high profile band's lower budget music videos, the third or fourth release from an album, so they were a little less protective because it wasn't the big release for the first two songs that would be blowing all their budget. I did a few of those too, and naturally they tend to get scrutinized more, or you can't get away with quite an as out there or an as interesting idea. My first feature film, *The Hallow,* was kept at a certain budget range, which wasn't ultra-low, but it wasn't too big. And luckily I didn't get any real interference and the producers on it helped protect me and the project, not that the financiers were ever trying to steer it in a different direction. Again it's down to what the project is, what the budget level is and who the collaborators are.'

Reflecting on what kind of notes are most useful, he asserts, 'For me, specific notes are better than vague notes. When I'm giving notes as a director or showrunner working with writers or editors, I'm finding myself to be ultra-specific. For instance, when I'm working on *Gangs of London* with the scriptwriter and script team, on my own episodes as well as the other episodes that I'm overseeing, and also when working on the edits, you only have so much time to dedicate to everything you're doing; so I find myself being hyper-specific about what I would recommend would improve something, which may also be connected to the overall season or relate to the continuity of the other episodes. And so I expect that from the other people I'm working with. Some people give more of a general feeling note, which is OK if it is more of a question that needs sharpening. But I find that the less specific the note, the less helpful it is, because ultimately you're trying to hone in on precisely what's missing or what would improve the story or the character, or whatever it is the notes are about.'

Corin outlines some of the process he's developed for giving notes: 'I've been giving a hell of a lot of notes over the last years on *Gangs* and on my feature films, so I find myself getting into a very specific way of presenting my notes to the writer. As a director, there's no real benefit from being vague and not just cutting exactly to the chase, whilst also respecting who you're working with. I've got into doing notes a certain way, partly from lack of time. Say I'm working on six scripts at the same time, six projects with six different writers, some I'm collaborating with, some I'm overseeing. It's not like there's some mathematical way of presenting notes, but what I do is like a live stream. I'll read the script, and reading a script for me, if it's a hundred-page script therefore it should hopefully take you no more than two hours to read, but it'll take me four or five hours minimum, because I can't just whizz through something without trying to imagine how it'll be. Ideally I don't want to do that in two or three sittings, because that would break up the flow of it. I'd love to just read it and absorb the story, but then I'll find I'll have forgotten all the things I thought about, and I'll have to do the whole thing again. So now that's ten hours of reading that one script. So what I do is, as I read I'll have a Word document open, or the little microphone and notes app on an iPhone. The minute I've got any feelings about anything, it could be a small dialogue suggestion or whole scene or character, mythology or continuity, or structural adjustments, whatever it is, I hit the microphone and I speak it out loud, like

"Page thirty-two, scene thirty-four, where it says blah blah blah, I think we could improve such and such", or "Can we articulate more of a visual sense of the monster and define more clearly how the set piece goes here" or whatever it is, but I'll make a general note to myself, and keep going through the whole script, so it's like a real-time commentary. Then when I've done that, I'll go back through it and divide the notes either into the three or four acts or make a series of bold headlines accompanied with the page number, with all the suggestions that came to me as a kind of account.'

He explains, 'I've only crafted the way I give notes through constant experience on the job doing it, because I've never trained in any of this or in film school. It's just, I find, the most effective and efficient way of conveying my most honest instinctual responses to the script or outline I'm reading. My completely open, completely honest response as a director who's going to ultimately make the movie based on the script I'm reading. And usually the deeper you go, the more you ingrain yourself in the script and begin to understand the story you want to tell, or begin to feel the rhythm or detail out the rules of the mythology, the more incidental things, that you might not have initially planned on, start to emerge and can be improved as new thematic or emotional connections start to solidify. It's the same when you're editing. In some ways the closer you get to the final version the more you want to get it all just right in terms of how you see it, and you're honing it as you do it. So initially you can read a script and go, "Cool, this is a good script" or "That one wasn't for me", but then the more you're working into it, the more you're really addressing everything in it in relation to everything else, including how you plan on executing it, which also plays a part in changing it from the page. You get to know it, the arcs of the characters, the turns and twists in the pacing, the mythological reveals, when, where and how much and the internal, instinctive rhythm throughout the acts of the script. So it feels like a mistake if I read a script without writing my instant thoughts and notes down at that exact time of reading. Now, that's a long-winded process, but once I've done all that in a lot of detail, then I'll go through the notes I've made for myself and create a more structured notes document. I'll use my real time script breakdown assessment, with connections to the page note and scene. Then I'll plot out what I think the three or four most important headlines are, usually the overall pace, structure, characters or set pieces and any big issues that need looking at. Do them all as individual sections, and then go into more detailed page notes where I do my best to offer up any immediate solutions that came to me on the read. I try to keep the page notes as open as I possibly can, to capture my own primal response reading it and things that excited me, stuff I really liked. I think it is just as important to know what I really liked and loved to help align with the writer or co-writer. I'm more firm I suppose, with stuff I really, for some reason, can't see working, or don't buy into and want to weed that out as fast as possible or be convinced otherwise. I'm aware if I'm misunderstanding something and it could be me that's not getting it, in which case I still want it more clarified in the script.

He reflects, 'It comes down to how you work with the writers. It's always brilliant when you work with writers who are equally open and enjoy the back and forth and problem solving. Because it's that mutual respect isn't it? You want to get the best out of them, but also to be making the thing that you're envisioning. The way I prefer to work is being very open and trusting and to encourage that both ways. The way I feel it works best, is to get all my thoughts out onto that page, structure them as clearly as possible for everyone's sake, and send them to the writers first, then discuss with them together and then follow up with a call or meeting with the studio or other execs. Then at least they've got a chance to go through and digest what they do agree with, if they don't agree with something, or if they've got a different version of something to pitch back at me. That makes the process of that call much more creative and efficient. But I also feel much more secure having logged and processed all of my thoughts in the first place. That's the way I like to work, not everyone likes to work that way. Some writers like to keep themselves shut away, but I find it's better to be able to have that open thought process and honest back and forth.' He adds, 'It's interesting, because of the projects that I'm working on, for whatever reason I'm giving a lot of notes, and I don't think it is very helpful to just be negative and say, "Oh, this is shit" or "This isn't working" or whatever and not at least try and suggest a solution, if I've got one, or just be open and say, "I don't really know what the solution is here, but such and such isn't working yet and I know you'll come up with something", and hope that they do!'

And does he like getting the same kind of thing back? Someone making suggestions having identified an issue. He laughs, 'That's a good question!' He leans back in his chair as he considers, before reasoning, 'If you gave clear notes or criticisms accompanied by any helpful suggestions or solutions that are actionable, I'd be really happy, because that would help improve the script and save on time. But if it's more of a negative or vague note which might be difficult to address, usually this is to do with the tone or something, then it's less helpful. Though probably needs looking at,' he concedes.

As to how hard he likes someone to push a note if it's one he's initially sceptical about, he muses, 'It's a two-way process isn't it? It's about the collaboration. If we've been working together, and you have given helpful notes, even if there are some I don't agree with I'll think, "Venetia's got really smart points, and she's really keen on this particular one, so I should give it another look."'

If there's a note you don't agree with, he advises, 'You always say that you're going to look into it ...' He laughs, acknowledging what that implies – that look into it is all you're going to do. He expands, 'Early on in your career you might get frustrated by hearing a point of view and feel the need to defend your version, but the thing to do generally is to say: "That's really interesting, yeah, I'm definitely going to look into that" and then either you ignore it, or take a look and go, "Oh shit, they were right, that was a really good thought and I'm glad I looked into it." I try and remain as ego-less as possible and be open to good notes and good opinions. But pretty quickly you know whether someone's really smart and a great collaborator, or that they're not hitting it, or just giving notes because they feel they have to, and so you adjust accordingly.'

An artist as well as a director and writer, Corin frequently has a sketchbook stashed about his person. Sure enough, when the talk turns to how he uses drawing as part of his development process he pulls out not just one, but a fistful of carefully labelled sketchbooks. He fans them out like a winning hand of cards. He describes how visuals can be a useful tool for development and notes, enthusing, 'With sketchbooks, but also all forms of visualization, like concept art, storyboarding, rough doodles, or sculptures, I find from the writer side or the writer-director side it is so useful for sharing your vision. Conveying anything that excites me, or I feel strongly enough that I can articulate visually, then the minute I've got something, I'm sharing it in every meeting, with financiers, with crew. On *Gangs* we're having constant production meetings or core team meetings, and it's all about cutting to the chase at every opportunity to define the vision or overcome the problem, and drawings can be a really useful way of doing that.'

Flipping through one of his sketchbooks as he speaks, he holds up a page showing a jagged-toothed, haunted looking being, drawn in simple pen strokes. He reveals, 'This is for this Sam Raimi film that I'm doing. I don't quite know yet how it fits, but I like the vibe. So I'm banking it as an early thing. Right now I'm only sharing that with the writers.' He turns to a page in another sketchbook and holds up a charcoal drawing of two characters, one in a kitchen, the other lurking outside the window. The image evocatively conveys a foreboding atmosphere of unseen, intruding menace. He explains, 'Or on *Gangs* I did this as a quick doodle to explain the scene is in a kitchen at night and he's looking in a fridge and there's a man outside the window. I just think if an image makes me interested or excited, I know I've got something and sharing that with people like the production designer or DoP instantly permeates everyone's brain with a version of something that you might assume everyone is already visualizing but maybe they are not.' Corin holds up another page of the sketchbook, a kinetic drawing, from the perspective of someone firing a gun, as figures loom over them under a full moon. He continues, 'Or I'll try and draw an image that sums up a set piece, showing why it's exciting and sort of try and distil on the page why it will make for a great moment or sequence. In this case it's a man who's fallen into a grave and he's shooting his attackers from the grave whilst they're trying to cover him in dirt. Which immediately got me excited!'

In terms of the kind of note it's helpful to get back on images, he says, 'It's a funny thing to say, but it's just helpful to get a response. It definitely helps a lot with writers, when they go "Oh wow, I really love seeing that, and now I get it." Sometimes you get execs, not on any particular show or film, but they don't really respond or they don't express any opinion, which I find strange. I think it's sometimes because they don't have an ability to be able to visualize. Or sometimes perhaps a drawing might scare them because they're like, "Well, that looks like it's going to be fucking expensive!"' he laughs.

As he puts away his stack of sketchbooks, Corin illustrates why purely critical notes are less helpful. And less well received. He recalls, 'I remember getting pissed off with some notes before I shot *The Hallow*, from people I won't name, who were doubtful of us pulling off the ambition of the script. And it was at a point when obviously you're nervous and you're giving it everything you've got, but they weren't very constructive. They were just a bit like throwing a lot of doubt that we'd ever achieve it. Which made me even more determined to!' he laughs, before adding with characteristic fairness, 'But equally, if they're really experienced and they know you're a first-time director and you don't really know how you're going to pull something off, then it's important that they voice that opinion.'

He concedes, 'Horror's definitely a difficult one to pull off in a script. Because it's so visual and atmospheric and it's about the vision of the director to pull it off and create tension. It's really hard to read a script that conveys what the fear, horror and tension will be. But you can recognize it. Well, I can recognize it as a director, whether something's on the page and it gives me the opportunity to build it out. *The Nun* was a good example of a script that was not only a page-turning read, but a fun, enjoyable read. As a director giving notes to a writer, I want to make sure it's clear that you can see the opportunities to create tension, to sustain terror or a create an elaborate set piece with monsters; that there's an exciting predicament that has multi-opportunities for all those things. A good scriptwriter is able to ultra-describe that in detail, or to put in just enough information for the director to be able to highlight those opportunities. You want to understand what the key factors are that're going to lead to this being a very scary and original sequence or scene. I don't see horror as different to anything else. Other than that it's a lot harder to pull off a good horror movie and sustain the suspension of disbelief, tension, complex characters that you believe in throughout and create an atmosphere and a visual sensibility that supports the overall concept or mythology. It is, I feel, much, much, harder to make a great horror movie than any other genre. But equally you can make a really schlocky or bad one and it can be really enjoyable and fun! Those great horror movies like *The Shining* (Stanley Kubrick, 1980) *The Thing* (John Carpenter, 1982) or *Alien* (Ridley Scott, 1979) are because of the drama and the characters as much as the mood, tension or monster.'

He suggests the consequence of this for notes is that, 'Horror and anything more imaginative, action, anything that has set-pieces or scares or a strong design element, requires much more back and forth interpretation to get something on the page that's reflective of the final impact that you're going for. Obviously with horror the challenge is to try and keep the tension and the suspension of belief and the originality – so with notes, that's what I'm trying to coax out. If I read something and I'm like, "Well, I've seen this a hundred times, but I like the way in and out, how can we think about freshness? What if it took place in a different location or environment or we give it some additional rules or limitations that make it more interesting?"'

As he thinks, Corin toys with a small plastic chainsaw. He smiles, 'I'm just sitting here fiddling with my new Christmas Gremlin. And here's the Creature from the Black Lagoon.' He pulls another mini monster into view, explaining, 'Those are my screenwriting companions!'

Naturally, the talk turns to monsters.

Corin discusses notes around how much of your creature to reveal how soon, the balance of tantalizing without giving too much away. He says, 'It comes up a lot. Especially when you're making your first feature film, especially in horror and especially because everyone worries about what you can and can't pull off, which is a difficult thing to pin down. With *The Hallow* I did want to defy that, because I love creatures and I love horror. Everyone will bring up *Jaws* (Steven Spielberg, 1975) and go, "Yeah well in *Jaws* you never see the shark and it's much better as a result" and there's a huge story behind all of that, that's true. But also I love a movie where you do see the massive T-Rex and can commit to the vision. If you have the ability to pull off the effects, then it just depends what you're going for. But certainly on a lower budget, that question comes up a lot. It comes down to the story and what the reveals are and maintaining a way to always keep evolving it in terms of tension and intrigue and scare. Because you want to keep surprising the audience, and once you've shown your creature too clearly there's only so much surprising you can do. It also depends what kind of creature it is and whether it's a supernatural thing or a physical thing and what the rules are. So it tends to be dictated by the reveals in the mythology as well as budget. But I also firmly believe that just because you can show something, doesn't mean you should. I like to build in progression within the creature, so that you're never seeing the same thing twice. It's always going to either transform, evolve or progress. Just when you think you know what you're dealing with, there's a new factor to it.'

Thinking about notes around tone on *The Hallow* he says, 'I remember during the whole process of development there being tons of conversations about tone. Tone is probably the most important and hardest element in a film to define out loud. And it's one of the most important to establish as early on as you possibly can, because it is such a hard thing to pin down. You can establish the look of something – I can put ten visual references and go, 'That's the kind of look' and you go, 'Cool, I can totally see those Roger Deakins cinematography reference photos, that'll look amazing if you can shoot like that.' Or I can show my own creature designs, or references from other movies. Similarly when you read a script, you can establish the story based on the words. But tone is like an invisible thing, and everyone interprets it differently. The tone of what the film, story, TV show is and how it's going to be received, is in what world it's taking place in, what the choices of music are, how broad the performances are or how naturalistic it looks and feels. It's a combination of things. So to help articulate the tone, I put together tone sections within my master visual document or world bible. On *The Hallow*, the juggle was to do with how naturalistic, grounded or biological or scientific the tone was, compared to how mythological, supernatural and heightened it was. It was like a sliding scale. If it was too heightened, and too gothic it would have slipped into a slightly more fantastical kind of horror movie, which would be less relatable or believable than what I was going for. *Alien* was probably one of the main tonal benchmarks, where you have a film that is actually a B-movie horror in a haunted house with a monster at its core, but it's played out like it's real. It's grounded, everyone's performances are rooted in reality and quite a naturalistic one, and the design of the creature is all incredibly deep and thought out and biologically sound. Yet with *The Hallow,* if it was too naturalistic or too grounded or dry then it wouldn't allow for the mythology and the creatures aspect to come through without bumping. So it was a fine tonal tightrope to walk. I felt like if I veered too hard in either direction it wouldn't work. That was very much worked out with the producers, Joe Neurauter and Felipe Marino. I don't think we ever got any notes from any financiers about it, but we did establish, I think quite early on, that this is a horror movie based on fairy tale and folk horror, but it's not pushing to heighten the gothic side. I'd use other things for reference, so if *Pan's Labyrinth* (Guillermo del Toro, 2006) was a sort of fairy tale horror movie with a grounded reality and story that was maybe seventy per cent fairy mythology and thirty per cent reality, then this is probably the opposite of that, it's probably seventy per cent relationship drama in the real world and thirty per cent fairy tale mythology.'

Knowing and expressing what the intention is for the tone, helps clarify the direction for development of the script. Corin says, 'There were times early on when the script was way too weighted in mythology and fantasy, and that was when it felt wrong and like you might lose the audience you had aimed at. It felt if it was too fantastical, as much as I love fantastical elements, I want the fantasy to be part of the reality in it, not to change gear too much. Although if you watch *The Hallow* all the way through, there is a constant incremental gear change going on and it gradually takes on more and more of a classic fairy tale identity throughout the story and specifically becomes one in the third act.'

As we come towards a close, Corin says, 'Everyone would love to believe that someone writes a script, the first draft is perfect, it gets made shot for shot, it gets edited in exactly the same structure, and it's finished. Obviously, hopefully if it's a genius script and a genius director, it is close, but I'm always amazed at the amount of evolution, the transformation that happens across the length of the process, and in an edit suite particularly. Notes are a key part of the script's evolution, and they're incredibly important to be constantly honing your story into its final shape. It's the same with editing. Right now, I'm getting edit notes for eight episodes of *Gangs of London*. Each time you're delivering a cut, maybe you're delivering five cuts to execs and then broadcasters and you're getting notes from the execs and the broadcasters and doing phone calls on them all. That's me as a director getting notes from the networks and the execs. So I'll be giving responses back to all those notes. I try and not only read every note but be open to it, even if I'm like, "Fuck, I don't want to do this, but actually that's a really good note", so of course I'm going to do it. And I think it's helpful to let everyone know how you're responding. I'm doing it every day at the moment with the editors – we'll compile the notes documents from Sky, AMC, the execs, put them all in one document and then go through them. Go "Done" and explain what I've done, or "I don't feel the same, but we'll give it a go", or "That's interesting, I'll look into it." He chuckles at the implication that look is all he will do; reiterating, 'I just know – good notes are good notes; bad notes you don't need to do. It's sort of simple really. Good notes can be really frustrating, because you think you're there, but then someone sees something that unlocks the thing that you've actually been struggling to solve. Sometimes in the edit you can make one cut or change to a line using ADR and it can solve an insurmountable problem you thought you couldn't fix. So I remind myself that it's important to always remain open to notes. Even when it feels difficult or frustrating.'

He concludes, 'Storytelling is the greatest, simplest form of escape from our real lives. And should therefore be as immersive as possible. To pull off an immersive story that you can escape inside, whatever the genre, the story has to galvanize you. So a script needs to be written in a way that allows it to be the easiest bridge to becoming galvanized in a story. The script editor's role is key in finding ways to make the page read as enjoyably and fluidly as possible so that it can also transition into effective cinema. My general perspective on making movies, is everyone being open to improvement, at any time. And that involves making and taking notes, and ultimately deciding which ones to implement to improve the story.'

London, via Zoom, January and May 2022

Selected credits, awards and nominations

Butterfly: Writer, Director, Producer, Animator, Cinematographer, Editor (2003), [Film] UK: Mysterious Cat.
　　London Animation Festival award – Best Long Short (2006)
The Hallow: Co-writer, Director (2015), [Film] UK, Ireland: Entertainment One.
　　British Independent Film Awards nomination – Douglas Hickox Award, Best Debut (2015)
　　Screamfest award – Festival Trophy – Best Director (2015)
　　iHorror Awards – Best Foreign Horror (2015)

Strasbourg European Fantastic Film Festival award – Best European Fantastic Film (2015)

FrightFest award – Best Monster (2015)

FrightFest nomination – Best Film (2015)

Empire Awards – Best Horror Film (2016)

The Nun: Director (2018), [Film] USA: Warner Bros.

Gangs of London: Director episodes '*#1.2*', '*#1.3*', '*#1.4*', '*#1.9*', '*#2.1*', '*#2.2*', '*#2.7*' and '*#2.8*', Executive Producer series 2 (2020–22), [TV Series] Sky Atlantic.

BAFTA TV nomination – Drama series (2021)

Hollywood Critics Association Television Awards nomination – Best Cable Series, Drama (2021)

Tomm Moore

'A story well told makes us feel less alone. So if you communicate something honestly, you're giving a gift to other people who've been through that, or feel that. Any notes should be helping to communicate something essential that we feel we want to share with other people.'

10 Tomm Moore, photo by Shane O'Connor.

Tomm Moore grew up in Kilkenny, south east Ireland, where the town's medieval walls harbour a thriving arts scene, with festivals of music and crafts alongside the castle by the river. As a teenager, Tomm joined the Kilkenny-based Young Irish Filmmakers organization. Now, he provides opportunities in the town for the next generation – employing a host of artists at his multi-Oscar nominated animation studio, Cartoon Saloon, which he co-founded with director Nora Twomey and producer Paul Young. Tomm's deep Irish roots, love of art, nature and myth shine out of his films *The Secret of Kells* (2009), *Song of the Sea* (2014) and *Wolfwalkers* (2020).

On a hot late summer day, his wife out for the evening, the enthusiasm of that art-loving teenager is still evident in the Oscar-nominated director. When he appears on the screen for our Zoom, Tomm is full of unnecessary apologies for being a few minutes late, explaining he became absorbed in refining the drawing of a poster for *Wolfwalkers*. At the time of our chat, *Wolfwalkers* is due to come out in a few months and, unlike many other films scheduled for the autumn of the 2020 pandemic, goes ahead with a cinematic release. It becomes the third of Tomm's films to be nominated for an Oscar.

'Getting notes is probably one of the most painful parts of the process,' Tomm acknowledges with a rueful grin. 'I've had notes from people I respect, like Nora [Twomey, co-director of *The Secret of Kells*], that have left me ready to retire!' he laughs. 'And I've had notes from people where you just go, "Ah, I'm not even going to listen to this, because they don't know what they're talking about."'

He confesses, 'It's three or four years since I was in that painful place of getting the notes. It's probably good, as I'm not as bitter and angry anymore,' he half jokes, continuing, 'It isn't healthy to be like that, and it is an important skill to learn to take the notes, because it's a hard job to give notes.' Tomm advises, 'If someone takes the time to give you notes, respect that they've given you their time. It's easier for them to say "I don't have time to help." If they're giving notes, they're invested in the project. You have to start with a bit of an open heart, rather than being too resistant. Which is very hard.'

Contemplating how people react to receiving notes, Tomm says, 'There's a very experienced screenwriter working with Nora at the moment, who talks about there being three stages of responding to notes: "Fuck you", "Fuck me" and "What's next?" At first you're just angry at the person who gave the notes; then you're totally depressed that you feel like you're crap – if they're good notes, you start thinking "Oh man, I don't know what I'm doing. I'm an idiot"; and then you have to as quickly as possible move on to "What's next?" which is where you find ways to implement the notes – if you think they're useful or they can't be ignored. Though I have this amazing ability to hold the "Fuck you" at the same time as the "What's next?"' he laughs, 'I can stay angry while realizing I have to move on and make changes.'

Tomm observes, 'When you get notes you're in a very vulnerable place, and it feels like someone's criticizing you. It's good to get used to, because when you release the film there's loads of people out there whose job it is to write criticisms of your film. If you work in the post office or something it's only your superior who might give you feedback, but with a film it's just a free for all.'

Tomm outlines how the dynamics of notes can vary, depending on how the project is set up. He explains, 'There's different positions you can be in getting notes. You can be a director for hire who's been hired by a producer who has a project, and you're taking notes in a way to understand what they want you to do. Then there's the situation where you've created a project, you've written it on spec, it's been funded and there's this nervous thing where the people who're helping you to get it made by giving you the money want to have a say in it, but it wasn't theirs in the first place, it was yours in the first place. So you're like, "How much do I give to them?" If you're in a role where a producer comes with a book or a script and they give notes on what you're creating from it, you think, "OK, well, it was yours first, I'm going to try and keep ownership but respect what you wanted." Whereas the other way around where you're the original creator it's a different power balance.' He reflects, 'I've been very lucky, or it's been very important to me, that on my projects, where I came up with the project in the first place, that I've had the sort of final say.'

Tomm cautions, 'Keep in mind that if you take the bigger budget you may have less control. But again it depends on the set up.' As an example of the subtle distinctions he says, 'On *Wolfwalkers* I was a little nervous because we had taken the bigger budget when Apple came on, yet the project was already funded with our usual partners. I wanted Apple's notes. I wanted to make sure we made something they thought could be a success on their platform, but it didn't start with me going to them and selling the show, I was already making it and then they came on, so it's a slightly different position.'

Tomm emphasizes the importance of being selective about who you work with, and aware of the impact that will have on notes. He reveals, 'At one point The Weinstein Company were really interested in *Song of the Sea*. We had a call with Harvey Weinstein and met one of his producers in Cannes. And I was terrified. This was pre #MeToo, I didn't know about that then, but I was just terrified about this power. I talked to a friend who directed a movie Harvey was producing, and he said basically Harvey was so controlling that he had to fight every day for it to still be his movie. I thought, "I don't want those kind of notes." So I chose not to go that way, even though it might have been a fast way to get financed and it might have looked good on paper. So I think I avoided on purpose getting certain notes by avoiding the partners that would give those notes. If I ever had a project I felt was commercial enough for those kind of partners, obviously not Harvey Weinstein because he turned out to be a monster, but DreamWorks for example, I would be happy to get notes from them if I said at the start "I want to make a DreamWorks style movie, help me make it." I chose instead to have a lot less money, but not to have those kind of notes. So the notes I get are either notes that I ask for, or notes from partners that I've chosen, who I feel are on the same wavelength.'

Tomm recounts some of his search to find those partners on the same wavelength for his first feature, *The Secret of Kells*. The film is an animated imagining of the creation of the Book of Kells, an Irish illustrated gospel believed to have been made in the early ninth century. The story unfolds around a young monk, Brendan, in whose monastery the book is being illustrated, and interweaves Irish folklore and the perils of Viking raiders. Tomm recalls, 'During the process of looking for a production partner for *The Secret of Kells* we talked to a lot of Irish producers. I remember one very successful production company going, "Oh, we'll just throw it up in the air and see what lands", and we were much more protective or it, and maybe had a little bit of that youthful pride as well. There were a lot of people that liked the art and liked the idea broadly, but were ready to completely re-write the film, because they saw us as inexperienced and young. And they were probably right. But at the same time, it's a heavy load to carry an independent project for so long and I didn't want to completely scrap everything. Some of the notes were really dispiriting. I remember the Irish broadcaster asking "Why is this animated?" They just couldn't see it.' A small, sad, shake of his head expresses echoes of old despair and the struggle to make the film. He owns, 'It was hard. So I had to find a partner who was willing to help us make what we wanted to make, but I had to be open enough to listen to them.'

Ultimately, it was Didier Brunner, French producer of Sylvain Chomet's Oscar nominated animation *The Triplets of Belleville* (2003), who joined the *Secret of Kells* team. 'With Didier, Nora and I were able to keep what was important to us about it, but to re-write it with Fabrice [Ziolkowski] and with notes from Didier. I would say the best producer I ever met and worked with, besides Paul [Young] my business partner, was Didier Brunner,' Tomm enthuses, 'because he specifically wanted to make something that wasn't the easy option. It's too easy to be the producer who wants to be a mini Disney and copy what the big studios do. That's not really producing, that's just copying. But Didier had committed to producing something that was offering something different, and he pushed me to go that way. The notes he gave made a big difference. His first look at the script, and it's hard because it's a story set in a monastery, he said "There's no female characters here." I was like "Pangur Ban, the cat, is a girl", but Didier said "That's not good enough!"' Tomm explains how Didier's note influenced development: 'We didn't have the character Aisling at the time. Aisling then was just this ephemeral Galadriel type spirit in the forest. In Fabrice's first pass she became a love interest, and we decided no we can't do that, because Brendan has to be a monk and we don't want to go there. So we made her like a little sister. An annoying little sister, who's always better at everything. She went from being this forest goddess to being like a little girl. That all came from Didier's note, and it was huge. It was a huge part of the film and she almost took over the movie, because she's so many people's favourite character.'

Tomm mentions how notes fed into developing the look of the animation as well as the story: 'Another thing Didier did was with his notes on the design. He encouraged us to let go of the idea that this needs to look like anything else. He was always pushing for it to look different.' Tomm underlines the importance of finding people whose notes support a filmmaker's courage to make distinctive work. He asserts, 'A producer who really wants to do something different and pushes the director to be more brave than they might be, is the right kind of producer. If you have a producer who's nervous, and I've met producers like that, and I've been able to say no to working with them, anybody who's nervous, or says any of those Hollywood clichés like "Your hero has to be somebody you want to be or somebody you want to have sex with", you just think, "Get out of the room. Fuck off." Because those people are not filmmakers. They're just manufacturers. Who want to manufacture the same product over and over again. Those are the people you have to avoid. You have to find a producer who wants to do something different. And they're a special breed.'

Conscious of the benefits notes can bring, when they are from someone in tune with what you want to achieve, Tomm actively sought them out for his second animated feature, *Song of the Sea*. The film sees a young boy, Ben, adventure with creatures of Irish myth and legend as he seeks to come to terms with the loss of his mother, a Selkie – someone who can transform into a seal. Tomm explains, '*Song of the Sea* was very special in that I didn't have to take any notes. I didn't have any bigger producer than me, because there were five small producers and we were doing it for a small budget. I was in the lucky position of not being forced to get notes, but I went looking for notes from people that I thought would help, and then I could take what I needed from it. I'd made friends with a guy called Jim Capobianco over in Pixar. He was head of story in Pixar for *Ratatouille* (Brad Bird, 2007) and he worked very closely with Brad Bird. He was a really nice guy and a fellow Indie spirit. He gave me great notes on the script. I remember him saying "This is too long." People were reacting emotionally to the ending, which is almost a cheap way to get people to cry with the mum coming back from the dead, it was always going to work, but Jim said the tentpole is the storyteller, the sequence with the Great Seanachaí character in the middle of the film. Jim said you want to get to that moment as soon as you can, because that's the turning point for Ben's character. I learnt a lot from Jim about that, that you find a tentpole, and work towards it, then it carries you to the end.'

Describing how development contributed to shaping the film, Tomm says, 'On *Song of the Sea* we worked with Will Collins on the script, who I thought again was brilliant. Will is around my age and he's grown up in Ireland, so he knew all the poetic side of the storytelling that I wanted to embrace. Nora was the head of story, and she was huge. I would say it was Will, Nora and Darragh [Byrne, the editor] in terms of influence on the story. It was my original idea, I had an overall story that didn't change terribly, but mine was way too bloated and going in different directions. Will helped me learn to funnel the story down to its essence. I credit Will with paring it right down to just being about the family. And with making everything that was happening in the fairy world an echo of what's happening in the family, which was really good. Because there was lots of other stuff going in every direction before. It's like you start off the story like shoes with no laces in, in the script you put the laces in, and then with the editing and storyboarding you're pulling them tighter and tighter until it all fits really perfectly.'

Tomm illustrates how a key part of development is that shoelace tightening; honing and focusing the story. He recalls, 'In *Song of the Sea* on a couple of the drafts I said to Will "These are moments I want to see in the film, help me work them into the story." So it was visuals first, or images or moments first, and he was cool with that. And I was OK to lose one of those if they were never going to work story-wise. There was a long time during development that the fairies were trick-or-treaters going from house to house, "in disguise" as if they were kids dressed up. That got squashed right down.' Tomm stresses the importance of being bold and open enough to cut things during development in order to strengthen the overall story. He recalls examples of elements which, even though they appealed, were removed during development so as to benefit the story as a whole: 'There's always bits of folklore and history I'd love to fit in, but that we couldn't make work story-wise. I remember there were these characters I really loved the idea of in *Song of the Sea*, Formorians. When I read about them, they're described in that naïve, medieval way – monsters that'd always have one leg and one eye. So myself and Will had this idea that Formorians would be useless unless they worked together. So they were these characters hopping around on one leg with one arm and one eye.' Tomm bounces around in his chair, playfully illustrating the would-be monsters' motion. Continuing, 'And they had to put their arms round each other to make one monster-person to be able to do anything. It was like a neat little thing – they were going to teach the kids that instead of fighting all the time they needed to work together to solve things. We also had the Unseelies, which were these really nasty, dark versions of the fairies, and they had a much bigger part as the witch Macha's henchmen, they were really cool. And they just became owls in the end.' When I exclaim that the owls are terrifying, Tomm smiles happily, 'Yeah, the owls are enough, right?'

Tomm describes how development on the film continued: 'On *Song* I felt the script just before we went into animatic phase was pretty tight but a bit long. Which was hard, because we couldn't afford to make it the length that it was. Then the journey after that was we had a very good editor, Darragh Byrne, he brought a lot of story notes on both *Song of the Sea* and *Wolfwalkers*. Darragh and Richie [Cody], and the other editors on *Wolfwalkers*, had a lot to bring story-wise. I remember we had a sequence in *Song of the Sea* fully story-boarded, it explained in much more detail why Ben, the little boy, was so mean to his sister. It showed the growing resentment after the mum disappeared, and it was a good five or six minutes of screentime. I'd storyboarded it myself, I really loved it. And Darragh was brave enough to just lift it all out!' Tomm laughs in admiration. 'That kind of thing when you're like "Whaaaat?"'

Tomm demonstrates the value of both being open to notes, and of figuring out what they are really about. He says, 'We had a moment in *Song* when Ben said to his little sister, Saoirse, "I hate you." We'd even recorded it, my nephew did the voice for it. And we got conflicting notes on it – some people thought that was way too much, and some people thought "Absolutely, he has to say that." It was in and out and in and out for a long time, and I just had to make a call. Fifty per cent of people were saying it's ruined if you don't have that moment, and fifty per cent were saying it's ruined if you do have that moment! I would have said it to my sisters in the same way that I'd have said I hate broccoli or something, it wouldn't have meant that much. But to some people it just read as too much. The kid had gone too unsympathetic, there was no way back. It was really interesting.' He advises, 'Sometimes, if there's a note you don't like, you have to dig into it and go "Well, what is it overall that they're afraid of?" I realized that what they were saying wasn't so much about that line itself, but that Ben had become quite unsympathetic, maybe too much. So some of the stuff that Darragh lifted out helped, because it had been showing over and over again this dislike for the little sister, who was just so cute and everything.'

With notes on an animated film Tomm says, 'I think we have the advantage as animators, if you feel really strongly about a sequence you can go all the way to storyboard, do an animatic pass with music and voices and everything and really be sure they see what you have in mind for that scene, and then you've much more to talk about. Sometimes, even if in strict scriptwriting terms you're spending too long on a detail, it's interesting from the way it's happening animation-wise. I think it's really important that we don't start to think that animation and live action are interchangeable. Respect the medium and leave room for the medium in anything you're writing. Don't make a live-action film that happens to be animation. For instance on *Song of the Sea* there was a lot of stuff that people didn't like with the journey in the bus. They thought we didn't need the kids on the bus travelling into the countryside, they could pop out of the tunnel and just be at the holy well. But it was so important to me to get that journey in. It felt like a pause point, a moment of transition from the city. There was a lot of stuff in there, the being on the bus, the way they stopped the bus, the journey across the fields, that seemed ripe for the plucking. Similarly in *Secret of Kells*, the whole fun with Aisling in the forest before the oak tree seemed like something we could lift out. But they felt important moments to me. They were visual and musical and lots of things. So we could map it out and try it as an animatic to show people.' He adds, 'Also, sometimes people just forget! They've given the note back at script stage and then you show the animatic with it still in and you're sitting there sweating "What are they going to say about that bit?" and it just passes by and they have something else to say! It does happen, you can say yes to a note and then not really change it and people are busy and you get away with it!' he laughs.

In classic Zoom style my cat intrudes on the conversation, casually sauntering in front of the screen. Tomm warmly asks his name, I explain that he's Finn, confessing it's after Huckleberry Finn, because of being a vagabond rescue cat, rather than the Irish hero Finn McCool. 'My dogs are down in the kitchen' Tomm says, sounding apologetic that they're not here to say hello. 'The dogs are Rocky and Apollo, after Apollo Creed and Rocky Balboa. The guinea pigs are John and Paul. After the Beatles, not the pope,' he clarifies.

Getting back to notes, Tomm advises, 'One of the most important things to remember when you're giving notes is if you point something out and want to give an example of how it can be solved, give at least two examples. Because if you just say one thing it'll feel like "Oh that's what *you* would do." Whereas if you give a couple of examples of how to solve the issue and go in a couple of different directions, then the person feels "OK, I don't have to pick one or the other, I just have to do something like this." Try and keep the autonomy for the final decision in the hands of the director, so it doesn't feel like you're telling them how to do their job. It's the same as giving notes to actors, you don't do a line read for them, you go "more like . . ." Keep the notes like that. And be specific. Be really specific. If notes are vague, they're the most maddening thing ever. If someone says "Could it be a bit more, I don't know, fluffy?" You're just like "???"' He shakes his head and laughs.

As an example of how a specific note can inspire story development Tomm discloses, 'I've a friend, Elliot Cowan, who suggested very early on that Robyn didn't need to be a boy in *Wolfwalkers*. And it changed the whole movie. Making her a girl, everything started to click into place. It was genius. And maybe more than he realized, because there was a whole historical thing we could use about women's place in the 1650s. That was a good note. Elliot is an animation director and an editor for commercials, and on *Song of the Sea* and *Wolfwalkers* he gave great notes.' Tomm says warmly, 'I have a very small little group that I'm lucky enough to have, and I owe them all big time.' He confides, 'I've put them in the movies too, Elliot's in the background of some of the movies and so are other director friends that I've worked with in different capacities who I ask for notes. It means a lot to me. I know they know me and they know what I'm trying to do. A lot of the time when I go to my little 'brain trust', I'm essentially saying "I'm struggling with this. This little boy doesn't make sense, why isn't he allowed to go out with his dad? Why would he be against hunting when he is clearly wanting to be just like his dad?" and Elliot's note about making him a girl solved a lot of things.'

Tomm adds, 'The other thing I want to say that is really important about *Song of the Sea* and *Wolfwalkers*, is that both of those I would show the animatic to schoolkids. Their feedback and their reaction meant a lot to me, we took that on board a lot. That to me was more important than anything else, whether they understood it. If something wasn't clear to them I'd go back and rework it. For instance, it wasn't clear to the schoolkids in one of the animatics for *Wolfwalkers* that Robyn was from England. That was something we thought was really obvious. But it wasn't obvious to the kids and so we had to work on it.'

Pondering notes in connection with developing stories inspired by myth and legend Tomm says, 'It's been a challenge through all the films of how much do you respect the original story and how much do you change it? I remember getting an artistic licence from Eddie Lenihan, who is one of the last of the real old storytellers – he's who we based the Great Seanachaí character on, the storyteller in *Song of the Sea*. He's got a great long beard, he's really the druid of Ireland. He mixes up the stories for his audience. He'll tell a story about Finn McCool meeting Saint Patrick. Which is totally mad and wouldn't be 'academically correct'. But he feels they're our stories to retell, and you retell them for the audience who's listening. When we had that chat he made me feel much more relaxed. And I remember Fabrice describing it more as a shopping trip than being reverential. Going through the history and the mythology and plucking out what was the essence of what we wanted to talk about, then looking for things in the folklore and the history that serviced that story we wanted to tell. Back in the early days of my career I was a little bit nervous about it, even about I suppose an early version of cultural appropriation, I was afraid of it being embarrassingly too "Oirish", and those were two very good pointers which helped me with that.'

We discuss notes he's had asking him to put more explanation of a myth or legend into his films. Tomm says, 'Every one of the three films went through a phase where we were convinced we needed an opening like in *Watership Down* (Martin Rosen, 1978) – you know at the start there's this whole, lovely, animated aboriginal style story of how rabbits ended up in the position they were in. So we designed, and never animated, something like that for each one of those movies. We had written a whole intro that let people know what it was, and bit by bit it came out. My instinct is to go that Miyazaki way of throwing people in and just giving them enough to catch up. Rather than giving them a lecture before the film starts. Because I don't think anyone pays attention to those anyway. But we used to talk about for *Wolfwalkers* that we needed some kind of *Star Wars* (George Lucas, 1977) crawl of text up the screen or something, to explain the English Civil War, who Oliver Cromwell was and so on. In the end we realized, it doesn't matter, we won't even call him Cromwell. That note came from Nora. When you see the movie, people who know the history will go "Ahhhh, we know who he is!" and to people who don't know the history, he's just yet another British villain,' he laughs.

He acknowledges, 'I think it's hard for people who read the script, who are putting finance in; they are always going to ask for that explanation of what's going on, they're always going to feel that you need that. But it's almost like a failure if you need a narrator or an opening crawl, it feels like you've let everyone down. Jericca Cleland, who was a layout person in Pixar that I met, helped a lot on *Song of the Sea*, and on *Wolfwalkers*. She was massively helpful, and she was big on getting it all on screen. She said anything you need to know should come from a character. Trying to get it all in that way. A lot of American people, who are really talented, would always think "Oh you're in the world of lore and myth, people would like to have this laid out at the start" and I can see what they mean. And there is that kind of thing in most fantasy movies. Even in *Princess Mononoke* (Hayao Miyazaki, 1997), not in the Japanese version, but in the English translation of it that Neil Gaiman did, there's a whole bit at the start, "Long ago, in the time of . . ."'

One way Tomm dealt with notes asking for that mythological expositional scene setting was by trying it, then taking it off to show you didn't need it. Rigorously honest, Tomm admits, 'But I was also showing myself and my co-directors we didn't need it as well. We would have it there until we were sure we didn't need it. In *Wolfwalkers* there was a scene that was almost animated, it went as far as being key posed, that we took out very late and we were very nervous about removing. It was the mum of the little wolfwalker girl, at the beginning explaining what a wolfwalker is. And we lifted it out, bravely I think, because it means you only learn what a wolfwalker is at the same pace Robyn, the little English girl, learns about it. The other way was very safe, because you made sure the audience knew what it was, but it took some of the engagement with the main character away, because until the middle of the movie when Robyn herself found out what a wolfwalker was we all knew more than her. The actors had acted it out and it was beautiful, because the mum had all the symbolism that Bronagh in *Song of the Sea* had, where she was a selkie but she was also kind of Ireland. It had all this poetic double meaning where the mum was telling her daughter "We're dying out, we're the last of our kind, and we have to be careful", all this stuff that had a second meaning. But in the body of the film it was too heavy.'

Tomm relates how they arrived at the decision to remove it, prompted by a note during the edit – 'It came from the fact that we had to cut the film. The movie was too long. There were suggested cuts from lots of people, and that one was one of the most dramatic. I'd learnt from the previous films that the most dramatic cuts I almost like, because you're kind of "Oh, that's exciting!" So we tried it. And nobody was sure about it. We'd had Maria Doyle Kennedy, who's a famous Irish singer and actor, play the mum, and that was her biggest scene as human, the rest of the movie she's a wolf. Everyone was like, "Are you sure? It's Maria!" But I think I got a note from several people – "If you wanted to lift something, you could lift that", because it was exposition, you know.'

Reflecting on how people from different cultures can understand myths without needing expositional detail Tomm says, 'I'm more and more interested by the fact that not only do the myths have equivalence, but the archetypes have equivalence in all mythology. So no matter where you are in the world you'll recognize something. If you grew up on *Star Wars* you'll recognize the archetypes in mythology because it's in superhero pop culture. I rely on that a lot – that's there's a universal truth in all these characters and situations and themes and tropes that people will identify with. Which is why I think I find the Miyazaki stuff so interesting, because I didn't know much about Japanese mythology for a long, long time and it was his movies that made me go "Ohhh, this is interesting, this way of seeing the world."'

We discuss working with notes from historical advisors. Tomm says, 'Nora had that more on *The Breadwinner* (Nora Twomey, 2017), because it was very important to be culturally sensitive. I think I'll encounter that if I go outside telling stories about Ireland. If I was to do something about Greek myths or African myths or whatever, gosh I'd tread much more carefully and I'd have a lot more advice. But ever since I was quite young I was always a bit of a nerd for Irish history and mythology. I did get cultural advisors but I wasn't hanging on every word, I was more checking in with them. The person I was most nervous about was a man called Bernard Meehan, the Keeper of the Book, who took care of the Book of Kells in Trinity College. He was very generous and gave us access to material that we needed. He did comment on the script and the designs but we were taking it very lightly, he didn't have any particular power, but we wanted his blessing you know. It's an interesting thing that, the relationship we have with our national treasure, it is *our* national treasure, so I felt it was mine as much as his. But he was the expert. When we showed him the nearly finished film he shook my hand and said, "You did your homework", which I was really happy about. It was one of my favourite things! He's retired now, but they embraced the film, they showed it in part of the display about the book in Trinity College, and we had the premier there in the Long Room, and the fact that he endorsed it in that way meant a lot to me.'

Asked if he has any favourite moments from his films, and whether it arose from a note, Tomm laughs, 'God, I'm an awful egotistical person – when I think a lot of my favourite bits they were things that I wanted from the start! But give me a second, I'm sure there's a good example, well Aisling!' he says with delight, 'She's a brilliant character and she evolved from a good note. So there you go.'

Wrapping up, Tomm reflects on the importance of storytelling, 'The quote that I always come back to, and I think it was Brendan Gleeson said it to me, and he said someone else said it to him, is the idea that a story well told makes us feel less alone. If you communicate something honestly, you're giving a gift to other people who've been through that, or feel that. That's the most important thing. And any notes you get should be helping to communicate something essential that we feel we want to share with other people.'

As we bid our Zoom goodbyes, I ask what he has planned for the rest of his Friday evening. He lifts up his tablet to the screen to show the poster design he's working on for *Wolfwalkers*. It's an art nouveau style depiction of the wolfwalker girls, 'I'm trying to make it Alphonse Mucha style, so I'm trying to work in a lot of nice details. I'll spend the evening now doing lots of art nouveau fiddly details and listening to podcasts' he says happily. A few months later the *Wolfwalkers* poster, with its fiddly art nouveau details, dominates the centre of New York, painted huge on the side of a building, launching the film into the world from its origins in Kilkenny.

Kilkenny, via Zoom, August 2020

Selected credits, awards and nominations

The Secret of Kells: Director, Writer (original story), Co-producer (2009), [Film]
   Co-director Nora Twomey, Ireland, Belgium, France: Buena Vista International.
   Dublin International Festival award – Audience Award, Best Irish Film (2009)
   Annecy International Animated Film Festival award – Audience Award, Feature (2009)
   Edinburgh International Film Festival award – Audience Award (2009)
   Irish Film and Television Award – Best Animation (2010)
   Irish Film and Television Award nomination – Best Film (2010)
   Irish Film and Television Award – Rising Star Award (2010)
   Academy Award nomination – Best Animated Feature Film of the Year (2010)
The Prophet, segment 'On Love': Director (2014), [Film] Dir. Roger Allers USA: GKIDS.
   Jerusalem Film Festival nomination – Best Children's Film (2015)
Song of the Sea: Director, Writer (original story), Producer (2014), [Film] Ireland,
   Denmark, Belgium, France: StudioCanal UK.
   Academy Award nomination – Best Animated Feature Film of the Year (2015)
   European Film Award – European Animated Feature Film (2015)
   Galway Film Fleadh award – Best Irish Feature Film (2015)
   Melbourne International Film Festival People's Choice Award – Best Narrative Feature
      (2015)
The Breadwinner: Producer (2017), [Film] Dir. Nora Twomey, Ireland, Canada,
   Luxembourg, US: StudioCanal UK.
   Canadian Screen Awards nomination – Best Motion Picture (2018)
   Online Film & Television Association nomination – Best Animated Picture (2018)
   Academy Award nomination – Best Animated Feature Film (2018)
Wolfwalkers: Director, Writer (story by), Producer (2020), [Film] Co-director Ross
   Stewart, Ireland: Wildcard Distribution.
   BAFTA nomination – Best Animated Feature Film (2021)
   Academy Award nomination – Best Animated Feature Film (2021)
   Irish Film and Television Award – Best Film (2021)
   Irish Film and Television Award nomination – Best Director – Film (2021)
   Annie Award – Outstanding Achievement for Directing in an Animated Feature (2021)
   Stuttgart International Trickfilm Festival award – Best Animated Feature-Length Film
      (2021)
Greenpeace: There's a Monster in My Kitchen: Co-Director (2020), [Film] Dirs. Tomm
   Moore, Fabian Erlinghauser, UK: Greenpeace.
   Irish Animation Awards nomination – Best Short Film (2021)
   Annie Award – Best Sponsored Animated Production (2021)

Quick Fire Q&A 6:
How do you deal with rejection or critical notes?

'You've got to accept first of all that it is going to hurt. And that you're going to get cross. And it's having strategies for dealing with that. Often that's having something else to do, like another project you're working on anyway. I remember getting really cross once about something and kicking this football round the garden for a long time. Really smacking it into some walls.' – **Sally Wainwright**

'Dealing with notes is really difficult. There aren't many jobs where you're endlessly being told that you've got it wrong and you need to change it. That's not what the notes are saying, but that's how you hear it. It's really hard and it doesn't necessarily get any easier. I've got a set of notes sitting on my lap-top right now, that I've had for about four or five days and I just haven't opened them because I'm not actually in a place where I can sit there and be told what I've done wrong. Yet. You need a support network of other writers who understand. And you just have to try and toughen your carapace. The problem with writing well is that your emotional antennae have to be open – that's how you write a good script. You open yourself up to everything around you. Both intellectually and emotionally. And then somehow you have to close that off when people start sending you notes. There isn't anybody who deals well with it. You have to find your own way of dealing with it. I go to karate. I find punching things really helpful. Everyone needs to find their own way. There isn't a manual. You can go out and get drunk. Or you can put the notes in the fire. I do all of those metaphorically. But literally I do a really violent sport. And that really helps.' – **Simon Beaufoy**

'Go for a run. Write exactly what you want to say back and don't send it. And then just mine into it and see if there's anything in there that you genuinely think comes from a place of misunderstanding that you can correct.' – **Tomm Moore**

'I think you just have to figure out a way to make people see the light. And this is a tricky thing to say to writers – sometimes the script is not enough on its own. Sometimes you need to create something else to get the tone across. With *Shaun of the Dead* we had a lot of rejection from some companies who just didn't get it. And maybe this is tough for some people to hear, but even with people that did get it and wanted to make the film, such as Film4 initially and eventually Working Title, I think that if we didn't have *Spaced* (1999) to show them as examples of our prior work, *Shaun of the Dead* would never have been made. If it was just a screenplay doing the rounds, I think most people would have gone, "Hmmmm, no." But because we had a kind of proof of concept in the show – the tone, the humour and the performances – it was like having a showreel in a sense, so people reading the script could go, "Oh now I get it, it's going to look and feel like this." Even when you're more established you still have to do that. With *Baby Driver* (2017) it was really difficult to get across the execution of the movie. Beyond the screenplay I made sound mixes of the songs with sound effects in them, and then eventually made an entire reel of clips of other films cut to the songs with occasional bits of story-boards, and actors saying the lines which I spliced in from a first read-through I recorded around five years before I made the film. So then you had a screenplay and you also had this other reel that was effectively a tonal preview of the film. So it's tough. Obviously there are brilliant, brilliant screenplays that become very hot properties on the printed word alone. And then sometimes, when there's an element of tone or execution to it, you need a little something else as well. In terms of the rejections on *Shaun of the Dead*, I don't think I ever felt "The script is no good." It was more of, "How do we figure out how to sell this?" I think you just have to find ways to pick yourself back up again and keep going.' – **Edgar Wright**

'It depends how negative it is. I've not been in a situation where it's been so awful. But you reduce them down to their simplest essence and then see if they make any sense.' – **Ben Wheatley**

'If several people are saying the same thing, then it's a problem. But that's something I have learned more from picture editing when you have something tangible in front of you. If you have a strong conviction something will work on film it can be hard to explain in theory, but often these are the best ideas. If you feel strongly then keep it.' – **Lynne Ramsay**

'I'm a Black woman – many of us have had to face rejection from a very young age because of society, so it's something I'm very used to. I've had it from day dot. I'm more shocked if I don't get rejection or critical notes. I've learned to grow a tough skin, and to not be deterred – ever. The best thing you can do if you truly believe in something you are doing with a story is stick to your guns and as I've always said when it comes to nurturing your creative journey – don't take no for an answer, even when the rejection hurts.' – **Amma Asante**

'In terms of rejection, Ray Harryhausen once firmly told me, "You've got to be resilient" and coming from a man who has worked his way through centuries of cinema as an almost one-man army of creativity, it is inevitable that he must have experienced a substantial amount of rejection and difficulties in bringing his incredible visions to the screen. So I took those five words on board early on and always try, no matter how negative, disappointing or anger-making a situation is, to "be resilient", keep doing my best, water off a duck's back and tomorrow is another day. In terms of applying that to criticism in notes, I think it's really straightforward – you just take the good notes and don't take the notes you don't agree with. No stress. I will always process all the notes to fully examine and interrogate them and to use anything useful within them. You come to know pretty quick who gives good notes and who doesn't. But I'll read all the notes because I'll be open to anything if it's a good note, or a good germ of an idea is hidden somewhere within the criticism, and sometimes that may take time to uncover. If it's critical, but a good note, then it's great. In terms of being unable to solve a story problem that is holding you up, when I made *The Hallow*, my editor Nick Emerson and I got stuck on something we couldn't figure out a solution for and found playing aggressive Ping Pong was a great way to unlock the answer!' – **Corin Hardy**

'I try to tell myself to sleep on it and rethink tomorrow, and not poison the editing room with my hard feelings. But also I do things that are not very strategic. I really get insulted sometimes. I remember saying once to a producer, "You would never say something like that to Paul Greengrass!" and he goes, "Why Paul Greengrass?!" It was meant as a joke, but I must have felt a lack of respect, the kind Greengrass gets for very good reasons, though that probably comes from my own basic insecurity. Which is partly what I use as a filmmaker, often portraying insecure characters. So . . . It helps getting older. I worry less. But the worst thing that can happen is you don't care: "Sure, I'll change it, just for peace in the valley", I really don't want to be like that. I want to stay on fire about eighteen frames, not be a pragmatic fat cat.' – **Lone Scherfig**

'If you've had critical notes the most important thing is to not respond immediately. Read it, go away for the weekend, leave it alone, come back and re-read them. Notes can sometimes elicit a flight or fight response, which is completely natural because it's your baby. But sometimes you come back to those notes and they're not as bad as you thought they were. They're actually fine. Rejection is really hard. But you have to move on and do more work! Don't see it as lost work, you've gained experience, you might be able to sell it to someone else, you might be able to do something else with it. Basically, you just have to keep going.' – **Alice Lowe**

'There's no advice on that other than if you can't deal with that you're in the wrong job. Just get on with it. Have a word with yourself. If you can't deal with rejection, if you deliver late or if you can't follow a brief, get out of town.' – **Russell T Davies**

'It happens to everyone, so try and cultivate a masochistic streak. Sometimes I've gone into notes sessions embracing that I'm like a boxer that hasn't trained enough and I'm going to be beaten up, quite severely, and just accept your fate and know deep down that there's going to be a lesson in it – it's going to motivate you to work harder on the material.' – **Michael Pearce**

'Like a break-up – ice-cream, the warm embrace of friends, wine, perhaps sparkling saké; and then a couple of days later, man up, woman up, and just be "Yeah OK, I love my job, I'm going to go back to it."' – **Krysty Wilson-Cairns**

Amma Asante

'The best thing note-givers can do is contribute to a very honest environment. That means giving honest notes when the notes are necessary and being able to acknowledge when they're not.'

11 *Amma Asante – courtesy of Searchlight Pictures, photo by David Appleby.*

Writer and director Amma Asante's debut film, *A Way of Life* (2004), resulted in her becoming the first Black director awarded a BAFTA for writing and directing a feature. A Londoner with parents of Ghanaian heritage, who lives in Europe with her Danish husband; Amma's work frequently reflects the rich possibilities, as well as challenges, of cultural intersection; with complex social observations smuggled in under cover of affecting romance and period drama. The United Nations held a special screening of her second film, *Belle* (2013), as part of marking the abolition of slavery; her third, *A United Kingdom* (2016), was the first film by a Black director to open the BFI London Film Festival. She has directed episodes of acclaimed television series *The Handmaid's Tale* (2019) and *Mrs America* (2020). At the time of our interview she is preparing to direct a television series, *Smilla's Sense of Snow* and a feature film thriller, *The Billion Dollar Spy.*

It's somehow comforting that such an accomplished, and habitually glamorous, woman begins our mid-pandemic Zoom chat as her washing machine merrily reaches the crescendo of its spin cycle in the background. To find her balancing domestic duties and working from home, like so many of us during lockdown. But then, generating empathy with an audience is a hallmark of her work.

With a characteristic blend of forthrightness and quiet consideration, Amma begins, 'You can live on one or the other extreme of the notes-taking process. You can take everything lock, stock and smoking barrel, without questioning anything. You can believe everybody that gives you notes, feel you need to acknowledge every note and respond to every note. And that can be dangerous. At the other extreme, which can be equally dangerous, is rejecting everything and throwing the baby out with the bathwater – not really having the ability to listen and collaborate and deduce what makes sense and what doesn't. And that takes a moment to figure out. You can't always come in right away and say, "That makes sense and that doesn't." Or know if a note is eradicating a unique element of the kind of story you want to tell or not.'

Expanding on whether notes can risk eradicating or dulling a filmmaker's originality of vision, Amma says, 'Historically there has been an idea, which is only now starting to be challenged with any sort of real authenticity or weight behind it, that any experience outside of what has become the default experience – that is generally white, straight and male, or has the closest proximity to being white, straight and male, is wrong and is bad writing. An idea that existences outside of those narratives, based on what I call patriarchal storytelling, are simply not plausible. And that has been supported by the entire industry. Oftentimes when we talk about systems and we talk about institutionalized behaviours, there's broad far-reaching words that sometimes take individual responsibility out of the equation. But for me what it means when something is institutionalized or systemic, is that the people who initially planted the seeds don't necessarily need to be the ones who execute the actions. Because it's so systemic, everybody does it. In other words you don't have to be a white male to give out notes to writers that say "This doesn't work" if it doesn't fit that patriarchal type of storytelling. Because we've all been taught the same thing. Layers of the system back up that kind of premise – that A is plausible and B isn't; from studio executives and production development executives, all the way through to film critics, who all traditionally have been white and male. When women have been allowed to step into those roles, every once in a while a woman is allowed at the table, sometimes they also apply the same measurements of what is plausible and what isn't, because that's what you do to get it 'right'. That's what you've been told by father patriarchy is right and correct. To be in the gang, at the table, you must speak the same language.'

Amma explains, 'If you've been raised within that system, as a writer it's sometimes very, very difficult to find your voice; because the minute something authentic comes out, which you feel is the authenticity of your life, or the lives of others that you want to put down on paper, you can be told "That's not plausible, that wouldn't work." And so the question that you're asking – is there a danger of notes blanding things out? – absolutely, one hundred per cent.'

She reflects, 'It is being challenged. I woke up this morning thinking about the ten-year gap between my first film and my second film, and thinking that that is now a little bit less likely than it was back then, for a writer who is Black or of colour, or a woman, who experienced the kind of success I experienced in the beginning then had all the doors closed for the next ten years.' Digging deeper into it she continues, 'There is a different story for women of colour, than for instance for male directors of colour. Which goes back to proximity to patriarchy, proximity to the 'default' story. Anything that is closer to white, anything that is male has more proximity. So people who are most distant from patriarchy are people who are Black and at the intersection of being Black and female. Then you add other layers onto that, the furthest you can get from being white, male and straight is to be a Black female who's gay. So those authentic stories that could have been coming from those arenas for years, there's absolutely a danger that people who belong to groups that didn't fit into the 'default' would have their identity and uniqueness, their power and the real crux of their value, sort of worn away by notes if they're forced to fit into the shape and the flavour that has been more comfortable to those who have been the gatekeepers.'

Amma says, 'I think the world is changing slightly because of some of the mould-breaking projects and audacious storytelling that have managed to be told, infrequently, in the last few years. Not infrequently because people haven't been trying to tell those stories, but infrequently because those are the ones that have been let through. And if you're lucky it's not a trend, it's not a fad. It's actually culture shifting and evolving our planet and our humanity and our existence.'

Turning to how she handles notes herself, Amma says, 'Unless it's really outright racist – and I have had out of order notes before that should be challenged; my way forward has always been to sort of nod, take the note down and go away to try and understand the note. When the note works it's great! When the note doesn't work, I go back, either before delivering the next draft, or when delivering the next draft, to say "Look, this is what I tried and this is why it didn't work and here are the reasons why it didn't work, and these are the different versions of it I tried that didn't work. Have a look at this and see how it feels. I've addressed five out of your eight notes." Sometimes I find that a note that felt very uncomfortable at the time of being given it, two or three days later you realize actually is a really good note. A really useful note that actually is pushing my narrative forward. That's how I measure if notes are good or not, by asking myself, "In terms of the authenticity of my world and characters, is this maybe a different way of me getting to the essence of what I'm trying to say? Maybe it's a different pathway, but ultimately does it get me to the same place or further?" Sometimes a great note-giver, a great executive, can give you a note that further cements your vision, which I guess is what everybody's hoping for.'

She continues, 'It really just depends on whether or not the note takes you in a completely different direction from the story or the point or what it is you're trying to say. And whether you genuinely think it takes you in an utterly different direction when you properly sit down and think about it. Or whether actually, it simply further cements what you're trying to say. Sometimes when we deliver a draft we've had our head buried in the work so deeply that it's very, very difficult for us to come up for air and listen to what somebody else says, or to break down the four walls that we've kind of built for ourselves as we try to tell this story. And sometimes there's something deeply thrilling and freeing about somebody else coming in with a different voice. When they're good, they're coming in trying to build on the story that you've told them you want to tell, the story that they've bought into in the first place. I've had that more times than not. And I've had that not just in the screenwriting process but also in the editing process, which is also where notes are very important.'

Amma emphasizes, 'I've never attempted to make a film or a show that I didn't want my producers and my executive producers to be as proud of as I am. I'm not one of those filmmakers who just wants to deliver my view. My view is really important, and you must have a vision, but it's really important to be collaborative with the people who have decided they want to invest in your vision and your story. There needs to be an honesty and an openness. The best way for me, what I work towards all the time, and mostly achieve, is to find how I can take the note and express what the executive wants, while still maintaining the sanctity of my vision. That is where you want to get to as a screenwriter who needs other people's money to make your work.'

Before becoming a screenwriter and director, Amma was an actress. Mid 1980s audiences in the UK could have seen her as one of the regulars in hit children's television series *Grange Hill*. By her late teens Amma concluded acting was not for her. Her mother encouraged her to learn to type so that she would always have secretarial work to fall back on. As Amma worked to improve her typing speed what instinctively came out from her fingertips was a sit-com. Shyly using a pseudonym at first, she sent it to people she knew from her time working as a young actress, for their notes. Receiving positive feedback, and gaining development deals with both the BBC and Channel 4, she began writing in her own name, eventually co-creating and writing television series *Brothers and Sisters* (1998).

Looking back to that time Amma recalls, 'Because I had both of those deals with Channel 4 and the BBC, I was dealing with different sets of note-givers and I remember learning fairly quickly that notes are not always to be responded to immediately. And that notes aren't necessarily easily implemented. They're not something you can just "do". I remember understanding very quickly that the note-giving process can be a really useful process or a really bad process – depending on who's giving you the notes. The earliest thing I learned was to try and take notes, to try and be collaborative, to try and really engage with the process. And understanding that unless they're really, really good, advanced, note-givers, oftentimes a note is given to you not really understanding the impact it's going to have on everything else around it. So you have to decide how long it's going to take you to do the next draft addressing the notes. Oftentimes in your contract it says when you have to deliver the next draft, but oftentimes you decide at the end of the meeting when you'll deliver the next draft. I understood relatively quickly, I'd say within months, that I had to really address how I gave a timescale, because it wasn't just addressing a note, it was addressing everything else that note impacted, seeing it all the way through the script. I had to learn how to say, "No, that doesn't work" and how to be big enough to say, "Yes, that did work, and it's really made a huge difference to my script and I'm really grateful that I got the note and had the time to interpret it." Both of those things are very hard.

'For both the writer and note-giver there's a whole emotional and psychological process that both sides are having to go through,' Amma reflects, 'Any writer puts a whole load of themselves inside any screenplay. So on their part it's really hard not to take it personally, but you have to find a way to do that. The process for note-givers is really tough too, because first and foremost we know it's your job to give notes. We know that you often have to earn your position. But we can tell when notes are being given for the sake of giving notes, as opposed to because they're really meaningful. The note-giver needs to be able to get themselves into the space where they understand that a blank page is a blank page and a writer comes along and fills it with a whole load of words that gives the note giver the ability to give notes. In other words, without that page being filled there is no ability to give notes.'

Amma advises, 'The best thing note-givers can do is contribute to a very honest environment. That means giving honest notes when the notes are necessary and being able to acknowledge when they're not. I really appreciate and feel more comfortable and more trusting around note-givers who are able to say every now and then, "I love it. It's fine as it is." Therefore I'm much more trusting of them when they say, "This actually needs work here because of a, b and c." Then I'm never leaving a meeting thinking you gave a note for note's sake. On the other side it means us writers being able to acknowledge that we can't always see the value of a note until we've had chance to sit down and work it through. We've got to take our guard down in order to be able to do that. But also to have the confidence to come back and say, "I tried it and it didn't work and this is why it didn't." Then it gives the note-giver chance to explain in a different way, or to say a bit more about why they suggested in in the first place, or maybe there's a whole third way around it, that gets you to where you want to be.'

There's a brief pause as Amma quietens her washing machine's attention-seeking end of cycle beeping. She resumes, 'The best thing I ever experience from a session of notes is a breakthrough moment when somebody just asks a great question and leaves me to go away and find the answers. The worst experience I've had with notes is when I've created a scenario or a situation or a theme or an idea that I've put down on that blank page and then the note-giver comes up with a word for it. In other words they're giving the note back to the writer asking them to create something the writer has already created; it's just that they've come up with a marketing word for it. For example, let's take a scene out of *Damage* (Louis Malle, 1992), which is one of my favourite films. Somebody has written a dinner scene with a group of characters around a table. It's fraught with psychological tension, when a bottle of wine spills on a white tablecloth and the camera focuses on that. In the script, it might have said something like "We focus on the red wine as it seeps into the white tablecloth." And then the note-giver will say, "You know, what's really happening in this scene is blood is being spilt metaphorically and we want to know that." And the writer says, "But that's what I gave you! I just didn't write 'blood is being spilt' because if I did you would say 'that's very on the nose'!" We writers know when a note-giver doesn't have any notes and they're just sort of churning over what we've already given them back at us. So honesty in the process is really important. We don't want to be in a world where note-givers are too afraid to give their notes or feel embarrassed about giving their notes because I'm saying writers can see right through you! I'm not saying that. I'm saying we know the difference between really powerful notes and notes which are only there to sort of justify the title you've been given at the production company. We don't say it, but we know it.'

Amma continues, 'Because we're all individuals, I don't know that across the board there is a "right" way to give notes. But I can say for myself, I don't like prescribed notes. Sometimes you're stuck in a situation with someone who doesn't know how to ask questions. They only know how to prescribe notes. In that case I try and understand what is beneath the note. What is underneath this prescription? What are they trying to get at? Then I will work out my own version of that.' She adds, 'In the same way that I can sense a cinematographer who's a frustrated director, I can sense a development executive who's a frustrated writer. I've no interest in somebody who hasn't delivered something that has literally been a hit as a writer themselves prescribing notes and saying "Do it like this". And frankly, even if they have had a hit as a writer, it'll be different. We know that if you give two directors the same script you'll end up with two different movies, and if you give two writers the same book to adapt you'll end up with two different screenplays. So I'm respectful, but there's never a right to say to somebody "Why don't you do it like this?" Amma emphasizes, 'There can only be one directing voice in any room. You can't have a directing cinematographer, you can't have a directing editor, you can't have directing producers. You can only have one directing voice. And depending on whether you're in TV or film, you either have the director's voice or you have the showrunner's voice. When I'm giving notes myself, as a director to a writer, obviously I know how to write, I know how to tell a story, but I don't necessarily know how to tell *their* story from that writer's point of view. So I attempt to place my notes in the context of questions. That's what I try to do (not always successfully) and that's also what I like to get back.'

Amma expands on how she gives notes to a writer on a project she's directing but not writing: 'It depends on my relationship with the writer, and it really depends who's been brought on to create the vision. Sometimes you're brought onto a project and it is very much the writer's project. First of all you only say yes to that if you feel that your vision and the writer's arc so much in unison that there's so much harmony between your vision and their vision that you're not going to compromise yourself as a director who also creates content. That's really important to me. I'm not a gun for hire at all. So I will have big opinions, bigger than perhaps a script executive should have, because I am part of the creative vision of the story. In that case it's about amending what I do as a writer who, as I said earlier, doesn't ever want to deliver a story that my producers and exec producers are not proud of, so I find a way to take their notes and still achieve my vision. I sort of flip that on its head when I'm working with a writer. Which is, how do I take what it is they want, the way that they want to tell the story, and how do I ensure that I still get my vision out of it without making them feel that they've compromised or harmed their vision in any way? How also do I make them think bigger, bolder, more audaciously about how we tell this story? How can I trigger their imagination from a visual point of view, to get them to think differently about how they express an element of the story that they want to express, but so that it fits in with the ambition and scale, whether that scale is small, big or medium sized, so that it can hit all of its potential? I feel that my job is to sort of knock those walls down, unclip those wings, and say "Wow, we can fly with this! Imagine if we told the scene in this particular way." I'll try to present it in a visual way, not in a "Imagine if she said this to him and then he said that and then she said that back" – not writing it at all, but asking, this is a really crass version – "If this was set on top of a mountain and the sky turned purple, what then? What would happen? What would the characters be saying to one another?"'

Turning back to her own writing, she considers how early in the process it's useful to have notes. She cautions, 'Inexperienced note-givers will often try and trip in and intrude while you're still in your research process. While you're still pulling your vision, or your point of view together. The best producers, note-givers and executives leave you alone until you've got something to deliver. So for me that means leaving me alone while I research. Leaving me alone while I pull together the initial treatment or bible. It's once I've delivered something on paper that I want your notes. Because two things – firstly, I think most writers, if they really think about it, will agree that when we talk to someone else, an executive, a script editor, a note-giver, about what we're intending, we have fifty per cent of what we're thinking in our head and it's only the other fifty per cent that we're saying aloud to the person we're talking to. But we think we're saying a hundred per cent. There's a whole load of context that is innately there in our heads that we may or may not end up vomiting out onto the paper. If you are getting notes back before you've even attempted to vomit all that out on the paper it can snuff the light out on really strong elements of the vision. That said, there's the other version when you put it down on paper and you still haven't put down the full context that's going on in your head. And it's the script editor, if they're really savvy, who will say, "There's more here than you've put down on paper." Through their questions and their probing a good script editor will draw out the wider context.'

Amma continues, 'Secondly, there's also what you do subconsciously as a storyteller. I remember reading a book many years ago, *Directing Actors*[1] by Judith Weston, I still read it before I direct every single film, it's so damn good,' she enthuses. 'When I read it before directing my first film it talked about whether or not you're directing your own work or directing someone else's writing, all writers make subconscious connections. Or have subconscious elements in their story. Your job as the director is to pull together the connections in those subconscious elements. Even if you're the writer and you're directing your own work, you have to find the subconscious elements that you have brought forward as the writer. I think that's very much the same for script editors and development. They have to find what's going on in the subconscious of the writer. That's what the most brilliant ones do.'

The conversation turns to the detail of how Amma works, how she'll sometimes focus on individual story elements in particular drafts and how notes can be valuable feeding into that process. Taking an example from her film *Belle,* which explores the life of a bi-racial woman raised by her aristocratic relatives in eighteenth century England, Amma explains, 'Essentially, in the first draft I try to lay out the footprint of what my vision of the film or the TV show is. All the elements that are going to be in there. So, who are the people that populate the world? What is the gaze that we see this through? All that will be there in the first draft, then it's about really digging in deep and finessing. I sometimes get a young writer say to me, "It seems so simple, but it's so complex,

[1]Weston, J. (1996) *Directing Actors: Creating Memorable Performances for Film and Television,* California: Michael Wiese Productions.

there are so many elements that you're entwining together, how are you doing that?" And I will say I could never dig into all the elements so deeply all at the same time, I can't juggle in that way. So I have to create the footprint of who they are, their lives, their arcs, who's the lead, who's not the lead, who's the second lead. What do I want to learn about a person's story? In that first draft it might only be a very thin shell for a particular character, sort of pointers towards the fact that I want to go there, or sometimes I'll think that's it, that's her story, and then I'll get a note. For example, I had a mixed-race script executive on *Belle*; after my first or maybe second draft, where I had everything that you can essentially see in the film, he said to me, "I don't understand Dido Belle's existence as a mixed-race woman. It's not touching me, it's not reaching me. I don't understand what the unique obstacles are." And that was when I deliberately went in and did a draft that purely focused on her intersection. Purely focused on what it was like to be raised and not be able to hang your hook on the legacy of your mother, because you don't necessarily have the privilege of having the woman in your life who can guide in how to navigate life as both a person who is Black and woman all at once. So what does that look like? What does that feel like for her? It was a global note and it required me to look at absolutely everything, at everything that showed what Dido Belle was and was not.'

Amma declares, 'The cleverest notes for me are those that are a comment or a question. So the comment the executive made about not being able to really feel the sense of what it was specifically like for Dido Belle as a bi-racial person in that time, was for me his way of saying "What are the social aspects? What is the social commentary aspect here to her being a mixed-race female?" That was the biggest question for me. Obviously the story had the Zong in it, the ship transporting enslaved people which the court case in *Belle* was about. And all of the elements which the history itself brought forward – what is the price of a life of a man? What is the place of a woman in society, even a very privileged woman? History brought together those two social elements – what it was to be a woman and what it was to be arguing the realities of who could be deemed as human and who could be deemed as cattle. History gave us that. The script executive's note on what is this experience for Dido Belle made me realize I was telling her story as a Black woman, but I wasn't telling her story also as a bi-racial woman. That one comment from the script executive opened up a world of drafts for me. It was really important that I told that story of what it is to, like Belle, come from both the oppressed and the oppressor. This is where the social commentary was; that's what we experience as people who are bi-cultural, in other words we might be mono race, I might be a full Black girl, but I'm born and raised in Britain and I've got parents who were raised in a previous British colony in West Africa, and that may be similar for those people who are bi-racial. You may both belong and 'dis-belong' to the worlds of the oppressed and the oppressor. What happens when today you are living side by side with the people whose ancestors once enslaved your ancestors or colonized your ancestors? What happens when you're living side by side with them in that community, in that culture, in that environment? There's a lot of interior stuff and material that can be drawn from that. But essentially it all comes from a note. That's what a good note does, it opens a window onto a focus.'

Amma considers how to handle any notes asking for more historical explanation or context. She says, 'You try and listen. You try and make that work, because the one thing you don't want to do is pour your heart into a story and then have fifty or seventy per cent of the people who might go and see it not really understand it. The one thing you don't want is for a note to be correct and you've ignored it. I'm definitely not so complacent to think that doesn't matter. It's also why I try things out on people, and it's why we have test screenings. The most fundamental notes we get are when we have test screenings, because that's audiences. They give us notes and we go back and we follow those notes. They give us notes by saying what they do understand, what they don't understand, when they got bored, when they didn't get bored, what they think is pointless, what they think took too long to get to. Those are really fundamental notes. Films pay a fortune to companies who can then pull together a report, and apart from reading that report I always read every individual note as well. Every single form the audience filled in. With a test screening everybody fills in a form, all two hundred, six hundred, however many people were in there, fill in their forms answering all the questions. Then we have a focus group of about twenty-five people afterwards, who for another hour sit and have a discussion and answer questions, which are led by a company which specializes in doing that. And I'll sit there at the session. They don't necessarily know. Now they know me so I'll not necessarily be there, but in the beginning they wouldn't know who I was. You'd be sitting there listening, listening to some very harsh realities about what doesn't work about your film. They are a sample of the demographic that your film will go out to, so you have to work out when you get back to the edit what you listen to and what you choose not to, what you choose to take a chance on.'

As we come to a close, me a little guilty about the load of unhung out washing that's been quietly crumpling in Amma's machine, she concludes, 'The importance of telling stories is to explore who we are. To explore who we are as cultures, societies, individuals. Storytelling for me is about either reflection, challenge or escape. And even in the stories that allow us to escape, we are still exploring who we are as a culture, how we respond to those stories, what interests us, what's in the zeitgeist that's going round at that time. Whether it's straightforward reflection or whether it's escapist mythologies, it's still speaking to who we are as a culture and as a people. I think that it's an important way of exploring discourse and facing who we are and honouring who we are, challenging who we are, challenging ourselves to do better as well as acknowledging how far we've come. Stories, reflection, self-reflection, are important to any society. That's why storytelling is something that goes back to day dot. Cultures have always told stories to each other. Always.'

Denmark, via Zoom, February 2021

Selected credits, awards and nominations

Brothers and Sisters: Head Writer (1998), [TV series] BBC.
A Way of Life: Writer, Director (2004), [Film] UK: Verve Pictures.
　　London Film Festival award – UK Film Talent Award (2004)
　　San Sebastián International Film Festival award – SIGNIS award (2004)
　　BAFTA award – Carl Foreman Award for Most Promising Newcomer (2005)
　　BAFTA Cymru award – Best Director – Drama (2005)
　　Miami Film Festival award – Grand Jury Prize – Dramatic Feature – World Cinema
　　　Competition (2005)

Miami Film Festival award – FIPRESCI Prize (2005)

London Critics' Circle Film Awards nomination – British Newcomer of the Year (2005)

Belle: Director, A film by (2013), [Film] UK: Fox Searchlight Pictures.

Miami Film Festival award – SIGNIS Award (2014)

Washington DC Filmfest award– Audience Award, Best Feature Film (2014)

Palm Springs International Film Festival award – Directors to Watch (2014)

Women Filmx Critics Circle Awards nomination – Best Movie by a Woman (2014)

Black Reel Awards nomination – Outstanding Director, Motion Picture (2015)

Image Awards (NAACP) nomination – Outstanding Directing in a Motion Picture (2015)

A United Kingdom: Director (2016), [Film] UK, USA: Twentieth Century Fox.

Black Reel Awards – Outstanding World Cinema Motion Picture (2018)

Women Film Critics Circle Awards nomination – Courage in Filmmaking Award (2017)

Where Hands Touch: Writer, Director (2018), [Film] UK: Vertical Entertainment.

Black Reel Awards nomination – Outstanding World Cinema Motion Picture (2019)

The Handmaid's Tale: Director, episodes 'God Bless the Child' and 'Useful'' (2019), [TV Series] Hulu.

Mrs America: Director, episodes 'Betty' and 'Shirley' (2020), [TV Series] BBC.

Smilla's Sense of Snow: Director, Executive Producer (in development), [TV Series].

The Billion Dollar Spy: Director (in development), [Film].

Empire Awards – Inspiration Award (2018)

Lone Scherfig

'The most important thing to bear in mind when you're giving notes is trusting that people can solve it, but that they may not solve it in the way you imagine.'

12 Lone Scherfig – courtesy of Creative Alliance, photo by Robin Skjoldborg.

Sitting in her white-walled office in Copenhagen, Lone Scherfig exudes calm. A serenity that arises from a merry humour combined with a rigorous work ethic. Especially impressive calm, since she is about to go into production on her maternity-ward set TV drama series, *Dag & nat* (2022). Lone created the series, is the head writer and is directing the final two episodes. 'I've had I think thirty-two sets of notes on it in one year!' she exclaims with a smile.

The internationally feted Danish writer and director came to prominence with the much-loved *Italian for Beginners* (2000). It was part of the Dogme 95 movement, along with films by Thomas Vinterberg and Lars von Trier. Dogme films adhered to a set of rules, such as only using sound recorded on location, which aimed to keep the focus on story and actors. Since then, she has worked extensively in the UK, as well as America and Scandinavia. Her films, including *The Riot Club* (2014), *Their Finest* (2017) and the triple Oscar nominated *An Education* (2009), capture peculiarly British subtleties of class and humour. She smiles and laughs often as she talks. The rhythms of her native language sneak into her impeccable English, resulting in distinctive patterns of emphasis that add further charm to her words, which hold you as entranced as her films.

One of the central tenets of the Dogme movement was to turn obstacles into blessings – if it rains on the day of the shoot for a scene written for sunshine, see if the scene can be more beautiful, have deeper meaning, in the rain. Lone Scherfig tilts her head up to the ceiling as she contemplates whether it is also the way she views notes – as obstacles to turn into blessings. 'Notes have been sometimes helpful, sometimes destructive,' she reflects; advising, 'the best way is if you can turn the process into a dialogue where you come with each your expertise. That it is not criticism, but an exchange about how to develop the best script. Notes you've asked for are much nicer than notes you haven't asked for,' she laughs. 'The best case is when you are given notes by people you really respect and you believe can diagnose problems. And then, although they maybe will not always come up with the cure, at least they will tell you what they feel in a way where they trust that you will find solutions. But it's demanding. I don't know any directors and very few writers and editors who actually enjoy it and are curious to see what people feel.'

'The most successful film I ever made, *Italian for Beginners*, had no notes,' Lone observes, 'I just wrote the script, shot it, worked on the post and went home. Of course that's not the best starting point for entering a culture of more criticism and more control' she acknowledges with a smile. Thinking back to *Italian for Beginners,* she recalls, 'Whatever advice you got along the way was from people you had asked for help, and that is so rare. I think only four or five of all the Dogme films had that privilege, and it was to do with the financing. Because when you're on such a small, small budget then you get freedom. I can completely understand, because I'm both a writer and a co-owner of a production company, that you can't ask anybody to invest in something that they haven't yet seen or heard without them having something to say about what they can read. There are really good producers who will help you and are able to see things from a distance and come up with advice and know the process. I feel very thankful to those – the people who have given me useful notes, given the project useful notes. The thing is, directors are a combination of super-sensitive and very controlling. But filmmaking is a collaborative art form. You let everybody come up with ideas as long as you're the one who can decide which ideas are good and which are not. Directors are not exactly typecast to receive notes; because the things that make you a good director are the same things that make you bad at sitting there listening to other people's not always super-smart opinions. But as I get older I'm better at actually asking for all the help I can get.'

Lone admits, 'When I first came to work in the UK I did find the notes culture there a bit of a shock.' She says, 'When I talk to younger directors now, I'll warn them about it and tell them what to expect from the different types of meetings, so they don't feel overwhelmed or criticized or painted into a corner. Because, coming from an auteur-oriented film upbringing, I really didn't know what to expect. But things did change over those years, the UK became more inspired by the American way of working. The past ten or twenty years the whole film world has become more professionalized in Scandinavia as well, and note-giving is part of it. It is integrated in the process and the planning. You even sit at meetings where you talk about the process, saying, "OK, we know that that company comes up with their notes quite late, so we need to have a week there where we're just waiting for them" or in the editing – "Yes, but it's going to take a full work day if they come and visit the edit and then another bad morning the next day where you sit and get rid of your bitterness", she laughs ruefully.

Lone outlines practical ways she addresses the realities of working with notes: 'At the moment I'm show-running this hospital series in Denmark, and we agreed with the TV station really early on to optimize the process. Meaning that we stick to all deadlines so they know exactly when we're going to deliver what, and have space in their diary at that time. That was in order to have a very speedy, smooth process. When I get a script from the writers I'll read it straight away and answer them straight away. That was first of all to have a more enthusiastic, respectful workflow. But also so this whole note-giving thing hurts less and feels like more of a vitamin injection rather than somebody sitting down in a controlling way going, "OK, will we go one step further with this project?" So that's worked. We've also tried to get all of the conversation out of the editing room, saying "Let's not stop the editing process whenever you have some decision-makers coming in and watching." That's in order to get more out of your editing time. Because the frustrating part of all this note thing is you want to get on with the work. You feel that you very quickly have understood what they've said and you want to get on and do it instead of having to sit like a schoolgirl waiting for all the details you already think you've understood,' she laughs.

She advises, 'I think there's no way to get around it in the British film community. Unless you work on a really, really tight budget and have complete creative control. So I think you have to look at it as a collaboration. It helps a lot if it's people whose judgement you believe. Often I like if it's combined with audience testing, because you have a third party which is the audience, where you can turn thoughts into numbers. Especially if you test with at least four hundred people; those anonymous people may actually give you reliable advice, or at least information.'

Lone sums up, 'So no, I don't like notes. They are my least favourite part of the process. But I've also experienced again and again that the films do get better when you sleep on them and get on with it, and look at the work as a collaborative project.

'Just try them,' she advises, 'most notes are really quick to do, try them. If you tried it and it didn't work, or even if you can show it and people may go "Yeah, you're right, it doesn't work", then it becomes a nicer dialogue. Or you try it and then you come up with a third version. When you get to that process, if you have time enough for it, there is a real chance that your film will improve. Because there are phases in both scriptwriting and editing where it's a good thing that somebody questions things and shakes the tree and sees things from the outside. Also you get to moments in the process where you think, "Now I actually need advice, we're just moving commas here, we need someone to come in and challenge this." It could be they say some detail about a scene and once you're looking at the scene you go, "Hmm, and while we're at it, why don't we change that line? And hold that shot a little longer?"' Smiling, she says, 'You get inspired to go back and revisit things and again that marginally improves it. But the big improvements I do think you get from testing. It sounds crazy, but I've had times when I've asked if the testing could please be in my contract, because it's expensive to do it and I wanted to make sure it wouldn't be cut in the budget or lost in the planning.'

Thinking back over her work she reflects, 'There are things in the films where I think the notes were really wrong and I can still wake up in the night saying "Why didn't I put my foot down? Because they were wrong." But the opposite is the case too. Lots of things, big and small, in all the recent films, that I have to thank somebody else for.' Practically she says, 'It can be a case of who writes the most notes and who is the most exhausted – and who takes the biggest risk. Because during the edit at that time when everybody comes in full of vitamins, you as a director are running out of battery. Every day the film gets a tad better, but that tad gets smaller and smaller and smaller throughout the post-production. I think it's maybe the same thing when you are scriptwriting – that in the beginning you make really big improvements but then they get smaller and smaller and smaller.'

She recalls, 'When we did *Their Finest* it was a really fruitful process. For instance, Amanda Posey, one of the producers, is very meticulous. Which is something I've been protesting a lot against, but I see myself being more inspired by it now that I'm the head of a group of writers. Her very British insistence that you keep going and going and going – it's pursuit of excellence.

I think it might be not just her personality, but a tradition from Oxford and Cambridge, which is where a lot of the decision makers in British filmmaking have studied. Lionsgate's testing was also so helpful. They tested that film right down to how much people laugh on a scale of I think one to a hundred on exactly what moment. That was a tough, but interesting process, and the last few weeks the film became a lot better. Also I was more experienced. I had learned to navigate in this environment, how to interpret and be inspired by the notes, and how to not take things personally. Also not just to interpret them, but to see how one note on an element may expose a problem that's sitting elsewhere in the film – that people point something out that could be about something else. Which is why notes that are really clear, like "I felt bored here and here" or "I was confused by this or that" or "Please don't touch that because it's so moving" are so useful. It's something I do a lot with writers, pointing out what I like best. Because I've also done comedy, I tell writers to not get tired of their own jokes, because eventually from draft to draft they begin to delete them. It's important to also reassure people when you're giving notes.'

Lone says, 'The reason people keep going with giving notes is not necessarily desperation, it's the hope it gets one or two per cent better every day. And it's also their jobs. That's what I have to remind younger directors about: you have to live with it because they don't do it because they want to be destructive, it's because that's what they were hired to do. Or because they've invested money and time, even if they, unlike you, do not risk their entire work every time they present a film. Also, I'm often the one on the other side of the desk, being the one who gives notes, and I know that it always comes from a good place; that you really want to inspire that things get different or better or wilder, or that people investigate and find out it was the best version that we had already.

'The most important thing to bear in mind when you're giving notes is trusting that people can solve it, but that they may not solve it in the way you imagine,' she advises, 'and to remember that you're talking to a person who knows the script or the film better than you do. If you pose questions rather than come with statements then it more easily becomes a dialogue that's fruitful. If instead of saying, "She shouldn't have all her rooms blue", you ask, "Why are all her rooms blue?" then you actually get an answer that explains it. Or the writer might go, "Oh that was a mistake, I meant all her cabinets were to be blue." It's not the best example, but asking the writer or editor questions shows what needs to be clarified, but it also opens up for a better version of what there is.'

Lone advises, 'Important qualities to have when giving notes are sensitivity, curiosity and precision. Though sometimes you have to be vague, it could be: "I feel that whenever we're in the office those scenes somehow feel heavy" – that would be fine and useful to a writer or director. Mere criticism is not useful at all. Pointing out mistakes that are too late to correct, especially after the film is shot, is just destructive. But very few people who give notes do that. They all say "Use the notes you like." And they probably mean it,' she says, smiling warmly as though remembering individual past conversations. 'I do the same thing when I give notes, or rather ask questions, telling people: "I'm never going to go back and control whether you did what I suggested or not." I also sometimes ask people how they prefer to get the notes. Usually you write or get very general notes, and then there are so-called page notes, which are more specific. But sometimes I would even write notes in the script itself. Isn't it easier if I put my notes directly into the script? Saying, "What if this scene was longer?" or "I don't understand why she says that" or "This is so witty, don't touch it" or whatever. I'd never do that if I hadn't asked first. It's very intimidating, but then again it's very fast to fix it as a writer if you get notes directly into the script. Because then you can sit and go, "Oh, yeah she's right, I'll try it."' Lone's fingers mime typing cheerily at a keyboard. She adds, 'Or they can simply delete your notes from the script. I wouldn't want to recommend that way of working, but some writers think it's fine and I don't mind it either.'

Contemplating who she receives notes from she muses, 'It depends a bit on the project, who I would ask. Maybe I should be better at asking people, friends who I trust. We do a lot in this country [Denmark], ask fellow writers or directors,' she pauses, scrunching up her face as she scours the truth of that further, 'but often we don't do it until we've already shot the film, so I guess I should do it more. Because we used to. It's kind of died a little bit here, the film school culture where you used to show your friends your script. But I am the co-owner of a company where we do it. Where you know that the people around you, just like the decision makers in the UK, want the same as you do, which is to make the best possible film out of the idea and the resources.

'Some note-givers are really good at small, relevant details, logic mistakes for instance; others are better at giving broad strokes,' Lone observes, 'Some may say, "I know I have a sweet tooth so I would like this or that" – in other words, a lot of it is a matter of taste. It's important for a note-giver to be aware of that – that it is sometimes merely a matter of taste. And it's important for them to spend time actually getting to know the script. Because there are a lot of times when someone gives a note and you think, "But it is sitting there! Why haven't they seen it?" Giving good notes is a lot of work.' She cautions, 'There's also a thing of when to give which note. Sometimes you, as a reader, can think, "I'll see if that's still there in the next draft and then I'll comment on it." I guess also as a note-giver you have to choose your battles. The better you know the script, the more precise you are, and better questions you ask, the more you'll be respected and people will want to address your notes. Because you can't dismiss them as, "Well, she certainly hasn't read the script has she!" In the UK people really make an effort. No matter which level they're working at. There's very little sloppiness. Which is one of the things that I really like about working there. Everyone's so thorough.'

The talk turns to *Their Finest,* directed by Lone and adapted by Gaby Chiappe from Lissa Evans' novel. Lone recalls some of the development of the film, 'I read the book and then the script. That's part of starting a collaboration with a writer, to not go, "Yes, but I'd like to make not that film that you've written, but this other version of the book." And I did like the script, but the first version of the script was quite long, as first drafts often are, so I came up with suggestions of where to trim the script. I also revisited the book a couple of times to make sure that nothing had been flushed out with the bathwater. I read the book again one last time before the script was locked, to re-read all of the Ambrose Hilliard lines, the character played by Bill Nighy, and check that none had been lost. And there weren't. Gaby is very careful about detail. And she is incredible at receiving notes, because she's worked in television for so many years. This was her first feature film, but she was so experienced from television. She is someone who really can accept if something is questioned or criticized. She goes home and comes back with a solution that's better than what you suggested. She really knows the art of receiving notes and processing them and answering them. Also, she knew that if I thought there was doubt about something, then it's her decision. I decided that is how it would be on that film. First of all because I think she's really good, but also because it was based on a book, and because she was on board before I was. And because again, it's sometimes just taste, and hers is good.'

Looking back to another project, the BAFTA winning, triple Oscar nominated *An Education,* directed by Lone with a screenplay by Nick Hornby adapted from Lynn Barber's novel, Lone observes, 'I remember someone giving notes on *An Education* praised Nick Hornby for addressing notes so seamlessly. And I thought, well, yes, but you're sometimes meant to actually change things because of notes! Not just address them so you can hardly see it was done, so everybody feels they did their job. It was a wonderful script, so Nick wasn't ever really challenged by notes that said, "Actually, there might be a completely different version of this." We never got to that because there was no reason to. But "addressing notes seamlessly", I never understood what that praise was about! I think the tradition in the UK is very much oriented towards the written words, because many of the people who read your scripts have a literary rather than cinematic background. So they think if you've tweaked the dialogue so a certain piece of information has been emphasized, then you're A-OK, you can tick the box that that story element was told. And that's not the same thing as it being in the real fabric of a film.'

Considering adaptations and notes from the book's author, Lone says, 'Lissa Evans gave notes on *Their Finest*, also Lynn Barber on *An Education*. The new film I'm working on next, which is also an adaptation, I've asked that the novelist reads it. Because first of all you want to be loyal. And also they may come up with something that you hadn't seen.' She advises, 'Even if they don't have any legal rights to have a final cut or final decision on the script, it's the right thing to do. To give them a chance and to listen to them. They'll have a point, because it's their brainchild and they know it even better than anyone.'

The Riot Club, directed by Lone, was adapted by Laura Wade from her own stage-play. The film explores the behaviour and attitudes of a group of privileged young men belonging to a fictional Oxford University private dining club, which could be read as being inspired by the real life Bullingdon Club to which UK government figures, including Prime Ministers David Cameron and Boris Johnson, belonged while at Oxford. Lone recalls, 'When we did *The Riot*

Club the interesting thing about that film in terms of notes, was that the conversation was to a very high degree political. It was questions like should we have added a happier ending, where Max Irons' character wins, and for instance Lauren, the young girl, forgives him? That might have been a more commercial film, but it wasn't the film that everybody wanted to make. Because they thought no, it should be like it is in reality, that the posh, even if they're the bad guys, win. I'm still on the fence wondering if we had made a more satisfying, romantic and hopeful ending, more people might have seen the film? But that's a political discussion. Do we really want to lie to the audience?' Her face expresses revulsion at the idea. She weighs up, 'To put in something that's against the core of the film, or would we rather have a film that's seen by less people? I'm still debating. And still it is one of the things I am confused about and I would love to go back and shoot a new ending to that film!' She chuckles at herself for wanting to do that. 'Because there is so much good material in that film,' she enthuses, 'A fantastic cast. It's ninety-five per cent there and the last five per cent has to do with that people walk away being confirmed in the reality – that Boris Johnson won,' she finishes sadly.

Lone's films are frequently full of humour, characters finding bright moments even in the midst of dark circumstances. We discuss notes on comedy. She says: 'I remember with *An Education* I had a meeting with Nick Hornby to go through the script so that I was sure that I had found all the jokes that were in there at that point. As a writer I have experienced that directors didn't see the jokes in a script. Where they're just mystified. And once you have to start explaining, then it's not working. You can do a bit of stage directions to indicate them. The cast on *Kindness of Strangers* (2019), which I wrote, could see the jokes immediately. There weren't any questions – "Is this meant to be a joke or not?" But I remember on one film stamping my feet, saying "I am the humour police on this film!"' She laughs at the memory of her passion, before continuing, 'And then we tested it with an audience and I conceded, "OK, nobody liked the joke. We'll turn it around, or edit it differently and see if it works in a different version, or lose it." But I've experienced many times that the audience laughed much more in the cinema than the producer had expected. But I've also experienced when a joke in a script could be better. I cut them out all the time, as they might read as if they're a good joke, but they actually aren't. Stylistically humour can change a lot, what's fun now wasn't fun five years ago, and vice versa. Actors who don't have a funny bone have a hard time playing comedy, it's maybe the same with people who give notes, that some will see the jokes and some won't. Sometimes they're right. Sometimes it's just not a very good joke. Or I am highly amused but nobody else is. Because if they don't like it, a lot of other people won't like it. And then you're down to who do you want to please? Is it more important that filmmakers get their film or that the audience gets theirs or the producer gets theirs? You're trying to make the film that's the best seen from any of those chairs.'

Reflecting on notes from producers, Lone says, 'Whenever you go to a party and you sit in the kitchen at 3 am with other directors, there are a lot of sad stories about bad work experiences and underqualified producing,' she laughs at the picture she's painting, acknowledging, 'Maybe it's the opposite thing with stories where producers sit in the kitchen at 3 am! There is a built-in dilemma there and the happiest collaborations I've had with producers, or with writers, have been when one pushes the gas pedal the other presses the brake. You take turns. You inspire one another but you can also say to one another, "That joke just isn't good, I don't know how else to say it." Being the humour police is not necessarily protecting myself, it's also protecting the writer, saying "Please can we watch it with an audience, because she did write a really funny line" – be it the novelist or the scriptwriter. It's not just fighting my own battle, it's also fighting for the writers.'

When it comes to her own scripts, she says, 'I now like to share them later and later in the process. I was more generous with it earlier on. More excited to share the joy.' She beams fondly in recollection of her eager younger self. 'But that was not so much about wanting someone's notes on the idea, it was more about "Look!"', she opens her arms wide, like a ringmaster presenting a treasured act, 'To engage people. At that point you're only ready to receive praise. As a note-giver you should remember that this is part of the process, times where all you should do is support. But that's early on. Or to just suggest things like, "When you move further with the script, why don't you try and go a little in that direction?" but that's all. Support and understanding and somebody being interested is enough early, early on. Or some stylistic things where you can say, "Oh, I think that this has a Guillermo del Toro element to it" or something, which is a big, big note actually. Because it says why don't you move to a more surreal tone, why don't you forget about authenticity, why don't you open up for bigger imagery?'

I wonder if her writer-self gives her director-self notes or vice versa, and if so, who gets the final say. She laughs, 'They collaborate. When it's something that I've written myself it tends to be underwritten because I know that I'm going to direct it. But if I write something for other people it's also often a bit underwritten, I have to go back and give a bit more information in prose because I had assumed people would see it. There is this horrible saying,' she switches into an entertaining old school Hollywood mogul style accent, '"If it ain't on the page it ain't on the stage." And I underestimate that all the time.'

So have notes ever helped her get something out from her head that she thought was on the page but wasn't actually there yet? Unhesitatingly, she answers 'Yes. Or they ask me to elaborate on things, because I am a bit shy and not too keen on emotions and conflict, and you should be – you have to torment your characters and stay in the conflict. I have a tendency that if it gets serious I either start employing some humour or ending the scene. So sometimes some of the best notes I get as a writer is somebody going, "Can you stay with this a little longer? Isn't there more to be milked out of this moment?"'

She says, 'Notes during editing are worse because it's, "No! She cannot all of a sudden have a hairstyle you might like better, because we shot the entire film already!" You can get notes during the edit where people tell you a thing they don't like and there's nothing to do about it. So you just sit there every time you watch the film thinking, "Yes, that person didn't like that hairstyle and maybe it indeed is hideous."' She lifts up her palms in a gesture half shrug, half despair. She illustrates, 'We had a note in *An Education*, somebody who didn't like that the film has a greyhound race in it. They thought it was immoral to show these dogs.' Lone clearly still feels this deeply. She muses, 'You could say, "Yes, but they also smoke in the film, and this is what they did in that period." The racetrack in Walthamstow is no longer there, and it's not that we are *for* greyhound racing that it's sitting in the film. But every time I see the film and I get to that moment I get disturbed. That's a proof that I'm too sensitive and listen to people's criticism. But it's also an example of someone saying something at a point when there's not anything you can do about it. Because of course if we were to cut that out it has a knock-on effect to other scenes. It is the big evening in the film when the character David proposes to Jenny.'

In contrast, Lone praises fruitful, helpful notes during post-production: 'Editors are very good at giving notes because often they have an ability to remember all the shots and do complicated edits in their heads like players of blind chess' she says, the admiration and respect clear in her face. 'They can almost, like a hoover, absorb everything and then go "What about that close-up in reel six? Maybe that could be useful in scene thirty-eight?"' Her expressive hands motion like the grabber claw in a seaside box of delights, slowly and precisely reaching for the best toy. In terms of the overall edit process she says, 'There's a horrible expression now where they call it Director's Cut which is after you've had I think ten weeks in the editing room, and I'm so against that. Because a Director's Cut is traditionally the director's, often longer, version of for instance *Apocalypse Now* (Francis Ford Coppola, 1979) that they've had to cut down in order to meet a distributor's needs. So calling the first cut the Directors' Cut is a big, insulting, misunderstanding. But when you are through the film once, you start being at a stage where it is good to have someone come in, because then you are at a point where you really can't see the forest for trees. Also people are curious. It's their film as well, they're responsible and they want to see something early on. I'm producing now, and I try and preserve the first cut for the director, but of course I want to see what's going on and of course I already have a lot of ideas – I've seen the rushes and have an idea where the good takes are, where the best performances are and where there's something where I think "Please don't let that end up on the editing room floor." But on a normal, medium budget film you need ten to twelve weeks before you start being capable of listening to anybody's ideas and advice.'

She ponders the broader question of making work within a system that involves notes, 'Not in my case, because I think one of the reasons that I thrive quite well – I complain wall to wall, but I also really thrive with it – is I haven't worked with any producers I wouldn't want to work with again, or investors or financiers for that matter. But in theory there could easily be talent which is not developed because they can't work in that environment. I think Tessa Ross, while she was at Channel 4, you see proof that she had the ability of really supporting and developing very original talent. Enabling them to work in this quite critical environment. That she somehow managed to protect them so they've later done one film after another. Because you knew she came with the approach of saying: "They may be saying all that, listen to it, but it's *you* that I trust", Lone points an emphatic finger down the lens, 'She sent that signal very clearly. And some of her legacy was built on believing in people like Steve McQueen, so that they came back again and again. Because she managed to navigate being head of this note jungle.'

As we come to a close, Lone emphasizes, 'I think the most important thing note-givers should do is support originality. And look to see that there's some sort of truth there. And relevance. There are a lot of projects circling around that are absolutely fine and will be fine films, but where if you start questioning the originality and truth and relevance then they may not make it as high level. I think the most important thing is that you feel seen as an audience member. Films are culture in its essence, no matter the genre. The best thing you can do, is to support a writer's voice.'

Copenhagen, via Zoom, August 2021

Selected credits, awards and nominations

On Our Own: Co-writer, Director (1998), [Film] Denmark, Sweden: All Right Film.
Italiensk for begyndere: Writer, Director (2000), [Film] Denmark, Sweden: Zentropa
    Entertainments.
    Danish Film Award – Best Screenplay (2001)
    Danish Film Award nomination – Best Director (2001)
    Berlin International Film Festival Jury Prize – Silver Bear (2001)
    Berlin International Film Festival – FIPRESCI prize (2001)
    Warsaw International Film Festival – Audience Award (2001)
Wilbur Wants to Kill Himself: Writer, Director (2002), [Film] Denmark, UK, Sweden,
    France: Nordisk Film.
    Danish Film Award nomination – Best Director (2003)
    British Independent Film Award nomination – Best Screenplay (2003)
An Education: Director (2009), [Film] UK, USA: Entertainment One.
    Sundance Film Festival – Audience Award World-Cinema Dramatic (2009)
    British Independent Film Award nomination – Best Director (2009)

BAFTA nomination – Best Director (2010)

BAFTA nomination – Best British Film (2010)

Danish Film Award – Best Non-American Film (2011)

One Day: Director (2011), [Film] UK, USA: Film4.

The Riot Club: Director (2014), [Film] UK, France: Universal Pictures International.

A Serious Game: Writer (2016), [Film] Dir. Pernilla August, Sweden: Nordisk Film Distribution.

The Astronaut Wives Club: Director, episodes 'Protocol' and 'Launch' (2015), [TV Series] ABC.

Their Finest: Director (2017), [Film] UK, Sweden, France: Lionsgate UK.

Göteborg Film Festival – Audience Award, Best Feature Film (2017)

The Kindness of Strangers: Writer, Director (2019), [Film] Denmark, Canada, Sweden, France, Germany, UK, USA: Vertical Entertainment.

Berlin International Film Festival nomination – Best Film (2019)

Dag & nat: Writer, Director of selected episodes (2022), [TV Series] YLE, Creative Alliance.

Danish Film Award nomination – Best TV Series (2023)

The Movie Teller: Director (2023), [Film] France, Spain, Chile: HBO Max.

Quick Fire Q&A 7:

What's a common problem that tends to come up during development?

'Well, it's always problematic and a massive undertaking to get a film made. But also magical. I think it's translating your vision as clearly as you can without over analysing it to the degree you kill it.' – **Lynne Ramsay**

'The beginning. The clarity. The combination of people wanting to make the film more user-friendly, but at the same time making it more conventional. It's that balance. There's a word, "streamlining", which I detest. It's meant to describe making the plot clearer, but in doing that getting rid of originality or interesting digressions. It's how as a writer or director to stay original in a process that basically wants you to shape things so that they look like other things. But the really good notes you get from people who'll help you find depth and inner logic.' – **Lone Scherfig**

'There's always a bit where you go, "Does the character have any agency? Are they a good person? Do they act for themselves? Is there enough of them?"' – **Krysty Wilson-Cairns**

'The first script will be way too long. Get it over with. Get the vomit draft out, get it done, so that you can start refining it.' – **Tomm Moore**

'Sagging in the middle is always an important one to address.' – **Amma Asante**

'It's always about reducing time, speeding up pace in the first act, getting to things sooner, the characters' set up and motivation being clear enough. It's always the same and everyone's kind of aware of it and normally that is just a natural part of the process that evolves as you go through development. So it's something to be aware of, but nothing to be scared of. That and in terms of the kinds of films I make, usually it's solving or clarifying the "creature mythology", the rules by which the monster abides, which can take some back and forth to establish a way of articulating what you do and don't need to know about a demon or a monster's origins and usually the unique way in which it can be defeated (and how that taps into the journey of the protagonist).' – **Corin Hardy**

'I wouldn't say it's a problem, but my process means that I work on creating three-dimensional characters only after several drafts. I find that I want to create the story-frame first, and during that process the characters are close to being archetypes, but I can only do the deep exploration into the character once I know where the story's heading. I know some people do it the other way around, they create their characters, and follow them on their journey. But then you would have a different problem, and that would be creating a compelling narrative momentum, which is hard to accomplish on a first draft if you don't know where you're going.' – **Michael Pearce**

'This is more within the studio system: if the script is in some way unconventional, people still talk in act structure and beats. So you might dismiss the Syd Field, Robert McKee or *Save the Cat* approach, but it's often how most Hollywood Studios think. So you're essentially trying to sell them on something fresh while also adhering to the formula. It's almost a way of subverting the formula, so you get the best of both worlds. Maybe you can do something which on paper hits all the beats that they need, but then there might be a Trojan horse element where you're bringing in something that's more subversive or different. Overall it's about selling it to those people, because they do think in those terms. So it'll always be the same notes, such as "Ah, it feels like act one is too long" or "I don't feel like there's a hard mid-point in the middle of act two." But it's always a length thing, and I think some of that is just about perception. I'd wager a lot of producers flick to the last page asking themselves, "Is it over a hundred and twenty pages?" And if it is, that sets off alarm bells before they've even started reading it.' – **Edgar Wright**

'One of the hardest things when I'm constructing an episode is the logistics of getting everybody, all your characters, in the right place at the right time. I remember talking to my script editor on *At Home with the Braithwaites*, Anna Davies – she was a really good script editor, brilliant and lovely, we worked really well together. I rang her up because I'd got stuck and thought "I can't finish this episode." She was trying to talk it through with me, and I said "I feel like all my characters are running round and I can't pin any of them down, into specific scenes, into specific conversations." I remember having this image of little Braithwaites running round, underneath my desk. I had a glass on my desk for trapping insects so I could release them out the window, and it's something like that – they're all there and I know where they all are, and what they all do but I can't scoop them up in a glass and get them into this scene and that scene. In the *Braithwaites* I always had a birthday or a wedding – they're very useful for getting people together. All the series of *Last Tango* have finished with a wedding!' – **Sally Wainwright**

'One thing I give as a piece of advice, and I follow all day long, every day, is page count. It's the duration. If it's a sixty-page script – deliver sixty pages. Don't deliver ninety pages and say "We'll sort that out with draft two" because actually deciding what stays inside the sixty pages – that's the drama. It's not just about page count, you're fundamentally deciding what's important and what's not. I stare at that page count all day long, it's my driving force. Don't ignore it. Don't ramble.' – **Russell T Davies**

Edgar Wright

'The best script editor or development person is not there to be negative, they are there to help the writer, or writers, make the best version of what they want to do.'

13 Edgar Wright, photo by Adrienne Pitts.

Cheery, bright eyes under a floppy fringe – Peter, a miniature Schnauzer, is hanging out on the sofa with his clearly beloved buddy, award-winning writer/director Edgar Wright. Edgar's work is held in such affection that among fans it takes only a warning 'Swaaaan!' or observational, 'You've got red on you' to conjure up *Hot Fuzz* or *Shaun of the Dead*. As well as feature films, Edgar has directed television series, commercials, music videos and documentary *The Sparks Brothers* (2021). All possess a kinetic, uplifting energy married to impeccable comic timing and choreography. He is a devoted cinephile, his passion and depth of knowledge shining out from every frame of his work.

Edgar began making films as a teenager. Aged seventeen he appeared, together with friend and fellow director Corin Hardy, on an early 1990s children's television programme which showcased both of their work. By the mid-1990s Edgar was directing episodes of television series. The success of *Spaced*, directed by Edgar from scripts by Simon Pegg and Jessica Hynes, led to Edgar directing, and co-writing with Pegg, *Shaun of the Dead*. It was hailed as the world's first zombie rom-com, now a cult classic.

In the last couple of years alone he has completed and released two films, *Last Night in Soho* and *The Sparks Brothers*; launched his own production company, Complete Fiction, with writer-director Joe Cornish and producers Nira Park and Rachel Prior; and become a governor of the British Film Institute. Peter the Schnauzer is keeping quiet about what Edgar has planned next.

In one of Edgar Wright's films, *The World's End*, omnipotent alien, The Light, tries to explain to some humans that its actions are really for their own good. To make things better. The free-spirited humans respond 'Quit Starbucking us', asserting their right to be a non-homogenized mess if they want to. I put it to Edgar that sometimes people might fear notes could be like that – an attempt to control and change things to a preconceived notion of what's better. Eradicating things that diverge from their idea of the norm. He throws his head back, laughing in recognition. Then he confides, 'Sometimes innovation and things that are fresh and different or subversive, some of that stuff you have to try to sneak in.' Explaining, 'If you're working with a studio, they're always thinking about how they could sell it. I think studios sometimes think in worst case scenarios; that if the movie is bad, at least we have this actor in it, or if the movie is bad at least we can cut together this trailer. I feel that's sometimes the way they approach filmmaking, with these fail safes. Obviously, everyone thinks they want to make original films, but anything that's really original or really different would have a tendency to make some people nervous. So if you're doing something that is completely "out there", you're either going to have to make it in a very, very independent way so you're not answering to anybody, or you're going to have to find a way to work with that.'

If notes question something perceived as 'out there', Edgar advises, 'When there are things that you have a really strong idea about, you just keep having to sell them at every stage. Usually in all of my movies there's some scene or sequence that at a producer level or a studio level they just don't get. So they question "Why do we need this sequence?" In *Shaun of the Dead* it was the sequence called The Plan, where Shaun lays out a plan and then Ed shuts it down and then there's a second plan and Ed shuts that down and then Shaun outlines the third plan, which is what they go for. At script stage, where this partly becomes a budget thing, they're thinking, "Why do we need this scene?" And this scene to me is the raison d'être of the movie. This is the thing that we can do in this zombie movie that isn't in other zombie movies. Sometimes with the execution of a scene visually or tonally, or even the way that the visual effects will work, people don't really understand it until it's done. It isn't until you've finished the sequence, with the music, with the editing, that people go, "Oh, I get it."'

Edgar observes, 'It takes real fortitude to keep arguing the toss about why a particular sequence is going to work. Then it comes down to other elements such as, "We can't afford the sequence, you're over budget and over time, you have to cut out this sequence." In *Last Night in Soho* it was another sequence that's one of my favourite bits in the movie, which was questioned. Towards the end of the movie, there's a stairs sequence where you see Eloise escaping.' Ever conscious of creating maximum movie-going joy for everyone, he's careful in how he describes it: 'I don't want to ruin the movie for people who haven't seen it, but it takes place in two dimensions, in the present day and in this semi-dream state. It was a very strong idea I had, very early on in the first draft. But because it involved visual effects it really wasn't fully realized until it was done. And Eric Fellner, one of the producers, was always saying "Do you really need that half of the stairs? Can you please try, just one time, cutting out the alternate dimension part?" Then when he saw it finished, he went, "Oh, now I get it." Edgar laughs, appreciating the trust of his long-term producer to support him to shoot the sequence despite his reservations. He adds, 'This is something where you're fighting for an idea for years! You can picture it clearly in your head, and think to yourself "If only I could show you what's in my head" and sometimes it's difficult to get that across on the page.

'On a script level there's always times where you cannot win the argument with the screenplay alone,' Edgar notes. 'Sometimes it'll be a proof of concept aspect of the development. On *Baby Driver* there was always an issue where some people, even if they wanted to make the movie, didn't quite understand how some of the set pieces were going to work. I had to do a whole presentation of the action to the studio so that they could greenlight the movie. This is way beyond the script now, we've done the script, done an audio version like a radio play, have all the music, have all the storyboards, animatics, and then you're starting to demonstrate some of the stunt sequences on video. A lot of the time, you're just trying to find ways to sell your idea. And it's always difficult when a movie, similar to the ones that I've made, is more than just what's on the page. You're trying to convey a sense of that in the screenplay, but the screenplay is not the entire story. There's a whole other level. So it is an interesting challenge, and one which continues to this day.' He laughs, fully aware it's a challenge created by his own artistic ambition.

When responding to notes from studios, Edgar says frankly, 'Sometimes it comes down to a very binary choice between the movie getting made or not getting made. For *Baby Driver,* the original ending was much less ambiguous and more obviously a dream. Tom Rothman [Chairperson of Sony Pictures Entertainment], in that way that studio heads have an idea of how things are going to be sold and how things are going to be received, said, "You cannot make a movie like this and end it on a dream." He's saying it in absolutes. And I want to make the movie. I'm not going to let the movie die by saying "No, it has to be a dream! And I don't care if that means it doesn't get made." Of course I want to get it made. So instead I say, "OK, let me have a think." If there's a situation that is a really black and white choice between something being made and not being made, then yes I will have a look at it! To Tom's absolute credit what is in the movie now is better than what was in there before. The current film is ambiguous. I think it's nice that people can read it in whatever way they want, and I'm never going to say they're wrong either way. It could be read as Baby dreaming in prison, or it could be read that he's out after seven years and reunited with Debora. And whichever way you think it is doesn't matter, it could either be read as a happy ending, or it could be thought of as the dream of what he wanted to be in the future.'

Edgar ponders some of the challenges of navigating notes: 'The trickiest thing is when you get notes that are in direct opposition to the film that you want to make. Having to deal with that and try to move past it. On *Scott Pilgrim* (2010) there was a big note that kept cropping up about one of the things that defines the movie, which is that we never explain in *Scott Pilgrim* how people can fight. It just happens. Similar to how in a musical people suddenly sing and dance, in *Scott Pilgrim* they suddenly fight. But early on there was always the question of "Can we show him training? Can we explain how he's a great fighter?" And because that wasn't in the source material, my feeling was that that's a different movie. I don't want to make *The Karate Kid* (John G. Avildsen, 1984), I want to make this magical realist epic. But it's still a hump that you have to get over. In a way, you have to sell them on everything else. To give another example, there were several things going on before me and Joe Cornish left *Ant-Man* (Peyton Reed, 2015), but the key one was that in our screenplay, at the start of the film Scott Lang was a real criminal, and by the end of the film he had redeemed himself. That was straight from the books; in the comics he is a career criminal and a burglar. I felt it was a more exciting arc if you take a criminal and make him a hero, he redeems himself through the movie. But we were asked "Does he have to be a criminal? Could he be somebody's who's wrongfully accused?" And that eventually became a really contentious note, because I felt it's stronger if he has a redemption arc, rather than being a nice guy at the start and a nice guy at the end. So, in that particular case, it was something that eventually we couldn't move past. It becomes a difference of opinion. And then it becomes enough of a difference of opinion to say "I'm not going to direct the movie anymore." Obviously there's always those things like with *Scott Pilgrim* where they said "Oh, we'd love it if you could explain how he can fight, but ultimately we support what you want to do with the movie" and they let me make it. In the other case it's more akin to unstoppable force meets immovable object. It can't be resolved, so somebody has to either fold or walk away.'

Thinking about handling notes generally, Edgar admits, 'I'm probably not good at receiving notes because I immediately get very defensive. I've had to learn to give it at least twenty-four hours before angrily responding. Because usually in that twenty-four or forty-eight hours, you calm down and then see the sense behind the notes.' He laughs, then advises, 'The big mistake is to get notes and respond immediately. Because even if your natural response might be "Oh my God, you're so wrong, why do you not understand?" you have to just calm down. Either it might be a really great note, or even if it's something that you disagree with, such as "Does it have to be zombies?", you have to find your own way of selling what you want to do with the film. I try to be a bit more Zen about it and give myself a moment to let the notes really seep in. Then you might think, "No, I disagree" or "No, this is not how I see it" and it might unlock something else. It's always said about notes from studios – "What's the note behind the note?" The same thing happens in focus groups and test screenings, you might get a response to something but it might be something else that is the issue. George Miller told me this analogy – in the same way a doctor talks about referred pain, the thing that everybody zeroes in on as the problem might not be the problem, the problem might be somewhere else. And sometimes it's more of a butterfly effect issue.'

Edgar illustrates with an example from *Scott Pilgrim vs. the World*: 'There's a scene where Scott Pilgrim goes into a coffee shop and sees Aubrey Plaza, and she's furious at him and starts swearing and there's a black box that comes at him every time she says the F word. Eventually he says, "How are you doing that with your mouth?" And I thought that was a really funny sequence. But originally in the first cut of the movie in an earlier scene, Scott Pilgrim says the F-word to Ramona Flowers. He's talking about Puckman, the original name for Pac-Man, and he says, "They were worried that if they called it Puckman people would vandalize the P into an F, you know, like Fuck man." In the first test screening with that edit, Scott's earlier line got a mild laugh and then the later scene with Aubrey Plaza got nothing. And it's like what George Miller said with referred pain – it's not a problem with the coffee shop scene, it's a problem with the earlier scene. So we edited that Puckman scene so he doesn't say fuck, he just tails off. As soon as we did that, the later scene got big laughs.' He concludes, 'So if you disagree with a note, think what's the note behind the note? What's making them say this? What's the other thing that could be changed? If there's something you disagree with, maybe there's something else in the script you can improve that's also going to improve your case for the bit that you don't want to lose. But mainly, the thing is to at least walk around the block. Don't respond immediately. Don't get super defensive.' He adds laughing, 'I say that, and yet I can't take my own advice. I get defensive. Good advice that I myself do not take!'

Reflecting on how notes and development can enhance a script, Edgar gives an example: 'I'm not sure if this was a note or whose idea it was, but it was a genius idea. The first draft of *Hot Fuzz* was long. It was maybe a hundred and fifty pages or something crazy, it was a bit like reading a novel! It had even more characters in it, there's a big ensemble in the movie as it is, but previously there was Nick [Frost]'s character Danny Butterman, and there was also a romantic interest for Simon [Pegg]'s character, Nicholas Angel. A girl who worked in a cake shop, Victoria Flowers. We had a whole sub-plot in the movie about Nicholas Angel meeting somebody new in Sandford. We did a read-through with the long script, and Alice Lowe actually read the Victoria Flowers part. But the script was long, and it felt like with Danny Butterman and Victoria Flowers you essentially had the same B-plot twice. I don't remember who came up with this note. Maybe me and Simon [Pegg] did it ourselves, but basically, we cut the Victoria character completely and gave all of her dialogue to Danny.' He guffaws in delight, partly at the audacity to do it and partly at how well it worked. He observes, 'People sort of detect it. Where people have said of *Hot Fuzz* "Oh it's like a romance between the two guys." I often think to myself, "Well, you're not wrong!" because we took the romantic sub-plot with this female character and gave all of her stuff to Danny. There's lines in there which are simply directly transposed to the other character. For instance, when Nicholas Angel comes back to Danny's for coffee, there's a bit where Danny says something about "You just don't know how to switch off that big melon of yours" and I think that was literally a Victoria line given to Danny. And it just seemed to work. I forget whether anybody gave us that note or if it was something that Simon and I came up with, but it was a great way of conflating two things to make the whole thing fresher.'

Edgar illustrates how such positive development can be inspired by notes at a later stage too, and can help a director crystallize or articulate their thoughts. During the edit of his documentary, *The Sparks Brothers*, Edgar recalls, 'At a certain point I showed it to my friend Phil Lord, who is also a big Sparks' fan, and he said "Oh I love it, I have one note, I just want to hear a bit more of the songs." And I said "You're not wrong! I totally agree." And then it became a matter of how can we do this without adding too much more runtime? Because you have to manage it between what is the movie that Sparks' fans would want to see and what would a person who's never heard of them before like? How much would they watch? It was a good note, because I was feeling it subconsciously even if I hadn't said it out loud myself.'

Edgar considers times he's been on the other side of the table as the one giving the notes: 'I was a producer on one of Ben Wheatley's films, *Sightseers*. Because there was a great script and Ben was on board I came into play not so much as script editor but more giving notes once the movie had been shot. As a lot of people say, the edit is the final draft of the script because you have an opportunity to keep writing in a way, which is partly through editing and sometimes it's through writing new material, which can be done via a reshoot or ADR. Either way, there's lots of opportunities for you to tweak things afterwards if something is not clear. I'd watched the first cut of *Sightseers*, I wrote some notes to Ben, and in an interview once, and I'm really glad he said this, Ben said, "The best notes I ever had were from Edgar Wright because he did what most producers don't – he also included a list of the things that he loved!"' Edgar roars with laughter, but underlines the importance of the point and why it's so valuable to a director by adding, 'Because usually notes are negative.'

In his own directing work, one of the things for which Edgar is celebrated is his use of music. In passing I admire the exquisite precision of his placement of the line 'Call the cops' from a Happy Mondays' track in *The World's End* just as Gary's car is pulled over by the police. He beams with delight, 'Oh, I'm glad you noticed that! I don't think anybody's ever said that to me before, thank you!' Which of course has me beaming with delight also, but more to the point reflects the extreme care and attention to detail he takes with his work. When music is so integral to a film, how does that fit into the notes and development picture, if there are particular tracks that a writer-director might want in a scene? 'It's a tricky one,' Edgar agrees, 'and this is something for first time writers to beware: you've got to be really careful about putting songs in scripts full stop. So two things: you've got to have B choices ready, and if you're writing a low budget script I would advise against putting in too much existing music, because the producer might look at it and go, "Hmm, this is going to be expensive." It's difficult. With *Shaun of the Dead* I think we had the Queen song 'Don't Stop Me Now' written into the script, but because it was my first proper feature, we didn't know for sure whether we could clear Queen. So during pre-production we had a B and a C choice song as well. The B choice was 'Rasputin' by Boney M. and I think the C choice was something like 'Bye, Bye Baby' by the Bay City Rollers. But of course Queen was the one we really wanted. And it was to the credit of Nick Angel, the music supervisor, that before we started shooting we got an agreement from the band. On the flip side, *Sightseers* the screenplay didn't have any songs written into it. And that's probably a more sensible way to approach it, because then people aren't reading it and going, "Oh, this is going to be expensive!" or "What happens if we can't clear that?" It's a very dangerous game to play and I think you also don't want to use songs as a crutch. If the film is going to live and die on a particular song. Would *Shaun of the Dead* still have worked without the Queen sequence in it? Sure. Obviously it's still a bit that elevates the movie and in some people's case is their favourite bit in the whole film, so we'll forever be grateful that the band let us have it. Because they could have quite easily said no. So you've got to be careful at a screenplay level that your entire project isn't standing or falling on you clearing a track. Don't put in something that without it you don't have a movie, because then you could be in trouble.'

Edgar addresses the realities of how long projects might be in development, sharing some of his own experience. '*Shaun of the Dead* – from first talking about it to making the movie – took three years, maybe a bit more,' he recalls, 'We first discussed it in the summer of 1999, then started to think about it more seriously in terms of this is what we're going to do next in 2001, after the second series of *Spaced* finished, and then we started filming it in spring of

2003. At the time, that felt like a long time. A long time between projects when I wasn't really working. I couldn't do other stuff that easily. I could maybe do the odd commercial or music video, but doing a whole TV series of something, which I did get a lot of offers for after the second series of *Spaced*, wasn't feasible. I knew that if I took a series it would be bye-bye to *Shaun of the Dead* for six months or more, and the momentum would be lost. That felt like a long time. But then when you talk to other people they say "Oh, three years is fast!" Some people are trying to get their movie off the ground for ten years or more. The thing is, you can't be disheartened by that. It's not indicative of the project itself, or you, it could just be what's in the ether, what's happening in the business, what people are looking for and not looking for. And with film, especially British film, it could just be the state of the industry in terms of how flush it is with development money. It might be a period when things are really bad, and not many films are getting made. It's never entirely about your project. So you should never really take it personally. It's the way the chips fall. For example, we developed *Shaun of the Dead* with Film4 in 2001 and I think in 2002 they even announced it at Cannes as part of their slate. Then, as you might remember, Film4 went bankrupt and stopped making movies. They've come back since, but at that point, people assumed that Film4 was over for good. And we had a film that we'd developed with Film4 and it suddenly became "Now what the fuck do we do?" Fortunately, because Nira [Park] had a relationship with Channel 4 through *Spaced* and *Black Books,* she managed to convince them to let us put *Shaun of the Dead* into turnaround so that we could take it elsewhere. Otherwise, it would have just been sitting there as an asset of the – at that time – defunct Film4. So it's a credit to Film4 that they were the first people who gave us development money to write the script, but we then had to get it out of there, and that was the period when we had to go round with our cap in hand which was also when we got the most "No"s. And to their credit, Working Title, which was the biggest of the companies we approached, were the ones who said yes. Lots of other people said no.'

Edgar concludes, 'The best script editor or development person is not there to be negative, they are there to help the writer, or writers, make the best version of what they want to do. If they can help with the execution of something, whether that's helping them refine what they already have or giving them an idea that they may not have had, then that's what it's there for. Development and script editing is a different thing from submitting to a studio, where you might send something and they say "Hard pass."' His hand chops through the air with the sharp finality of the decision. 'But if you're working with a script editor or development people who like the idea already, then they're there to nudge you in different directions. Or even nudge you in the same direction you want to go and just try and make it better. And sometimes the resistance to a note will just make you double down, as a writer or a director, on "OK, I think this is a genius sequence, clearly I'm not communicating what it could be, maybe there's no way of doing that on the page, but I'll find a way of selling this sequence." And there are plenty of cases where there have been bits in my movies where people have asked "Why is this in here?"' He puts his hands over his face, half laughing, half embarrassed, adding, 'It's such a fascinating process. Having occasionally been on the other side of it, (A) writing for somebody else and (B) being either a script editor or a producer, I always want to be as helpful to the creatives as the best people I've worked with.'

Wrapping up he says, 'The most amazing thing about this medium is that, and I think it's a quote from Roger Ebert, who says films are an empathy machine. There's a thing where people will often say "write what you know." You can make something very personal, or you can make something personal in a metaphorical way. Me and Simon [Pegg] had never been in the middle of an alien invasion, but *The World's End* is our most personal script. What's great about film is you either go to see something that you relate to, or it takes you into a world that you would never be able to visit in your lifetime. Either to go to other worlds or cultures and learn or experience something through that or to create a world that doesn't exist. I think the thing that's always fun and interesting is how you can put a personal stamp on the most outlandish film. It always seems funny to say that *Shaun of the Dead*, *Hot Fuzz*, *The World's End*, *Baby Driver* even, and *Last Night in Soho*, are really personal. People would ask, "What's personal about an eighteen-year-old Cornish fashion student coming to London and having supernatural experiences?" and I'd be like,

"Well, a lot! I'll break it down for you, but in the meantime – enjoy this movie!"'

He laughs once more, revelling in the rich delight that is filmmaking.

London, via Zoom, August 2022

Selected credits, awards and nominations

A Fistful of Fingers: Writer, Director (1995), [Film] UK: Wrightstuff Pictures.

Asylum: Co-writer, Director (1996), [TV Series] Paramount Comedy Channel.

Alexi Sayle's Merry-Go-Round: Co-Writer, Director (1998), [TV Series] BBC.

Spaced: Director (1999–2001), [TV series] Channel 4.
    BAFTA TV nomination – Situation Comedy Award (2000)
    BAFTA TV nomination – Situation Comedy Award (2002)

Shaun of the Dead: Co-writer, Director (2004), [Film] UK, France, USA: Universal Pictures.
    British Independent Film Award – Best Screenplay (2004)
    Fangoria Chainsaw Award – Best Screenplay (2005)
    BAFTA nomination – Best British Film (2005)
    Empire Awards nomination – Best British Director (2005)
    London Critics' Circle Film Awards nomination – British Screenwriter of the Year (2015)

Hot Fuzz: Co-writer, Director (2007), [Film] UK, USA: Universal Pictures International.
    Empire Awards nomination – Best Director (2008)

Scott Pilgrim vs. the World: Co-writer, Director (2010), [Film] UK, USA: Universal Pictures International.
    Empire Awards – Best Director (2011)

The Adventures of Tintin: The Secret of the Unicorn: Co-writer (2011), [Film] Dir. Steven Spielberg, USA, UK, France, New Zealand, Australia: Amblin Entertainment.
    Annie Awards nomination – Writing in a Feature Production (2012)

The World's End: Co-writer, Director (2013), [Film] UK, USA: Universal Studios.
    Empire Awards nomination – Best Director (2014)

Baby Driver: Writer, Director (2017), [Film] UK, USA: Sony Pictures Releasing.
    SXSW Film Festival award – Audience Award (2017)
    Empire Awards nomination – Best Director (2018)
    International Motor Film award – Best Drama Feature (2019)

The Sparks Brothers: Director (2021), [Film] UK, USA: Focus Features.
    NME Award – Best Music Film (2022)
    International Documentary Association nomination – Best Music Documentary (2022)

Critics Choice Documentary Awards nomination – Best Director (2022)

Critics Choice Documentary Awards nomination – Best First Documentary Feature (2022)

Last Night in Soho: Co-writer, Director (2021), [Film] UK: Universal Pictures International.

BAFTA nomination – Outstanding British Film of the Year (2022)

Fangoria Chainsaw Award – Best Director (2022)

Hollywood Critics Association nomination – Best Original Screenplay (2022)

Hollywood Critics Association nomination – Best Horror Film (2021)

BloodGuts UK Horror Awards nomination – Best Original Film (2022)

BloodGuts UK Horror Awards nomination – Best Director (2022)

BloodGuts UK Horror Awards nomination – Best Screenplay (2022)

Venice Film Festival nomination – Best Film (2022)

Empire Award – Inspiration Award (2011)

Empire Award – Visionary Award (2018)

Quick Fire Q&A 8: What's your advice to someone wanting to start out in, or further develop a career in script editing or development?

'Well – they should read this book! And I would say consider the factory of a soap opera. Simply because of the high volume – five scripts a week that have to have notes given very fast. And then you move onto the next five. So you learn a lot from that. But, that's only for people who love soap operas. Don't go into those serial shows if you don't love them. Theatres have readers and some production companies have readers. I think maybe the answer is, everyone is giving notes all the time, so start to listen to them. When your mates are coming out of a movie saying it wasn't quite as good as the last one – work out why.' – **Russell T Davies**

'What I really value is somebody who wants to be a script editor. As opposed to somebody who's using it as a stepping stone to something else. Real script editors are gold dust, they're rare. And people who really understand what that job is and who can do it are few and far between. The best ones, like Anna Davies, she didn't want to be a producer, she wanted to be a script editor, and that's what she knew she was good at. I've got a few students I try and help, and

I don't think I'm very good at analysing people's scripts and telling them what's wrong with it and telling them what they should do. I think I'm really bad at it. I'd be a really shit script editor. I'd be one of the annoying ones who gave far too many notes. And because I know I'm not good at it I really appreciate other people who can do it. Who can be succinct, who can be clear. A good script editor is someone who for you will bypass that thing of having to put a script in a drawer for six months till you've forgotten it and can look at it fresh. Somebody who can do that for you overnight. So it's somebody who knows that that's what they want to do.' – **Sally Wainwright**

'Most importantly remember when you're talking about somebody's script you're talking about them. Try and get inside their heads to understand what they're writing and why they're writing it and the direction they're going. The people I sit really well with, we just understand each other. It's a relationship. You have to be a psychologist on some level and see why they want to write the stuff they want to write. And help them. It's like a relationship – if you try to fundamentally change someone it's not going to work.' – **Simon Beaufoy**

'Be brave. Helping someone do the best they can to create is really rewarding. It's not about egos but about the project. There is no boil in the bag answer, it's just really fun playing with ideas and helping getting the boat over the hill.' – **Lynne Ramsay**

'Don't always feel obliged to have opinions on everything. Not every element needs notes. Really know structure. And not just the traditional Anglo-Saxon dramatic structure, but also have knowledge of other sorts of dramaturgy. The overall structure, but also structure within a scene – who knows what at what point, the grammar of how a scene is built and can be rebuilt. Develop an ear for dialogue, and not just dialogue in the sense of "That's how I would have said it." And enjoy tormenting the characters. There's a lot of love for characters, but there also needs to be a lot of sadism towards them and respect for surprising acts or reactions from them. And then to keep reading literature. We read so many scripts, and I think whenever you read proper literature you are reminded about language and layers, abstractions and omissions.' – **Lone Scherfig**

'Try writing something yourself. If only to see what it's like and to see what being on the flip side of that is like. Practically, I didn't have a conventional route, so I don't even know what training you would do! You just have to hang around in the industry long enough that people realize you've got a flair for notes.' – **Alice Lowe**

'Don't do it if you're a control freak, you will be outed within hours. I once had a script editor/producer who went through my script with a real red pen and ruler and put double red lines through single words and phrases she didn't like. And then re-wrote a treatment I had written and delivered it to the broadcaster with my name still attached to it. When I found out what she had done, needless to say I left her project on her desk and she never heard from me again. I later heard I wasn't the only one she had done that to. I don't know any writers who go back to work with that person twice, because her control freak-ness is not conducive to working positively. So I'd say, don't do it if you're a control freak. Do it if you love writers and you love the reward that comes with facilitating writers in reaching their potential. It's a sort of thankless task, and you have to be able to live with that. People rarely hear the script editor's name, in the same way that we often hear the actor's name, but we don't hear the writer's name, it's another level for script editors. I remember a writer getting up on stage at the Women in Film and TV awards to accept an award and her entire speech was "Manda Levin, Manda Levin, Manda Levin", who was a script editor at the time. Essentially what she was saying was "None of this without her." It was the first time I'd ever heard a script editor's name called out. And I went on to work with Manda Levin because of that. So it's a thankless task, but it's a rewarding one if you're doing it for the right reasons, if you love writing and you love supporting writers and you absolutely understand the value of what a good script editor brings, just go for it. That's what I would say to anybody who wants to do anything in life, the door simply does not open from the outside.' – **Amma Asante**

'Both with writing and script editing, the obvious thing is – read, read, read, read, read. Not just stuff that's out there, but classic scripts as well. It's always interesting to look at films that you really love and then read the screenplay and see, "Well, how did the Coen brothers get this across? How did Quentin

Tarantino get this across?" Read writers that have managed to imbue their personality into their screenplays. In terms of script editing, it's similar to writing in a sense, except here you're on the outside trying to help this writer, or writers, make the best version of this script. But the disciplines are not that much different really. As a script editor it's all of the same skills as being a writer, only you're coming at it objectively with a view of how you approach it as an audience member, and how you can help them reach the goal they're trying to achieve.' – **Edgar Wright**

'I would encourage burgeoning script editors to go on some formal training. When I was on the script development programme on the Torino Film Lab the script editors learnt an incredible amount. They worked across four to six feature scripts over the period of a year, and worked alongside an experienced script editor who supervised the sessions. I would try to get into a programme like that (there are others) so you are working on debut films and are learning from an experienced practitioner.' – **Michael Pearce**

'Retain a sense of wonder about the eternal possibilities of storytelling and bring that with you into the work. Really love movies. Love watching movies and TV, and presumably you do.' – **Corin Hardy**

'Don't do it if you're a frustrated writer. Do it because you're good at it. Do it because you're talented at that, you've got a special skill at that. Do it because you love it. And the same way that I wouldn't write anything that I wouldn't watch, understand you have to pay your mortgage and earn a living and eat, but try your very best to do stuff that you like. Or work with people that you get on with, that'll further your dream. Don't go into it because you've missed out on your glory, go into it because it's the glory.' – **Krysty Wilson-Cairns**

Notes from the Note-givers

'You must listen to notes, but you must know when notes are bad. That's the tricky thing, because how do you do that? I think the first ten or fifteen years of your career are figuring out who to work with. Working out who you trust.' – **Russell T Davies**

How do note-givers become one of those trusted, respected voices? To become, as Peter Ansorge describes, 'crucial to the creation of television drama and film – to help draw out from the writer or director what it is they want to say and to ensure it is coming across.' To avoid being the annoying, prescriptive ones, the negative ones, the picky ones, the ones giving a note for the sake of it to boost their ego or justify their job, the ones barely disguising that a note-giver wants to write themselves and is attempting to do so by re-writing someone else's work rather than creating their own. But to be the ones who, as Lone Scherfig puts it, 'turn you into a better writer or director than you knew you were. And turn the film into a better version of the film than you had in mind.' To be the ones people want to work with.

How can all the hours of reading and analysis, the years of studying and practice, the four in the morning breakthrough thoughts about someone's script that swim up from the subconscious and are hastily mistyped in the dark into a phone note app before they slip away, be translated into valuable notes? Notes people want to hear. Notes that inspire.

With a deepened understanding of what writers and directors look for, here voices from the other side of the note-giving table share advice of how to put such insights into practice. In the following pages, distinguished script editors, story developers, producers, executive producers, development executives and commissioners offer their thoughts in response to the question: 'What's your best piece of advice for enabling a successful script editing, development or note-giving process?'

David Puttnam CBE, Oscar and BAFTA winning producer (credits include: *Chariots of Fire* (Hugh Hudson, 1981), *The Mission* (Roland Joffé, 1986), *Midnight Express* (Alan Parker, 1978), *The Killing Fields* (Roland Joffé, 1984), *Local Hero* (Bill Forsyth, 1983)):

'Giving notes to a scriptwriter can be quite a delicate process. I have always found that openness and susceptibility are key to the exercise. To cultivate these sentiments from the writer, you first need to first establish a sense of mutual trust and respect: get to know as much as possible about the person on whose work you're commenting; listen carefully to what they have to say, and wherever possible, offer context from your own work and experience – good *and* bad.

'Then, when you do come to review their script, ensure you have a sense of what they are trying to achieve, whilst being totally confident in offering your own opinion and convictions. Accept that your "conventions" may not be theirs. At all times be rigorous and be honest. Is the plot credible? Do the characters come alive? Does the language they use sound authentic to whoever is delivering it? Does the story and dialogue "flow"' or is it in any sense uncertain or inauthentic?

'Your job is to create a safe space for everyone involved – *especially* the writer and actors – allowing them, without fear of embarrassment, to modify and craft the text throughout the creative process.'

Eva Yates, Director of BBC Film (credits include: *After Love* (Aleem Khan, 2020), *Aftersun* (Charlotte Wells, 2022), *His House* (Remi Weekes, 2020), *Rye Lane* (Raine Allen-Miller, 2023)):

'The best development begins and continues with honesty – it establishes a trust, and a shared understanding and destination. It's asking questions in a framework of positivity and possibility, and closing the gap between a writer's intention and a viewer's perception.

'It's also having the courage to say when you think a script isn't working, or you don't understand, or feel a dramatic friction in something. Moments of disagreement are inevitable, surmountable, and sometimes even affirming for the writer.

'Execs are often considered hurdles instead of crutches, but by having conviction in a writer and an idea, we can make it less lonely, more expansive and roll up our sleeves together.'

Pippa Harris DBE, BAFTA winning, Oscar nominated producer, co-founder of Neal Street Productions and BAFTA Vice President for Television (credits include: *Empire of Light* (Sam Mendes, 2022), *1917* (Sam Mendes, 2019), *Call the Midwife* (2012–23)):

'Accentuate the positive! Even if you think there is a lot of work to do on a script, you should always kick off a note session by telling the writer what excites you about the draft. Which elements are working really well? Which scenes make you laugh or cry? Bowling straight in with a list of criticisms is a recipe for disaster and guaranteed to make any writer feel defensive.

'Also, don't sweat the small stuff in an initial meeting. Going line by line can be soul destroying as well as guaranteeing a very long session, which nobody will enjoy. Concentrate on giving a few, key, general notes either about structure, story or character and allow enough time to discuss them properly, rather than necessarily presenting your own solutions.

'Finally, don't be afraid to have no notes at all! Too often, script editors and development execs see their job as coming up with as many pages of notes as possible. It's not. It is just as important to know when to say nothing instead of continually micromanaging the process.'

Nicola Shindler OBE, multi-BAFTA winning producer and executive producer, Quay Street Productions (credits include: *Nolly* (2023), *It's a Sin* (2021), *Ridley Road* (2021), *Stay Close* (2021), *Years and Years* (2019), *Last Tango In Halifax* (2012–16), *Happy Valley* (2014–16), *Queer as Folk* (1999–2000)):

'My advice on script editing is always – better not different! Our job is not to suggest changes to writers for the sake of it, our job is to try and help writers make their scripts better. The worst notes are those which suggest how we, the script editors, would have written a scene or a character. We need to understand what the writer intends, hear their voices in our head and then help solve any issues. That isn't to say that everything a writer delivers is right. The script editor's job is incredibly important both for creative development and production. Sometimes writers think they have a character on the page that isn't there, so it's our job to help them put on the page what they are thinking.

'Also script editors need to make sure they are an integral part of production. There can be a division between development and production, but the script editors need to make sure they are at the centre of all the decisions being made and listening to all issues that arise from production.

'And to remember the mantra – the script is our bible – at all times.'

Andrew Ellard, writer and script editor/producer (credits include: writer – *Nova Jones* (2021), *Deep Heat* (2022); script editor/producer – *Detectorists* (2017), *Chewing Gum* (2015), *In My Skin* (2018), *Red Dwarf* (2012)):

'Listen. And ask questions. It's easy to treat note-giving like it's about declaring your opinions to a writer. But the best notes processes come as much from asking questions, and listening to the answers. My job as script editor is to understand what the writer wants a script to achieve, and then to help them achieve that. Maybe they *want* a scene to be less funny, or slightly confusing, or very expositional – these are only flaws if they're accidents. Sometimes there's virtue in each. Your job is to find out, so you can calibrate your feedback to suit the writer's needs.

'If I can, I try to watch things they've written before. Which helps answer the question "How do you see this script translating to the screen?" It gets you familiar with some tonal aspects the page won't always give you. And that process of curiosity carries on throughout – "How do you see this character? Where do you think the audience's sympathies lie at this point?" It builds trust. Not to mention the sheer difference between saying, "You've not even had these two characters meet, and they obviously should" and "Hey, do you think there might be value in getting those two characters together for a scene . . .?"'

Hannah Farrell, executive producer and Creative Director at Fable Pictures, formerly Head of Development at Ruby Films (credits include: *Hullraisers*

(2022), *Rocks* (Sarah Gavron, 2019), *Suffragette* (Sarah Gavron, 2015), *Saving Mr Banks* (John Lee Hancock, 2013), *Jane Eyre* (Cary Fukunaga, 2011), *Tamara Drewe* (Stephen Frears, 2010)):

'Writers bare their heart and souls on the page to share with us, and we must be mindful and sensitive to that. As note-givers we have to go with our gut instincts of course, about the story, the characters, the plot – but we are collaborators and need to be a friend to the project as well as an interrogator of it. The hope is the writer will see you as an ally – someone who can help problem solve and elevate, so trust is also a really important gift to earn in that process. You can, and at times must, challenge the script but always remain open to the process and that whilst the note may always have merit – there are also a hundred ways in which to solve it and you have to help the writer find their way.'

Tessa Ross CBE, producer and executive producer, Co-CEO of House Productions, and former Controller of Film and Drama at Channel 4; awarded a BAFTA for Outstanding Contribution to Film (credits include: *Sherwood* (2022), *Brexit: The Uncivil War* (Toby Haynes, 2019), *Life After Life* (2022), *The Wonder* (Sebastián Lelio, 2022), *12 Years a Slave* (Steve McQueen, 2013), *Under the Skin* (Jonathan Glazer, 2013), *Room* (Lenny Abrahamson, 2015), *In Bruges* (Martin McDonagh, 2008), *Four Lions* (Christopher Morris, 2010), *Slumdog Millionaire* (Danny Boyle, 2008) and *Billy Elliot* (Stephen Daldry, 2000)):

'If you're involved in some way in making a piece of art, the exciting journey is the one into the unknown. A journey led by an artist with an original vision.

'So not only does that diminish the importance of notes – it also means embracing the moments when your notes are wrong. They might well be wrong because they're influenced by what you've read, steering a piece of work to be a facsimile of another; to be derivative. But the reason you're working with this writer or director is because what they do isn't derivative.

'Putting it less loftily: you should always have respect for the writer, for the time and energy that's gone into the work already – and engage in what they're trying to do on their own terms. When you give notes you should be tentative, show kindness, and be encouraging. Honesty is wonderful, but only if everybody is asking for it and is ready to hear the truth.

'But really, if you think you have the answer, there's a great big chance that you don't. Being shown a new way by a writer or director is the best part of the job. When you're lucky enough to come across it, it's important to recognize it. Give yourself up to the privilege of working with people you admire.'

David Sproxton, BAFTA winning producer, executive producer and co-founder of Aardman Animation Ltd (credits include: *The Wrong Trousers* (Nick Park, 1994), *Chicken Run* (Peter Lord, Nick Park, 2000), *The Curse of the Were-Rabbit* (Steve Box, Nick Park, 2005), *Flushed Away* (David Bowers, Sam Fell, 2006), *Shaun the Sheep* (2007–10), *Arthur Christmas* (Sarah Smith, Barry Cook, 2011), *Early Man* (Nick Park, 2018), *A Shaun the Sheep Movie: Farmageddon* (Will Becher, Richard Phelan, 2019)):

'By definition "notes" are a critique of the work in question but not of the person creating the work, they are being given to make the work better. So notes shouldn't be taken personally by the creator of the work!

'If several people are giving notes, then have someone collate all of them before they go to the creator, this reduces their workload and also highlights more easily where more thinking needs to be applied. The notes can be grouped into subjects and topics and addressed more easily that way. Also it will show clearly where there is a consensus in the note-givers. The creator should be clear about what areas they are seeking advice on. Is it plotting, character, theme, etc. The work will of course be work-in-progress and there may be areas which are very rough because they are still being thought through. It may not be worth giving notes on those areas and the creator should point out that they aren't seeking thoughts on those areas.

'It's very often worth seeing/hearing the work a couple of times, a few days apart, to allow gestation to happen, before notes are sent in. Thinking often happens overnight and it's often hard to give reasoned or well-articulated responses immediately after a presentation. Allow people time to mull over what they have seen or read for a day or two.

'Try not to give solutions to problems to the creator, but point out where you feel there might be issues. The solutions need to be seen in context of the whole work; it can be very easy to say "Why don't you do this . . ." when there is good chance that the creator may have already considered that solution but rejected it for good reasons to do with the bigger picture. Ask open questions and keep the bigger picture in mind. Does the narrative address the underlying theme or message and is that clear?'

Faye Ward, BAFTA and British Independent Film Award winning producer, founder and Creative Director of Fable Pictures (credits include: *Stan & Ollie* (Jon S. Baird, 2018), *Wild Rose* (Tom Harper, 2018), *Rocks, Suffragette*):

'Firstly, always appreciate the writing and say positive things before giving notes. Then, if there is a scene or an act that you feel is not working or you do not understand it, before diving in and critiquing it, I would always ask what the writer's intention is about that moment and act. To understand what is in the writer's head and get under the skin of the emotion or plot or what they want to achieve. There are normally more answers in that conversation than what is on the page.'

Ludo Smolski, script editor, story developer and screenwriting and script editing tutor (credits include: *Censor* (Prano Bailey-Bond, 2021), *Filth* (Jon S. Baird, 2013)):

'*Listen.* Learn to listen. Really listen. Read scripts. Learn to read scripts. Really *read* scripts. There is an art to listening and a science to reading and analysis. Both take practice. It is the first and only way to earn trust, to show your sensitivity to the writer and the choices they've made. There is no productive, creative relationship without trust. Learn how stories work, how screen stories work, know the conventions and generic expectations and look for where the writer might be subverting them in original and interesting ways. Weirdly, you also have to be able to read and listen at the same time: can you "hear" the writer's voice in the script? Can you articulate what it's saying?

'Learn to prioritize. What needs addressing first? Not everything will be solved in the next draft – in fact, it is often revealing of other routes to explore. Sometimes you work out what it is by working out what it isn't. The writer's relationship to the material may evolve, or crystallize. Trust the process. This is how you learn to ask the right questions, interrogate the script and challenge the writer and their decisions (respectfully, because you have their trust). And then you'll elicit useful answers ... especially if you really *listen*.'

Peter Dale, executive producer and former Head of Documentaries at Channel 4:

'I was on the receiving end of notes for over twenty years, and by and large it was a mixed experience. So when I first started giving them I wanted to be "helpful". It took me a while to realize that the most useful thing I could do was simply to react as the audience. So I always lead with what I really enjoyed, and then try to focus a conversation around the moments when I didn't understand something, or lost concentration. A bit basic, but my experience is that anything flashy or prescriptive is often more about the giver than the film. Oh, and I never take notes while I'm watching – used to drive me nuts.'

Basi Akpabio, Creative Director at Agatha Christie Ltd (credits include: *And Then There Were None* (2015), BAFTA nominated *The Witness for the Prosecution* (2016), *Ordeal by Innocence* (2018), *The ABC Murders* (2018), *The Pale Horse* (2020), *Why Didn't They Ask Evans?* (2022)):

'Script editing an adaptation is always an interesting exercise in that you're riding two horses – trying to honour both the intention of the original author but also what your writer is trying to do. My mantra is that I am in the business of adaptation not replication. It's not about directly translating the book to screen, but digging into what the text is about and helping your writer articulate that in a way that works both as storytelling for screen and speaks to the audience you're planning to reach.

'Hopefully your writer will be on the project because they saw something in the original material that they wanted to explore (and alarm bells should ring if this isn't the case), so keep this as your north star. Ultimately success is going to be about delivering a great drama that captures the truth of the source material rather than a version that's doggedly accurate but dull.'

Mia Pinto, Development Executive at Amazon Studios, formerly Development Producer at BBC Studios:

'To quote *Double Indemnity* (Billy Wilder, 1944) – "There's a widespread feeling that just because a man has a large office, he must be an idiot." I'm a woman with a very small office, but even so, I think it's important to recognize that this is how writers see us. Every writer you work with has at some point in their career received truly abysmal notes from executives, and now, however pleasant that writer may be to you, secretly, their in-built assumption is that your notes will be bad. Particularly on the commissioning side, if your notes put a heavy focus on questions of "clarity", "pacing it up", putting the subtext on the page, etc, writers will assume that your role as an exec is to dumb down their script to serve the lowest common denominator audience. To build a genuinely collaborative relationship, the onus is on you to prove their assumptions wrong, by showing the writer that you are not the cynical suit in the big office – you're protective of what makes the script great, you care about what they're trying to say, and fundamentally, you're on the side of the creative.'

Daniel Battsek, Former chairman of Film4, previously President of Cohen Media Group, Miramax Films and National Geographic, and Senior Vice President of BVI (credits include: *The Killing of a Sacred Deer* (Yorgos Lanthimos, 2017), *Three Billboards Outside Ebbing, Missouri* (Martin McDonagh, 2017), *Saint Maud* (Rose Glass, 2019)):

'Because of my background in distribution and marketing, my notes tend to aim at what the script needs to do in order to make it as audience facing as possible, without necessarily trying to over commercialize it. Even if I've been very closely involved in initiating a project, I tend to step back and wait until the script has gone through one or two drafts without my input. However, I will keep myself connected to the creative team who are providing feedback, so that I don't completely divorce myself from the development process. I don't think that my skillset is best suited to detailed page-by-page note-giving, instead I believe it's more productive for my knowledge and experience to be utilized at a later stage to finesse some of those things and read it from both a creative and commercial perspective.

'I am firmly of the belief that the creative process needs to be allowed to flourish as much as possible without having to be too aware of the marketplace, films made by marketing departments don't tend to be heralded as pieces of art that we're really proud of. So I will always try to strike a balance that allows for that freedom of expression whilst still being aware of the end user, which includes both the business environment as well as the eventual paying audience.

'Film4 has always been built on backing filmmakers with distinctive, unique voices, and those projects are often very challenging in terms of they don't necessarily fit into a typical commercial box. That doesn't mean they can't be incredibly successful, and it's quite often the case that the most challenging, the most "out there" projects are ones that audiences really support. They provide an antidote to their daily bread and butter dose of blockbusters or mainstream movies, which if you are a cinema lover, is never going to be entirely satisfying.

'I feel very strongly that it's important not to try to turn every project into a neatly marketable package. Auteur filmmakers by their very nature need to tell the stories that they want to tell in the ways that they want to tell them. And then it's up to everybody else to position them in such a way that they find an audience. So it's finding that balance: on the one hand giving that supportive note that leads a filmmaker to understand a different way of seeing their material that might be more palatable to an audience, on the other hand, making sure that you give those filmmakers the licence to be as artistic as they want to be. I wouldn't want to pretend that this is always a smooth process but the friction involved isn't by any means a terrible thing per se.

'At Film4 I tended to err on the creative side, but when I was running a studio, one tends to perhaps favour the other side. But each project is different and with the slate at Film4 we try to have a mix of commercial/arthouse/debut films with financial models that create sufficient revenue flows to build a sustainable business.'

Charlotte Moore, BBC Chief Content Officer, previous roles include Controller of BBC One and BBC Commissioning Executive for Documentaries:

'Don't give lots of notes – decide the three most important things you want to say that will really make a difference. Always start with the positives – so your notes are listened to and taken in the right context. Identify where a show or script isn't working and explain why, but don't feel you have to be the one to come up with all the solutions. The trick is to empower the filmmaker to own the changes.'

Anna Davies, Head of Scripted Development, BBC Studios Kids & Family (credits include: *At Home with the Braithwaites* (2000), *The Demon Headmaster* (2019), *Katy* (2018), *Phoenix Rise* (2023)):

'A strong set of notes can really speed up the development process, whereas bad notes have the potential to confuse or infuriate the writer! Notes should always be seen as a way to have a conversation about a project rather than a list of instructions. If you're new to writing notes there can be a tendency to write a more critical response – sort of show off a bit and write clever notes. But it's not about your notes; it's about the writer's next steps – whatever you can do to help them tackle the next stage. It's important to understand what the writer wants the project be, what the inspiration is, and what's most important to them. There's no point giving a detailed set of notes if it takes the script in a direction the writer fundamentally doesn't like.

'Clear structure is important. Start with the biggest stuff – the main notes and questions that affect the script as a whole. A writer should quickly be able to see what the major notes are – clearly set out in defined subject paragraphs. Major notes can be followed by scene notes, giving the detail on how you could apply any suggested fixes in the main notes, as well as other specific notes within the scene. Or if the headline notes are really big, you might just discuss these with the writer to begin with.

'Good notes are part of a good working relationship between the note-giver and the writer. What you're aiming for is a shared love of the project, a solid shared understanding of what the audience will get out of it, and a willingness to do whatever it takes to make this a success.'

Index

The letter *f* following an entry indicates a page that includes a figure.